D0858326

Peter F. Drucker on Business and Society

The Drucker Library

Peter F. Drucker on Technology
Peter F. Drucker on Business and Society
Peter F. Drucker on Management Essentials
Peter F. Drucker on Nonprofits and the Public Sector
Peter F. Drucker on Economic Threats
Peter F. Drucker on Globalization
Peter F. Drucker on Practical Leadership
Peter F. Drucker on the Network Economy

Peter F. Drucker on Business and Society

Peter F. Drucker

Harvard Business Review Press
Boston, Massachusetts

Printed in the United States of America
10 9 8 7 6 5 4 3 2 1

Library of Congress Cataloging-in-Publication Data

Names: Drucker, Peter F. (Peter Ferdinand), 1909-2005, author. | Drucker, Peter F. (Peter Ferdinand), 1909-2005. Works. Selections. 2007.
Title: Peter F. Drucker on business and society / Peter F. Drucker.
Other titles: Men, ideas, and politics | On business and society
Description: Boston, Massachusetts : Harvard Business Review Press, [2020] | Series: The Drucker library | Includes index.
Identifiers: LCCN 2020004739 | ISBN 9781633699632 (hardcover) | ISBN 9781633699649 (ebook)
Subjects: LCSH: Political sociology. | Economic history—1945-1971.
Classification: LCC JA76 .D76 2020 | DDC 306.2—dc23
LC record available at https://lccn.loc.gov/2020004739

ISBN: 978-1-63369-963-2
eISBN: 978-1-63369-964-9

The paper used in this publication meets the requirements of the American National Standard for Permanence of Paper for Publications and Documents in Libraries and Archives Z39.48-1992.

CONTENTS

PUBLISHER'S NOTE

This book is one of several volumes in the Drucker Library published by Harvard Business Review Press.

The essays in this volume were written between 1946 and 1969. When Peter Drucker collected them for this volume in 1971, he resisted, as he explained in a subsequent volume of essays, "the temptation to rewrite," contending that it was "only fair to let the reader decide how well the author's opinions, prejudices, and predictions have stood the test of time."

Some fifty years later, readers may find Drucker's language at times dated or inappropriate and some of his arguments controversial or utterly wrongheaded. But as editors, we too have chosen to resist the urge to tamper with the original texts, for we did not feel confident that we could always tell the difference between updating and censorship. Further, we believe that one of the many delights of these essays for current readers, who enjoy the advantage of complete hindsight extending over the entire period in which Drucker made predictions, is in judging how remarkably prescient and applicable so much of his thinking remains today.

PREFACE

Do the essays in this volume have anything in common except the author? At first sight they may look like random scatter without underlying theme or unifying thesis. An essay on "The New Markets," which treats the financial fads and follies of the 1960s as symptoms of structural change in economy and society, may seem a strange bedfellow for an essay on Kierkegaard, surely the least "market-oriented" thinker of the modern West. An evocation of Henry Ford as the "Last Populist," and simultaneously the fulfillment and the denial of the nineteenth century's agrarian and Jeffersonian dreams, might seem very far away from the internal stresses of the Japanese "economic miracle" or the pathos and bathos of "This Romantic Generation," today's educated young people.

Yet all these pieces, despite the diversity of their topics, have a common subject matter and a common theme. They are all essays in what I would call "political (or social) ecology."

This term is not to be found in any university catalogue. But the only thing that is "new" about political ecology is the name. As a subject matter and human concern, it can boast ancient lineage, going back all the way to Herodotus and Thucydides. It counts among its practitioners such eminent names as de Tocqueville and

Walter Bagehot. Its charter is Aristotle's famous definition of man as "zoon politikon," that is, social and political animal. As Aristotle knew (though many who quote him do not), this implies that society, polity, and economy, though man's creations, are "nature" to man, who cannot be understood apart from and outside of them. It also implies that society, polity, and economy are a genuine environment, a genuine whole, a true "system," to use the fashionable term, in which everything relates to everything else and in which men, ideas, institutions, and actions must always be seen together in order to be seen at all, let alone to be understood.

Political ecologists are uncomfortable people to have around. Their very trade makes them defy conventional classifications, whether of politics, of the market place, or of academia. Was de Tocqueville, for instance, a "liberal" or a "conservative"? What about Bagehot? "Political ecologists" emphasize that every achievement exacts a price and, to the scandal of good "liberals," talk of "risks" or "trade-offs," rather than of "progress." But they also know that the man-made environment of society, polity, and economics, like the environment of nature itself, knows no balance except dynamic disequilibrium. Political ecologists therefore emphasize that the way to conserve is purposeful innovation—and that hardly appeals to the "conservative."

Political ecologists believe that the traditional disciplines define fairly narrow and limited tools rather than meaningful and self-contained areas of knowledge, action, and events—in the same way in which the ecologists of the natural environment know that the swamp or the desert is the reality and ornithology, botany, and geology only special-purpose tools. Political ecologists therefore rarely stay put. It would be difficult to say, I submit, which of the chapters in this volume are "management," which "government" or "political theory," which "history" or "economics." The task determines the tools to be used: but this has never been the approach of academia.

Students of man's various social dimensions—government, society, economy, institutions—traditionally assume their subject matter to be accessible to full rational understanding. Indeed, they aim at finding "laws" capable of scientific proof. Human action, however, they tend to treat as nonrational, that is, as determined by outside forces, such as their "laws." The political ecologist, by contrast, assumes that his subject matter is far too complex ever to be fully understood—just as his counterpart, the natural ecologist, assumes this in respect to the natural environment. But precisely for this reason the political ecologist will demand—like his counterpart in the natural sciences—responsible actions from man and accountability of the individual for the consequences, intended or otherwise, of his actions.

An earlier volume of essays of mine, *Technology* (published in 1970), centered on what used to be called "the material civilization": business enterprise, its structure, its management, and its tools; technology and its history, and so on. The present volume is more concerned with economic, political, and social processes: the early diagnosis of fundamental social and economic change; the relationship between thought—economic, political, or social—and actions; the things that work and don't work in certain traditions, whether those of America or those of Japan; or the conditions for effective leadership in the complex structures of industrial society and giant government. But in the last analysis, the present essays, and those in the earlier volume, have the same objective. They aim at an understanding of the specific natural environment of man, his "political ecology," as a prerequisite to effective and responsible action, as an executive, as a policy-maker, as a teacher, and as a citizen.

Not one reader, I am reasonably sure, will agree with every essay; indeed, I expect some readers to disagree with all of them. But then I long ago learned that the most serious mistakes are not being made as a result of wrong answers. The truly dangerous thing is asking the wrong questions. I do hope that readers, whether executives in a business or administrators in a government agency, parents or their children, policy-makers or citizens, teachers or students, will agree that this volume addresses itself to right questions. And even the reader who disagrees heatedly with the author's prejudices, opinions, and conclusions will, I hope, find these essays enjoyable reading.

—Peter F. Drucker
Claremont, California
Spring, 1971

CHAPTER ONE

The New Markets and the New Entrepreneurs

I

THE THIRD MERGER wave to wash over the American economy in this century is receding fast. It leaves behind a landscape changed even more fundamentally in economic structure than its predecessors did, sixty-five and forty years ago.

The first merger wave, the one that reached its climax between 1900 and 1910, was the merger wave of the "tycoons," with J. P. Morgan's U.S. Steel and John D. Rockefeller's Standard Oil Company as their prototypes. In these mergers a dominant industrialist or financier tried to gain and occupy a commanding height in the economy by obtaining control of a major material or a major industry. They were "offensive" mergers.

The second merger wave, in the twenties, was, by contrast, one of "defensive" mergers. Its prototype, indeed its earliest example, was General Motors, put together between 1910 and 1920 as a merger of medium-sized car companies for common defense

---

First published in *The Public Interest*, September, 1970.

against Henry Ford's near monopoly. The aim of these "defensive" mergers was to create a "number two" who would be able to hold its own against the giants which the first merger wave had spawned. And while a good many of the creations of this period—such as General Motors itself—in turn became the leading company in their industry, the defensive mergers made for less concentration of power in the country's major industries and for more vigor and equality in competition. It often resulted in "oligopoly"; but it more often thwarted "monopoly."

The third merger wave, the one which has now peaked, began with defensive mergers, very similar to those of the twenties. Typical are the railroad mergers, such as the one which created the Penn-Central, and the new railroad system in the Northwest between Chicago and Seattle. It is no coincidence that the plan for these railroad mergers is forty years old, that it goes back to the period of defensive mergers in the twenties. But the mergers among the major New York banks in the late forties and early fifties—such as the merger that put the Chase Bank and the Bank of Manhattan together into the Chase Manhattan Bank, the National City Bank and the First National into the First National City, or the Chemical Bank and the New York Trust Company into Chemical New York—were also defensive. As a result, commercial banking in New York—and commercial banking internationally—has become far more competitive. There are fewer players, to be sure, but they are far stronger and far more aggressive. These defensive mergers of the last twenty years aimed, as did the mergers of the twenties, at creating enterprises large enough for a national or international market and strong enough to withstand competition on a national (or, as in the case of the banks, an international) scale. Mergers of this kind have been taking place also in manufacturing industry. The merger between two medium-sized forest products companies, Champion Paper and U.S. Plywood, created, for instance, a billion-dollar business producing all kinds of forest products, from saw timber and plywood veneer to fine paper. Still, the combined company is considerably smaller than the country's largest paper company, International Paper, itself created by mergers before World War II.

The Diversification Merger

But the typical mergers of the postwar period, and especially of the last ten years, resemble neither the offensive merger of 1900 nor the defensive merger of 1925.

To begin with, there were two very different and yet "typical" kinds. In the "diversification merger" which dominated the early years of the period, say, through 1964 or so, a large company, though distinctly not one of the leaders in its industry, merges with companies of the same kind, but in totally different lines of business. One leader in this kind of merger activity has been ITT—the initials standing for International Telegraph and Telephone. Originally this was a company operating telephone businesses abroad, especially in the Latin-speaking countries. It also manufactured telephone equipment for these companies. It was, in fact, originally the foreign counterpart to the American Telephone and Telegraph Company, the Bell System. During the last forty years, the company gradually gave up or lost one operating telephone company after the other. It became instead a world-wide manufacturer of electronics, very large in its total, but no better than third or fourth in every one of its markets or technologies. And then, in the last ten or fifteen years, it expanded through the acquisition increasingly of businesses that have nothing to do, at least at first glance, with its main business. It acquired Avis-Rent-A-Car, the Sheraton hotel chain, and Levitt, the country's largest mass-builder. It also acquired Hartford Fire Insurance, one of the large casualty insurance companies (though the antitrust division is still trying to undo this merger).

In a similar "diversification through merger," American Radiator & Standard Sanitary Corporation, an old and large, but stagnant, producer of plumbing and heating equipment, merged first with Westinghouse Air Brake, a large, and also rather stagnant, producer of railroad brakes and signals, then with Mosler Safe, a medium-sized and rapidly growing company, making mostly equipment for banks, and then with Lyons, a California-based mass-builder. In the process the company became "American-Standard."

Two of the many hundreds of diversification mergers exemplify the phenomenon. One of these is the merger in which Montgomery Ward, a large retail and mail-order chain, came together with Container Corporation of America to form a new company, Marcor. The other example is the acquisition of the country's second-largest medium-term finance company, Commercial Credit, by Control Data, the one computer manufacturer other than IBM (and very much smaller) who has so far shown any profits making computers. At first sight Montgomery Ward and Container Corporation have nothing in common, and the merger makes no economic sense. But both companies, while absolutely very large, are no more than "also-rans" in their respective industries with less than one-third of the sales of the industry leader (Sears, Roebuck and American Can, respectively). In their problems, their opportunities, and their strategic decisions, they may therefore be akin to each other. Similarly, producing big computers and providing installment loans to automobile buyers have, it seems, nothing in common. But the central problem of the successful computer manufacturer is to finance his machines which, as a rule, are leased rather than purchased. The central problem of a finance company, especially the smaller and weaker one, is a dependable and steady supply of high-quality borrowers. Again, there is a high degree of "fit" even though the respective businesses are as diverse as can be.

The Takeover Merger

Diversification mergers, though continuing right through the sixties, passed their peak around 1964 or 1965. From then on, for five years until the end of 1969, the mergers that made the headlines were something quite different, "merger by takeover." This merger is forced upon a reluctant, and often loudly resisting, management by organizing a stock-holders' revolt against it. And the one who "takesover" is almost invariably a very much smaller company, a total outsider, indeed, typically a brash newcomer who did not even exist a few years earlier. In the diversification mergers, both parties plighted their troth with the promise of "synergism" which would somehow make the combined business be more productive than the two alone. But in the takeover, the slogan is "asset management," that is, the maximization of the value of the shareholders' equity through financial management. In effect, the takeover is far less a merger of businesses than a *coup d'état*. A guerilla leader, himself owning practically no part of the company he acquires, gets the outside shareholders of large publicly owned companies to oust their own entrenched "professional business management" and put him into the saddle instead. And the more successful ones of these new corporate guerilla captains went from one takeover to another. Starting with nothing, they built within a few years "conglomerates" showing total revenues in the billions.

Among the takeover victims have been some of the oldest and best-known companies in the country—companies run by entrenched "professional management." They include two of the world's largest steel companies, Jones & Laughlin and Youngstown Sheet & Tube, both with sales around the billion-dollar mark. They were taken over, respectively, by Ling-Temco-Vought, controlled by James Ling and built by him in a few years from a small electronics shop into a medium-sized aerospace company with sales around $160 million, and by Lykes Bros. Steamship Company, a New Orleans-based shipping line which never in all its forty years of history had had sales of more than $70 million.

In another bitterly fought takeover, AMK, a company of whom a few years earlier nobody had ever heard, took over the old United Fruit Company in Boston—a company with over $400 million in assets and almost $400 million in sales. This was AMK's second leap; in the first one a year earlier, it had taken over one of the oldest meatpackers, Morrell—but its base had been a small company making industrial machinery. The United Fruit shareholders sided with the raider, not because management had failed, but because it had been so successful in its attempt to turn around and save an old and ailing enterprise that it had accumulated a large amount of cash. The most spectacular of these takeovers would have been the takeover of the country's sixth largest bank, Chemical New York, with assets of $9 billion, by a company called Leasco which was not even mentioned in the financial handbooks of 1966, two years before it made the attempt (albeit an unsuccessful one) to engulf a huge commercial bank into what had started out, a few years earlier, as a small computer leasing operation without any capital to speak of.

There thus came into being a whole new group of entrepreneurs. They are not "owners," but they know how to mobilize the vast multitude of shareholders of big publicly owned companies against management. They have been able again and again to unseat "professional management" in the name of "asset management," that is, by promising to maximize financial returns. And their aim is not the "synergism" (whatever that may mean) of "diversification." It is the "conglomerate" built by financial manipulation and based on financial control.

The New Growth Companies

Perhaps even more significant, however, is another development, and one that never before coincided with a wave of mergers. It is the emergence of yet another group of new entrepreneurs far more numerous than the asset managers, but perhaps a good deal sounder, though neither as colorful nor as spectacular. These are the men who have been building new "growth" businesses in very large numbers. New businesses are, of course, being started all along. But these new businesses were started as growth businesses, and from the beginning with large investments from the capital market. In every year from 1965 to 1969, eight to ten thousand brand-new businesses got going. Many new entrepreneurs went to the capital market for anything up to a million dollars before their business had even been started, produced its first product, or made its first sale. A year or two later most came back for another substantial sum of money, ranging from $1 million to $10 million apiece. These companies were still sufficiently small and their investors sufficiently few in number—and also what the securities laws call "sophisticated investors" (that is, primarily investment institutions)—not to have to register their securities with the Securities Exchange Commission. Yet they were sufficiently large already to have to apprise the Commission of their existence. All told, these new businesses raised about $5 billion to $10 billion each year from the "sophisticated investors" during the last five years.

"Science-based" companies, most nonfinancial readers will probably say. Indeed the science-based companies that sprang up in the fifties around Boston on Route 128 or on the Peninsula south of San Francisco were the forerunners. But while science-based industries such as "learning" or computer application are to be found among the new growth ventures of the sixties, they constitute a small fraction of the total. Among the "glamour" stocks for which the sophisticated investors bid were franchise restaurants, magazine and book publishers, nursing homes and hospitals, manufacturers of prefabricated housing and of mobile homes, and many others.

Some of these new growth companies are even to be found in finance, both on Wall Street and as managers of investment trusts. The first of these financial growth ventures—and the most successful one to date, Donaldson, Lufkin & Jenrette—was started ten years ago by a group of young business-school graduates and had become by 1969 the seventh largest Stock Exchange firm. Then it singlehandedly achieved what Franklin D. Roosevelt, with all the power of the United States government behind him, had failed to bring about thirty years earlier: to force the Stock Exchange out of being a "private club." When Donaldson, Lufkin & Jenrette outgrew its capital base in 1969 and threatened to quit the Exchange unless permitted to sell shares to the public—something always strictly forbidden by the rules which, in effect, limited investment in Stock Exchange firms to wealthy individuals—it had become so important that the Stock Exchange had to give way. Donaldson, Lufkin & Jenrette raised $12 million by selling shares to the public in April 1970.

Very few of these new companies can be compared with Xerox, the growth company par excellence of the American economy in post-World War II—a company having barely $1 million in sales as recently as 1950, still having less than $50 million in sales in 1960, and, in 1969, reporting sales of $1.5 billion. But a good many of these new companies grew, within a very short period, to very respectable middle size—$50 million, $60 million, $70 million, sometimes even $100 million in sales. An even larger number grew to the point where their founders could sell them at a considerable capital gain to older, staid, and less "dynamic" companies bent on "diversification," or could, in a few cases, become "takeover entrepreneurs" in their own right. Not since the railroad and banking ventures of the Age of Jackson has there been any comparable explosion of new ventures getting, from the start, broad financial support in very large amounts.

The Developments That "Could Not Have Happened"

And neither the takeover merger nor the new growth ventures could really have happened, according to "what everybody knows" about the structure of the American economy. This is brought out clearly by the cleavage between the actual developments and the magisterial announcement regarding what could happen—just when the actual developments were approaching their peak.

Nineteen sixty-seven was the year in which takeovers exploded and in which also the largest number of "new growth" businesses appeared on the capital market. It was also the year, however, which produced the all-time best seller by an American academic economist, John Kenneth Galbraith's *The New Industrial State.* The book has two fundamental theses. One, professional management in the big corporation is so firmly entrenched that it cannot be challenged, let alone be overthrown from inside or outside. The dispersed "public" stockholder is completely disenfranchised, to the point where management need not, and indeed does not, aim at maximizing profitability, but can run the business comfortably to perpetuate itself in power. Second, new businesses simply cannot come into existence in this economy of large corporations which manipulate the market, both that of goods and that of capital. Small new businesses certainly cannot possibly grow. So said *The New Industrial State.*

What makes the contrast between the theses of this best-selling book and the reality of the very moment when it appeared particularly significant is, however, that Galbraith in this book is not the innovator, the iconoclast, and the exploder of the conventional wisdom which he had been in his earlier books. The two theses of *The New Industrial State,* however provocatively phrased by Galbraith, were the most conventional and most widely accepted theses regarding American economic structure. They go back, indeed, to the years before World War I, when John R. Commons, the father of American institutional economics, first propounded them. They underlay, of course, Veblen's work in the years of World War I. They were given full documentation in the classic on American corporate structure, Berle and Means' *The Modern Corporation and Private Property,* which came out in 1932. They were restated in the three books which initiated, one way or another, the tremendous interest in and study of the American business corporation the last twenty-five years: James Burnham's *The Managerial Revolution* (1941) and my own books *Concept of the Corporation* (1946) and *The New Society* (1950). For once, in other words, Galbraith, in *The New*

Industrial State, was the very voice of the "conventional wisdom." But this makes it all the more apparent that something significant must have happened in the very structure of the American economy in these last few years.

Indeed, not even the diversification merger is truly compatible with the prevailing and generally accepted doctrine of "managerialism." The doctrine preaches that entrenched management in the large publicly owned company does not need the outside financial market altogether. Large, well-established companies, so said the received wisdom of the last forty years, are capable of financing themselves through "retained earnings." But if this were, indeed, correct, the diversification mergers would not, indeed, could not, have happened. The accepted doctrine also teaches that such a company does not have to compete for management. Management can perpetuate itself and can offer competent mediocrities safe careers. In these mergers one top management voluntarily abdicates; for, of course, the new, merged company needs only one top management. No top management, one would conclude, would commit suicide if immune to stockholder control, in the first place, and capable of providing itself the resources for its own success. And, indeed, none has ever done so, under these conditions.

Unlike the defensive mergers of yesterday, the diversification mergers do not strengthen a company in the markets for its products or in manufacturing efficiency. The only explanation why managements in companies that are apparently doing quite well—as did Commercial Credit and Control Data, Montgomery Ward and Container Corporation, Sheraton Hotels, American Radiator and Westinghouse Air Brake—might be willing and often eager to merge is that they find themselves under pressures they cannot neglect, that is, unable to attract resources they must have to survive and cannot generate just by being big and established. The diversification merger, like the takeover and the new growth entrepreneurs, was a seismic disturbance that argues some major structural shift some place deep below the economy's surface.

The Multinational Company

One more development, equally significant, occurred in economic structure during these last few years, and it, too, "could not have happened." Fifteen years ago all but a handful of the major American businesses were entirely "American" (or at least "North American," i.e., with a subsidiary in Canada) in their geographic distribution. Today the great majority of major manufacturing companies are "multinational," with 20 to 50 percent of their output produced outside of the United States. Indeed, as Jean-Jacques Servan-Schreiber pointed out in his book, *Le Défi Américain* (The American Challenge), which followed Galbraith's *The New Industrial State* as the international economics best seller for 1968, the American companies producing in Europe are the world's third largest industrial power, outproduced only by the United States and Russia, and in turn outproducing even Japan and Germany. Nor is "multinationalism" confined to manufacturing companies. The large United States banks, the Bank of America, the First National City Bank, and the Chase Manhattan, have today an even larger proportion of their business outside the United States than have most multinational manufacturing companies. Several stock exchange houses also, White Weld, for instance, are truly multinational and have become leading underwriters in the European capital markets. And then there are the "offshore" investment trusts, American-managed but domiciled outside the United States and confined, by law, to doing business exclusively with non-Americans. One of them, Investors Overseas Service, started only in 1956 by a former social worker from Philadelphia, Bernard Cornfeld, had, by the end of 1969, amassed almost $2.5 billion in assets and had become the leading asset manager in many European and Latin American countries.

This development began in the United States; and for the first few years "multinational" was synonymous with "U.S.-based." Around 1965, however, the move to multinationalism became truly multinational. The fastest growers these last few years have been the Swedes. Today three out of every ten men working for Swedish-owned manufacturing plants work outside of Sweden; a few short years ago the figure was one out of ten. Then the Japanese, around 1968, began to move. Every issue of the *Oriental Economist,* Japan's counterpart of the *Wall Street Journal,* reports a new manufacturing plant built by a Japanese company abroad, a new joint venture with a non-Japanese company to produce abroad, a new Japanese manufacturing subsidiary abroad. The development has been so sweeping that one student, Judd Polk, an economist at the International Chamber of Commerce, argues that we should replace the old theory of international trade, which deals with the "international distribution of the fruits of production," with a new theory of the international allocation of the factors of production. Another observer, Professor Howard Perlmutter of the University of Pennsylvania, predicts that, by 1985 or so, the bulk of the world's supply of manufactured goods will come from three hundred worldwide companies, producing in all the major countries, managed multinationally, and owned by shareholders from all the major countries.

More than half of the production of the U.S.-based multinationals outside of the United States has been added in the last five years. Yet five years ago, every economist "knew" that American multinational expansion had been stopped, that, indeed, the American multinational company was in for a sharp contraction. For in 1965 the United States government banned further investment of United States funds in American multinational businesses abroad, especially in the developed countries (other than Canada and Japan). The ostensible reason was concern for the United States balance of payments—though a major reason was surely also the desire to placate our European allies, especially de Gaulle, who were complaining loudly that the United States was using its payments deficit to buy up the European economies. The ban has been strictly policed and is faithfully observed. Yet every year since 1965, the United States multinationals have invested more in Europe.

The answer is simply that America never financed the European acquisitions and new businesses of American multinationals; the Europeans did it all along. They exchanged their holdings in their own national companies, trading in a restricted national market, for holdings in a multinational company world-wide in scope and management. Actually, during these last ten years Europe invested quite a bit more—a billion or two—in shares of U.S.-based companies than U.S.-based companies invested in production in Europe, whether through starting a business or through acquisition of an existing European one. The result of this is that Europeans, in the aggregate, now probably own as much of the leading American businesses—perhaps as much as 20 percent in some cases—as United States businesses own of major industries in Europe. So far no one has paid much attention to this. But predictably we will one day soon discover this; and then "foreign domination of American industry" is likely to become as much of a political slogan in this country as "American domination of French (German, British, Italian, Dutch, or other) industry" has become a political slogan in Europe.

The Swedish and Japanese examples are even more amazing. In both countries the government has all along exercised the tightest control over investment abroad. In both countries investment in manufacturing plants abroad was officially banned and currency for it was simply not available. The multinationalism of industry in these two countries is, in other words, also being financed by the multinational investors—especially the investor in the countries in which the investment is being made—who exchanges his ownership of a local business against a share in the ownership of a multinational one.

But this is as incompatible with the "verities" of international economic theory as the takeover wave or the emergence of the new entrepreneurs is incompatible with the received wisdom of the doctrine of "managerialism." It is not only Keynesian theory that assumes the fiscal and financial sovereignty of the national state; all economic theory these last fifty years has done that. But no sooner did the most powerful state, the United States, exercise this sovereignty than, totally unplanned, the "Euro-dollar market" sprang up through which the Europeans channeled their capital into American-based multinational companies, thus defeating the United States government and their own governments as well.

It can be argued that the new mergers, whether diversification or takeover, are "temporary phenomena" and also that many of these were neither sound nor desirable. It can be argued that the new entrepreneurs were simply the froth on a stock market boom. It can be argued—as General de Gaulle did—that the multinational company is an abomination and a flagrant violation of the immutable laws of politics and history. There is, indeed, little doubt that a good many of the conglomerates were jerry-built, the result of financial sleight of hand and "asset exploitation" rather than "asset management." A good many of the new businesses, the shares of which were eagerly bought up by "sophisticated investors," were certainly fad and folly, and little else. One need not be an ultranationalist to see some real problems in multinational companies who have revenues larger than the national income of some of the countries they operate in, and who make their decisions in headquarters that are far away from the countries that depend on them and far beyond the reach of these countries' governments.

But that these developments of the last ten years may not be to everybody's liking, that they may not all have been desirable or sound, and that not all their results may be enduring does not alter two facts. They happened; and they have fundamentally affected economic structure, domestically (in every developed country) and internationally. Whether one likes them or not—and I personally have great reservations—one must ask what explains them. And one must assume that such far-reaching changes, which, moreover, fly in the face of so much we considered "knowledge" in the field, must have their causes in major shifts in the structure of the economy and in the structure of the society.

II

The developments of the last ten years are, I submit, the first responses to the emergence of two new major "mass markets": a mass market for capital and investment and a mass market for careers for educated people doing knowledge work. Like all first responses, they were, in all probability, the wrong responses or, at best, inadequate responses. But they were responses to real new challenges, and the challenges will not go away.

Every economy, whatever its structure or its level of development, has three dimensions. One dimension is that of goods and services, their production, distribution, and consumption. It is the "here and now" of the economy. The second dimension is that of allocating resources to the future, the dimension that deals with the formation and investment of capital. Finally, in every economy, there is work, there are jobs, and there are careers.

Each of these dimensions, at whatever level the economy operates, needs some way of allocating resources.

But it is only when an economy has reached the stage where it produces, in each dimension, more than the merest subsistence that choices begin to become important. Only then can there be a "market" or "planning." And a "mass market" can come into being only when there is enough supply in each area for large numbers of people to make meaningful choices.

The mass-market level in respect to the first dimension, the production and consumption of goods and services, was not reached anywhere in the world until about two hundred years ago. This was the essence of what the textbooks in economic history call the "commercial revolution" of the early eighteenth century, concentrated, of course, until the Napoleonic Wars almost exclusively in England and the Low Countries. But even in England the well-being of the population was still measured far into the nineteenth century, indeed, until the repeal of the Corn Laws in 1846, by the fluctuations in the price of the standard loaf of bread. Even in England, in other words, the great mass of the people, until well into the nineteenth century, had very little choice in respect to goods and services and were not yet capable of forming a mass market. They were determined by the supply rather than choosing from it. In Japan, by the way, the price of the basic rice unit remained the standard measurement of economic welfare until the time of World War I.

The emergence of the mass market in goods and services in the eighteenth century explains why there suddenly arose a discipline of economics. For until there is meaningful choice, there can be no economics.

But early economics, whether classical, neoclassical, or Marxist, did not produce a theory of money, capital and investment, let alone a theory for the dimension of work and jobs. There was no need for this because supply in these two areas had not yet reached the level where there was significant choice except marginally. There have been markets for credit for many centuries. They go back all the way to the great fairs of the late Middle Ages. Still, as late as the early 1930's, when I was a young investment banker in London, then still the financial capital of the world, it was axiomatic that no more than one out of every three or four hundred people, even in a highly developed economy, had enough savings to invest in anything but those financial necessities, life insurance and the mortgage on his home. In other words, even in highly developed economies, as late as 1930 the great mass of the people, in respect to capital and investment, were determined by the available supply rather than capable of allocating it, to any significant degree, among choices. And all earlier economic theory, from Adam Smith through Marx to Marshall at the turn of the century, assumed essentially that jobs were, by necessity, scarcer than available labor supply, whether this was being expressed in Marx's *"Iron Law of Wages"* or in the far more elegant but essentially identical equations of "Marginal Utility."

Economics, right through the nineteenth century, could treat capital on the one hand and labor on the other hand as being determined by the "real" economy, the economy of goods and services, and thus having no autonomy and no dynamics of their own.

Keynes as a Symptom

In this perspective, the development of monetary economics, culminating in the work of Keynes in the early thirties, bespoke a major structural change: the emergence of the capital and investment dimension of the economy into a true market system in which substantial numbers of people have choices. For Keynes, and even more for such post-Keynesians as Milton Friedman today, the capital and investment dimension is the "real" economy, with goods and services as much dependent on it as in earlier economics capital and investment were seen as dependent on the goods-and-services dimension.

When Keynes published his great works, in the early thirties, capital and investment were still very much a "specialty mass market" of a small minority, though one very much bigger than it had been only a few decades earlier. When the New York Stock Exchange announced around 1945 that it aimed at "mass ownership of shares," it had in mind raising the proportion of share owners from some 1 percent to 3 or 4 percent of the American population. The figure now stands at 80 percent or higher. We have not "nationalized" capital, but we have "socialized" it in this country. The instrument through which the largest number of Americans own the "means of production" today are financial intermediaries—mutual funds and pension funds, above all. They are the real "capitalists." These institutions are, so to speak, the "professional buyers" for the great mass of financial consumers. They are meant when the Securities Exchange Commission and the Stock Exchange talk of "sophisticated investors." And they owned, at the end of 1969, between 45 and 50 percent of the equity capital of American business. As a result, financial ownership in this country is now distributed roughly in the same degree of equality—or inequality—in which consumption of goods and services was distributed in the early twenties in the first great "mass-consumption" boom. The wealthy, that is, the top 20 percent of the population, probably still own or control more than 40 percent of the equity in American business. The poor, the bottom 10 percent of the population, do not, of course, own any equity capital at all. The middle group, comprising some 70 percent of the population, owns directly or through its intermediaries about half of the financial assets. The rest, by the way, is largely foreign-owned, again mostly by institutions.

An example of this development and of its speed is the pension fund of the American college teachers, the Teachers Insurance and Annuity Association. It manages the retirement funds for 300,000 people—for the great majority of the college teachers in the private colleges and universities and increasingly for teachers in state and municipal institutions as well. Founded in the early twenties, it took Teachers fifty years to build up a pension fund of about $2.5 billion in conventional annuities, invested mostly in bonds, mortgages, and other traditional life insurance investments. Then, less than twenty years ago, in 1952, Teachers added a College Retirement Equity Fund, that is, a common-stock mutual fund, and began to offer it to its participating college teachers. Today this fund manages a portfolio of common stock of well over a billion dollars—at which, incidentally, it is still among the medium-sized rather than the large portfolio managers. And almost all the participants in the conventional fixed-payment annuity pension fund have also become common-stock investors through the College Retirement Equity Fund.

What is rarely understood is that this is not just a quantitative expansion of the pool of investors. This is a qualitative change in their character. They are not "capitalists." They are "investors." Their main stake in the economy is not through their investments, but through their job and the income therefrom. What they can invest in the economy is, so to speak, "extra." They are not dependent on it. And therefore they can afford to take risks with the money.

In fact, the most rational economic behavior for this group is to be a "speculator," that is, to invest for capital gains rather than for income and security. The middle-income group, earning between $8,000 and $20,000 a year, is perhaps most conscious of the tax burden of our steeply progressive income tax and least capable of easing it through tax loopholes and tax dodges, precisely because its income is wages and salaries. Additional income from investments, therefore, holds out little incentive to it. Growth, that is, the opportunity for capital appreciation, is worth almost twice as much for this group, in terms of real income, as additional income would be. And this group, which is in effect today's majority stockholder, is, therefore, singularly receptive to the promise of "asset management" and to "maximization of the value of the stockholders' investment"—and perfectly willing to accept considerable risk in order to attain capital gain and "asset maximization."

At first sight, this would not seem to apply to one large segment of these new investors: the pension funds. Traditionally, pension funds have been ultra-conservative investors, if only because they predictably need an income in the future to pay off their pensioners. But today's pension fund, especially the pension fund in industry, has been set up in such a manner that the one and only thing that is predictable is that the income needed in the future cannot be obtained from the contributions paid in the present, but must be supplemented by appreciable capital gains. In the first place, the typical American pension plan bases a man's pension on his income during the last five years of working life; and in a period of steadily rising wages. This means that contributions to a pension fund based on present average wages will not be adequate for future pension needs. In addition, pensions increasingly are being adjusted retroactively for changes in the cost of living or in the wage level of the men still at work. In a period of rising wages and inflationary prices, future pension liability must, therefore, greatly exceed anything that present contributions can provide. Pension funds, therefore, in order to live up to the responsibilities under employment and labor contracts, simply have to invest for capital gains. The greater the inflationary pressure in the economy becomes, the more will "speculative" behavior appear as the only truly "conservative" line of action for a pension fund, and what used to be considered conservative behavior will appear as reckless and, indeed, irresponsible "speculation." The only way in which the typical pension fund of today can possibly hope to discharge its obligations is by investing in growth and capital gains; the only way it can possibly be true to its trust is by backing "asset management."

Thus, the new mass market for capital and investment must mean something very different by "performance" or by "value" than what either the traditional capitalist or the professional manager means by these words. These new expectations may appear speculative in traditional terms. But they reflect the economic realities of the new financial mass consumer, the employed middle class. They may be unrealistic; but they are perfectly rational.

A Mass Market for Careers

Perhaps more important in the long run, and far less seen by the general public as yet, is the emergence of the mass market in careers for educated knowledge workers, that is, for people with a college education. Only forty years ago, on the eve of the Great Depression, there were very few careers in which one could really get paid for putting knowledge to work. Essentially these were the old professions, the ministry, teaching, medicine, and the law, to which, in the early years of the century, engineering had been added. The Yale graduates who were hired by Wall Street houses in the twenties to be bond salesmen were not hired for their knowledge; they were hired for their connections.

The supply of men and women with advanced education and prepared for knowledge work has increased almost twentyfold since 1920. But the supply of job and career opportunities for them has increased even faster. In the last ten years the career choices for knowledge people have seemed to be practically limitless. In fact, that the young people today have to make choices of this kind, and without any real information, is surely an important contributing factor to the unrest on the college campus. The young people are literally overwhelmed by all the opportunities that clamor, "Take me."

The emergence of genuine choice for careers and jobs is so novel that there is no economic theory of a genuine "job market" so far. But there is the first sign that the old assumptions are being discarded by the economists. For the last ten years the "Phillips curve" has found increasing application in economic analysis. Named after an English economist who developed it, this curve relates inflation and employment. It attempts to identify the minimum unemployment needed in a given country to avoid inflationary pressures. It assumes, in other words, unlike any earlier economic theorem, that a shortage of men rather than a shortage of jobs is the "norm" of an economy and that the labor market, far from being the corollary of the market of goods and services and of the market for money and capital, is in itself a major force molding the economy and shaping its other two major dimensions. But this is only a beginning. There is so far not even the first sign of a true economic theory of the market for work, jobs, and careers, let alone of anything comparable to Keynes's overarching model.

Seventy years ago it was still true even in this country, as it is still true for the masses in the underdeveloped world, that most people had no choice of occupation. Even where jobs were plentiful rather than scarce, the job available to a young man and his job from there on throughout his life was largely determined by his father's occupation and his family's economic position. For the great mass of people this simply meant that son followed father; and in most cases, of course, that son followed father behind the plow. A few very gifted or very lucky or very enterprising ones could break out of this pattern, and in that respect, of course, American society has always had more mobility than any other. But even in American society, such mobility was the exception.

Today, no matter how unequally educational opportunities are distributed, the majority of the young have access to a college education and, with it, access to mobility and meaningful career choice.

Again, this is even more a qualitative than a quantitative shift. It is a shift from "looking for a job" to "expecting a career," from "making a living" to "wanting to make a contribution." The first employee indoctrination brochures, written by the early personnel men in the boom years of the mid-twenties when labor was scarce, usually started out with the question, "What does the job demand of you?" Today's recruitment brochures usually start out with the question, "What can you expect from the XYZ Company?" Where it was assumed, even at the peak of an earlier boom, that men were hunting for jobs, it is now assumed that jobs are hunting for men and that, therefore, they have increasingly to satisfy the values, demands, expectations, and aspirations of the knowledge worker. And, of course, the young knowledge worker is also the typical "investor" of the new mass-capital market. This explains in large measure what to so many observers, especially the older businessmen, appears as total contradiction, indeed, as glaring hypocrisy, in his behavior. He loudly proclaims his "idealism" and his demand for a "career that makes a contribution." But in the next breath he asks the company recruiter, "And what stock options do I get and how much are they worth?" But given his realities, there is no contradiction in those two expectations to the young knowledge worker—or at least not more than most people can comfortably live with.

We have been told repeatedly during the last few years that the academician no longer owes "loyalty" to his college, but instead to his "profession" or "discipline." But this is true of all other knowledge workers today. They have shifted from focus on the "job" to focus on the "career." The young academician is only the most visible of the lot, or perhaps only the one most visible to other academicians who write books.

But to see the full impact of this change, we may best go outside the United States to Japan and where mobility has been taken for granted, way beyond its actual incidence. For in Japan, especially for professional and managerial people, a job has long meant "lifetime employment." The young man graduating from college was, so to speak, "adopted" into a "clan," whether government ministry, business enterprise, or university, where he then stayed automatically the rest of his life. Both leaving one's employer and being let go by him were as carefully circumscribed as is divorce in the Roman Catholic Canon Law. One could leave for only one reason: to take over the business of one's old or ailing father. One could be let go only for very serious misbehavior or actual crime. These are still the official rules, but they are no longer being observed by the young, educated Japanese. They do, indeed, expect the organization they join to owe them lifetime employment. But they themselves demand increasingly the right to move—with proper punctilio, of course. Increasingly they expect—which is even more of an innovation—a "career ladder" appropriate to their education and qualifications rather than advancement by seniority. SONY was the first Japanese company to realize this. Skillfully blending Japanese traditions and the new values of the young knowledge worker, it combines the security of lifetime employment for those who want it with an open hiring policy for those who wish to leave their old employers. It also combines pay and title by seniority with job assignments and career ladders according to qualifications and personal choice. This is probably the real "secret" of SONY's rapid growth and its success against determined resistance to the brash newcomer by the whole force of the Japanese "establishment." It may well be an example from which we, in the West, can learn a good deal.

The First Responses

The structural changes in the economy, at home and abroad, can be understood as first responses to the wants and values of these new mass markets in investment and careers.

The diversification mergers were defensive responses aimed at shoring up an eroding competitive position in these two new mass markets. In essence they hardly differ from the similarly defensive mergers of the twenties, except that what forced formerly independent companies to band together at heavy cost in management position and status was growing deterioration and weakness in the capital and careers markets rather than, as in the twenties, in the market for goods and services. Many of the public announcements accompanying these mergers said so very clearly. The merger was undertaken because the combined companies expected to have "greater ability to raise capital," or "greater borrowing power," or "high value for their share owners"—as well as "greater career opportunities for our managers," or "more scope for our young people." Indeed, that a company can finance itself out of "retained earnings" is, in terms of the rationality of the new markets, a major weakness rather than a strength. It does not mean that a company is secure, but that it is stagnant. It may offer income to its owners, but not capital growth. It may offer jobs for middle-aged functionaries, but not opportunities and careers to young knowledge workers (let alone tempting stock options). Many of the diversification mergers were, of course, only face lifting; the new merged company is just twice as old, twice as bureaucratic, and twice as "undynamic" as each of the original businesses was before the merger. But in a good many other cases the diversification merger did, indeed, provide the "synergism" the merger announcement talked about—but in respect to their performance capacity and ability to compete on the new mass markets, rather than in the markets for goods and services.

By contrast, the "conglomerate" created by the takeover merger is an offensive response to the realities and demands of the new mass markets. "Asset management" is simply another term for the design of a "product" that fits the values and demands of the new investors and of their new investing institutions. For asset management aims at increasing the value of a business by sloughing off the obsolete and unproductive old parts and adding on to it new parts capable of rapid growth. In effect, the men who built the conglomerates by takeover tactics and financial manipulation presented themselves to the new investor as experts in obtaining the largest capital gain in the shortest period, and promised continuing capital gain and asset growth year after year in the future. These men understood that the new investors believe they can afford to take risks and, indeed, want to take them. The conglomerate builders understood that "profitability," which used to mean "return on capital," has come to mean "price earnings ratio" for the new investors, at least for the time being.

At the same time, the takeover merger also "packaged" for the careers market, though by no means to the same extent. It offered a small number of people opportunities at high risk for great gain, through stock options, for instance. It appealed to a good many young people who, in their present positions in established, old, solid companies, had a "job" rather than a "career," let alone a chance to become entrepreneurs themselves.

Equally—indeed, more than equally—the new entrepreneurs with their new growth businesses also represented a response to the demands and values of these two new mass markets. They appealed to two quite different "consumers" in the new capital market, with different preferences and values. They first sold to the sophisticated investor, that is, to the manager of the funds of the new financial consumers, the promise of rapid growth and with it of great appreciation of values. But many of them also realized that old-established, large businesses with limited growth opportunities in their scope can afford to pay very high prices for "glamour," that is, for adding smaller businesses with high growth potential: it gives them marketability in the new mass markets. The new entrepreneurs, in many cases, therefore, based their whole strategy on selling out to a "giant" as soon as their venture had become profitable.

Above all, the new entrepreneurs represent a response to the new mass market for careers. They did not, as a rule, go after new graduates; they let somebody else train them and weed them out. They staffed their key positions—franchise owners, executives, editors, research managers, investment specialists, and so on—largely with men who had not found in their first jobs, whether in industry, in government, or in the university, the career opportunities that appealed to them. Indeed, these new businesses would not have been possible had there not been a large and growing number of men whose demands for career opportunities the existing secure, safe, and even well-paid jobs with the old employers could not satisfy.

The multinational corporation and the offshore investment trust are proof that these two new mass markets are not confined to America but, in varying degrees, are common to all developed countries. The U.S.-based multinational corporation which uses European capital to buy up European businesses packages investment for the new foreign investor just as the diversification merger or the takeover merger packages investment for the new American investor. It gives the European investor a chance for capital gain. It gives him marketability of his investment, where capital markets for most European securities in European countries are restricted to the point of being illiquid; and, perhaps most importantly, it gives him public disclosure of performance and results, first imposed on United States corporations by the securities legislation of the thirties—and thus the information for financial and economic analysis on which sophisticated investors, and especially fiduciaries for other people's money, must and do insist. It is no accident that the European and even the Japanese companies that have been going multinational have immediately had to adopt standards of disclosure which, while still inadequate by American criteria, are "indecent exposure" in a European, let alone a Japanese, business setting.

But, above all, the multinationals exploited the new career markets world-wide. Where, in Europe especially, business still looks upon jobs as favors to be handed out, i.e., still acts on the assumption that even general managers are "hired hands" of whom there is an unlimited supply, the multinationals had to recruit and had to start out with the assumption that they had to create careers attractive to highly educated young men who had plenty of career choices. On this their success rests in large measure. In many cases the multinationals have become within a decade the industry leader in many countries, not by acquisition, but by developing new businesses from scratch. This, it is now generally accepted, is a managerial rather than a technological or financial achievement; but this means, specifically, ability to attract good young people, to hold them, and to allow them to go to work productively.

III

Takeovers, conglomerate building, even new growth ventures, have lost their bloom and their attraction. They became the first victim of the stock market collapse of 1969–1970. Actually it was the investors' disenchantment with these darlings of the boom that set off the stock market slide in the first place.

The disenchantment was bound to happen; and this is not hindsight. It was quite clear from the very beginning that the investors who supported takeovers and went in for the new and untried growth ventures were naïve to the point of being gullible (as well as greedy) rather than "sophisticated." It is plain silly to believe, as they did, that anything, and particularly a business, can grow forever at a high growth rate. If there is one thing certain, it is that any growth curve will flatten out, and that it will flatten out the faster the steeper its initial rise. If there is one thing predictable in the case of a young and rapidly growing venture, it is a severe crisis, caused by the very growth of the business and the resulting strain on management's knowledge and ability to control. The faster a new business grows, the more severe will its "adolescent identity crisis" be. Until this crisis has been weathered—and that often requires changes at the highest management level—no one really knows whether the business is viable, let alone whether it can resume its growth.

Some of the conglomerates, though by no means all of them, have actually done quite well; some of the "asset managers" really managed assets and did succeed in making ailing businesses sound again and tired old businesses again able to venture, to innovate, and to perform. A large number—perhaps the majority—of the new growth ventures met and successfully overcame their growth crisis. But a faith in magic is not maintained by statistical averages. And the faith in the conglomerate, in the creation of productive wealth by financial manipulaton and takeover, and in growth ventures that will succeed simply because they are in the currently fashionable industry, was magic rather than sophistication. It could not survive even the slightest shadow of doubt, not to mention real setbacks.

As a result of this loss of faith, many of the conglomerates—all those that depended primarily on the "financial leverage" of a continuous rise in the price of their stock—are in deep trouble. The most spectacular performer of a few years back, Ling-Temco-Vought, has actually had to sell off some of its earlier acquisitions, and others will surely have to do the same. "Deconglomeration" may be the "in" word in the next few years. The most spectacular of the multinational asset managers, Bernard Cornfeld's Investors Overseas Service, despite its almost $2.5 billion in assets, ran into very heavy weather in early 1970, as investors in its numerous affiliates and subsidiaries began to lose faith and Cornfeld himself had to resign.

Even the multinational manufacturing companies, though mostly powerful, solidly built companies with a strong base in their home market, face difficult times. Resistance against them on the part of national governments is growing rapidly, with the United States government—Anti-Trust, the Congress, the Internal Revenue, currency and investment restrictions, etc.—even more narrowly restrictive, perhaps, than the openly nationalistic countries.

The Inventory Crisis in the Careers Market

The mass market for careers will, at the same time, also go through a period of readjustment—will, indeed, face its own first "cyclical readjustment"—not because of economic conditions, not because of any cutback in governmental funds, but because of demography. The *supply* of college graduates is, obviously, heavily dependent on the number of babies born twenty-two years earlier. The *demand* in one important market segment, teaching, is, however, heavily dependent on the number of babies born six to seventeen years earlier. Or to put it differently, young people have to be students and have to have teachers *before* they can themselves become available as teachers. If, therefore, there is a sudden sharp upturn in the number of babies born, there will be, a decade later, a sharp increase in demand over supply with a resultant "inflationary pressure" on the career market. And if there is a sharp downturn in babies born, there will be, a decade later, "deflationary pressures." In fact, demographics (to which economists pay normally no attention) are the true dynamics of the "career market."

The demographic pressures on the American career market are just about to reverse themselves. Ten years ago the available new college graduates were still the "babies" of the very low birth years of the late thirties. But since the post-World War II "baby boom" had exploded in 1946 and kept growing thereafter for ten years, the demand for teachers was at record height in 1960, with a resulting excess of demand over supply, especially for women graduates, that created severe inflationary pressures. Now, however, and for the next ten years, the situation will be the reverse: the supply will come from the very high birth-rate years 1946–1957—with the babies of 1957, the peak year, furnishing the graduating college class of 1980. The demand will come from the years after 1957 when the number of births at first remained even for a few years, and then, after 1960, began to fall quite sharply. Elementary-school enrollment, in other words, is already going down significantly. Junior high-school and high-school enrollment will start to go down in 1972 or 1973; college enrollment may well go down from 1977 or 1978 on; even to keep enrollment at its present levels would require a significant increase in the percentage of youngsters going to college. The career market of the last ten years was heavily influenced by one of the sharpest jumps in the number of births ever recorded: more than 50 percent from the 2.8 million babies born in 1948 to the 4.3 million born in 1957. The career market of the seventies will be heavily influenced by a drop (much less sharp, but still almost unprecedented) in the number of babies born between 1957 and 1967—a drop by one-fifth from 4.3 million to 3.5 million.

In some ways this is good news. For it means that other segments of the economy will not be as grossly undersupplied with educated people as they have been these last ten years; health care is the most important example. But in the first place, the total pressure on the career market will go down. Where there were several jobs hunting for a graduate these last ten years—when the number of graduates was still held back by the low baby figures of the thirties and early forties—graduates and jobs will more nearly be in balance the next ten years, even if there is a boom in the economy. Graduates will have to learn again to hunt for jobs. Above all, however, there is what in the goods-and-services economy is called an "inventory imbalance." Teaching, having had the greatest and most crying shortage, has been heavily staffed with young people. This is true not only in elementary and high schools but in college teaching as well (even though colleges, unlike elementary and high schools, can "stretch" the teaching supply by having large classes supplemented by "teaching assistants," where public schools have class-size limits imposed on them by law). William Baumol of Princeton, the leading economist of American higher education, points out that in the sixties American colleges hired five new and young teachers for every old teacher who retired or died. As a result, there will be a sharp drop in the proportion of teachers who in the next ten and twenty years reach retirement age or die, while the total number of students will no longer go up, at least not sharply. Baumol foresees that the colleges will have to hire only three new teachers for every one who retires and dies in the seventies, and only one for each vacancy in the eighties. In the lower schools the imbalance will be even greater. Geoffrey H. Moore, the Commissioner of Labor Statistics, and Conrad Taeuber, Associate Director of the Census, calculate that there will be 4.2 million women graduates between now and 1980 who will, on the basis of past experience, look for a teaching job—and only 2.4 million openings for teachers in elementary and high schools.

The present college students, undergraduate and graduate, are heavily, indeed preponderantly, oriented toward teaching, which is, of course, what the liberal arts degree concretely prepares for. They are not training for the jobs that will be there to be filled: health-care technology; professional and managerial jobs in local government (where most of the educated personnel came in during the Depression or the early forties and are nearing, if not reaching, retirement age); and jobs in business, especially the highly technical "systems" jobs needed for work on environment and ecology. The students today complain that college tries to fashion them for jobs in the "military-industrial complex." They would have a much stronger case complaining that they are being grossly misled—especially by the young faculty which, understandably, thinks that the last ten years were "normal" (whereas they were unbelievably "abnormal")—into preparing themselves for jobs that will not be available.

The shocked surprise in the spring of 1970, when the graduating class suddenly found that they had to go out and look for jobs, may thus have been the first sign of a typical "inventory crisis," which always takes everybody by surprise. Whatever the economic climate, the next few years will be years of sharp readjustment in the careers market. The career boom of the sixties is as much a thing of the past as the stock market boom in takeovers, conglomerates, and growth ventures.

But the new mass markets will remain the realities of the economy, in the United States as well as in all other developed countries. Indeed, more difficult times—times in which sleight of hand and manipulation are not readily mistaken for performance—will only make greater demands on the development and management of institutions to serve these new markets, their customers, and their producers.

The "fiduciaries"—investment trusts, bank-managed funds, and pension funds—will continue to grow as the dominant forces in the markets for capital and investment. Their importance is going to increase, rather than decrease, if the economy no longer can count on automatic inflation. For then the difference between the "sound" and the "unsound" investment, between the growth company and the stagnant or decaying one, between the well-managed business and the one run by chief clerks, really counts. And then the investor, who, being employed and working for a living, has neither time nor knowledge to pick investments for himself, needs an "informed buyer" far more than in boom times. He then has to insist on getting as his investment manager the sophisticated investor which so far, in a great many cases, has only been promised to him.

It is surely symptomatic that, when Investors Overseas Services ran into trouble in May 1970, the Rothschilds were offering to take over the floundering investment giant. For the Rothschilds have a unique record for turning into a permanent major institution a financial innovation when, as the Rothschilds had predicted from the first, the founder overreaches himself. This knack, demonstrated again and again in the 170 years of their history, is probably one explanation of the longevity record the Rothschilds hold as a major financial power, outlasting by a good many years such earlier money dynasties as Medici and Fuggers, not to mention the one-generation mayflies of finance—the Morgans, for instance—which America has so far spawned.

"Asset management" may be altogether more needed than before and become far more productive in periods of stable, let alone of declining, business. Then it is particularly important, for the health of the economy as well as for the welfare of employees, communities, and shareholders, that a company's assets be employed most productively. Then it is important, above all, that managements which, because of sloth, lack of imagination, or lack of competence, undermanage or mismanage the assets in their keeping, be replaced by managements that can restore a company's capacity to perform.

This new asset management would, however, not build conglomerates, that is, heterogeneous business empires. Rather one can predict it will redeploy resources—abandon unproductive activities, for instance; it will bring in competent management, and it will then turn back a sound company to public ownership. Indeed, some such new asset managers have already begun to appear: some buying a floundering and undermanaged company with the intention of reselling it eventually as a sound and profitable business, some working for the present owners on a fee or bonus basis.

Altogether, the trends that characterized the financial markets of the sixties are likely to become more rather than less dominant, even though actual forms may well change. The market is likely to be increasingly a market of investors rather than of capitalists, and that means of people primarily interested in asset growth rather than in income. It will also, predictably, become an increasingly competitive market, the more informed the buyers become. It is already in all probability more competitive—and certainly far less concentrated—than the market for many goods and services. Companies needing money (and that means eventually every company) will therefore have to work on making themselves "marketable" to this new mass market. It is most unlikely that concern for financial performance and financial marketability will decrease in the next ten or fifteen years. No matter what the New Left says (indeed, no matter what economic doctrine the country accepts), concern for profit will predictably not go down during the next decade, nor will concern with capital gains. The most we can expect is that a stable dollar and control of inflation may lessen the need of the fiduciaries, and especially of the pension funds, for continuing growth in the paper value of their assets.

Making the Careers Market Work

In respect to the second of the new mass markets, the one for careers, a period of "inventory adjustment" will create a need for institutions adequate to serve the market. The market needs institutions which will play a role analogous to that of the "fiduciaries" in the mass market for capital and investment, i.e., intermediaries who are the informed buyers for the mass consumer, the educated people looking for career opportunities, but also the informed buyer for the mass producers of job opportunities, the employing organizations.

These will have to be market institutions. The career and work dimension, especially as far as educated people looking for careers in knowledge work are concerned, is incapable of being "planned." Indeed, the Soviet attempt to plan for individual careers and to direct young people accordingly has been the most dismal failure of Russian planning—even greater than the failure in agriculture. In the first place, the lead time needed to "develop the resource," that is, to train and educate for specific careers, is much longer than the time span for which we can project future needs, which, in general, runs to no more than six to ten years. In addition, planning here runs up against a simple law of mathematics: the impossibility of predicting the unique event (e.g., the toss of any single coin) from a large-number probability (e.g., the distribution of 1,000 tosses of a coin). And individual careers are "unique events" far more even than tosses of a coin. Finally, of course, planning careers means coercion and regimentation of the individual, and there is, fortunately, little reason to believe that our young educated people would enjoy this for their entire lives any more than they have traditionally enjoyed such "planning" for the period of military service, which is, after all, limited.

Yet we need to be able to provide information, guidance, and placement. This is particularly important as eight to twelve years hence we may well face another demographic shift: higher birth years are almost inevitable as the babies of the baby boom who now throng our college campuses marry and have children themselves. Beginning in the late seventies, the number of children in school should thus start to rise again. But, judging by past experience, this will be precisely the moment when the present guides of young people, especially faculties, will have adjusted their thinking to the changes in the opposite direction that are taking place now.

There are the beginnings of such institutions. The last fifteen or twenty years have seen the emergence of the "head-hunter," or "executive recruiter" (to give him his official name), the firm which finds executives in mid-career for new jobs. These firms are most active in business, of course. But there are some who find academic administrators, some specializing in clergymen to fill vacant pulpits, and others working exclusively as head-hunters for hospital administrators. There are also, of course, the college recruiters of the major companies: something which was literally unheard of thirty years ago, but today is considered as much of a necessity in a large business as a research laboratory or a sales department. And there are a few firms which actually give career advice to the individual, and especially to the mature individual who wonders whether he is in the right career path or whether he should change. Yet these are only first beginnings, comparable to the first investment trusts as they developed forty years ago. They indicate what we need rather than themselves satisfy the need. Whether tomorrow's institutions in this new market will be "profit" or "not for profit," no one can predict; it may also not greatly matter. But the new "fiduciaries" who are the informed buyers in the careers market are likely to be a major growth industry of the seventies.

Altogether the market for careers, in the long run, will become increasingly competitive. It will be increasingly important for the "consumer," the educated knowledge worker, to be able to make informed choices. It will be increasingly important for any institution to be able to attract the kind of people it wants and needs and to offer them what they need and look to. It will increasingly be important for any institution, business or nonbusiness, to be able to "market" its job opportunities. It will, therefore, increasingly be necessary for organizations to match the available job and career opportunities to the needs, demands, and wants of the customers. Perhaps one can sum this up by saying that, during the last fifteen years, there has been great emphasis on "manager development" aimed largely at making managers better capable to serve their organizations, whether business, government, or hospital. In the future, we are likely to balance this with growing emphasis on "organization development" aimed at making organizations capable of satisfying the aspirations of their career customers, the knowledge workers.

IV

The new mass markets will predictably generate new problems of public policy. Three, in particular, are already clearly visible, and for none do we have an answer; we have not even tackled our homework yet for any of them.

The most *novel* of these problems will be the role and responsibility of the new financial powers, the "fiduciaries" of the financial mass consumer who are the real "owners" of today.

Majority ownership of America's (and Europe's) businesses will increasingly be in the hands of people who are neither owners nor managers, but trustees. What should their role be? It can be argued—in fact, it has been argued by some of the most thoughtful fund managers—that, being trustees, they cannot and must not interfere in management. If they do not like a management, they sell their shares in the company; but they have no authority from anyone to exercise control. But if these institutions do not exercise control, who does—or can? Either management is uncontrolled and uncontrollable, or the policing function falls to the takeover entrepreneur. Clearly neither solution is acceptable. Yet no new one is in sight.

But the problem can also no longer be avoided. Indeed, it has been raised—though, as is the rule with new problems, in the least expected form. Nader's Raiders—the young lawyers who work under and with Ralph Nader of automotive-safety fame—raised it when they asked, in the spring of 1970, that foundations, endowments, and other trustees withhold their proxies from General Motors management and vote their shares instead for a series of changes in the company's Board, its policies, and its management which Nader's Raiders hold to be in the public interest. Almost at the same time, though, of course, in a totally unrelated development, the Anti-Trust Division of the Department of Justice filed suit against a very large fiduciary manager, the Continental Illinois Bank in Chicago. What the Anti-Trust Division charged was that the bank's practice—and every major bank engages in it—of having different officers of the bank sit on the boards of directors of competing companies was in violation of antitrust, even though these directors did not represent "ownership," but the shares held by the bank in trust for very large numbers of individual beneficiaries. That, in effect, Anti-Trust attacks as illegal precisely the same exercise of control and the same interference the absence of which Nader's Raiders castigate does not affect the importance and seriousness of the issue, nor the fact that nothing in our economic experience is of much help in deciding it. But it will have to be tackled, and soon. It will—indeed, should—become a major issue of public policy for a good many years.

The Multinational Company Versus the National State

The most *important* problem in its impact will be that of the multinational business.

Professor Perlmutter's prediction that, in another fifteen or twenty years, the world's manufacturing production will be in the hands of three hundred mammoth multinational companies, while widely quoted, represents an extreme rather than the most probable trend. But it is not rash to predict that within every developed non-Communist country a fifth or a quarter of total manufacturing output will be produced by companies that are multinational in their operations. Indeed, this is reality rather than forecast in ten of these countries (the United States, Great Britain, Canada, Germany, Italy, Holland, Belgium, Switzerland, Norway, and Sweden), is fast becoming reality in an eleventh (Japan), and is not yet accomplished fact in only two (France and Brazil).* This means that in the developed countries a very big part of the economy is subject to decisions made beyond the reach of the national government. But it also means, conversely, that governmental decisions in most developed countries—France and Canada being the only important exceptions—have impact far beyond the country's own borders through the effect they have on the multinationals headquartered in that country. United States antitrust laws, United States tax laws, United States restrictions on trade with Communist powers, are held by United States government authorities to bind the subsidiaries and affiliates of U.S.-based companies everywhere. No other country is quite so openly nationalistic. But other governments, too, especially those of the big countries such as France, Germany, and Japan, like to look upon "their" multinationals as instruments

*Of these, incidentally, the United States, Holland, Switzerland, and Sweden are "headquarters countries." In Germany ownership of industry by companies based abroad—mainly United States, Dutch, and Swiss—and ownership of businesses abroad by German companies roughly balance. In Japan, where the joint venture predominates (i.e., a partly foreign-owned company doing business in Japan in partnership with a Japanese company) ownership or co-ownership of businesses abroad by Japanese companies is growing so fast that Japan may soon also be in "ownership balance." Great Britain, Canada, Italy, Belgium, France, and Brazil are far more "owned" than "owning."

of their own economic policies in the world, while at the same time bitterly resenting that the subsidiaries of "foreign" multinationals on their soil are, in some measure, beyond their complete control.

This is not a problem of "capitalism." Indeed, the same ambivalence characterizes the economic relations within the Soviet Bloc. Quite clearly the multinationals which the Russians have been trying to build throughout Eastern Europe are resisted primarily for political reasons. They remove a part of the Polish, Czech, or East German economy from the decision and control of the Polish, Czech, or East German governments. Multinationals, whether "capitalist" or "Communist," put economic rationality ahead of political sovereignty.

De Gaulle's opposition to the multinationals was therefore not "anti-American." He not only opposed non-American multinational attempts, e.g., that of the Italian Fiat company to merge with Citroën, France's ailing automobile manufacturer, as vigorously as he opposed the Americans' coming in. He equally forbade French companies to become multinational themselves and to move beyond France. Indeed, de Gaulle's insistence on the congruence of political and economic sovereignty is completely consistent and the only rational policy for the problem worked out so far anywhere by anyone.

It was, however, a total, resounding failure. A larger part of the advanced sectors of French industry—computers or pharmaceuticals, for instance—is controlled by foreign multinationals than in any of the large developed countries other than Canada. France's own capital, at the same time, is paradoxically, more heavily invested in multinationals than the capital of any other of the "majors," but not in French-based multinationals making their decisions in Paris—for there are none, thanks to de Gaulle—but in the shares of foreign-based multinationals, i.e., American, Swiss, Dutch, and Swedish. And at the same time, there is no country where so many of the ablest young executives, researchers, and managers work for foreign-based companies. What defeated de Gaulle, in other words, was the pressures and preferences of the two new mass markets, especially perhaps that of the new consumers of the career market: the young, educated knowledge people.

Yet de Gaulle, with his usual clarity, at least saw the problem. The multinational corporation is by far our most effective economic instrument today and probably the one organ of economic development that actually develops. It is the one nonnationalist institution in a world shaken by nationalist delirium. But it is not a political institution itself and must not be allowed to become one. Yet it puts economic decisions beyond the effective reach of the political process and its decision makers, the national governments. This may well be exactly what we need to de-fang the nationalist monster. But national governments and their organs, whether legislative or executive, are unlikely to see it this way. And how we accommodate this tension between economic rationality and political sovereignty in the next few years will have a tremendous impact on both the economy and the working of government all around the world.

When Concentration Is Competition

But the most *difficult* problems posed by the emergence of the new markets and the new entrepreneurs are those of concentration and competition. In the other two areas, we have to find new answers. In respect to concentration and competition, we have to unlearn old ones. And that is far more difficult, especially as the old answers are being held with almost religious fervor and have become sacred chants for large groups of economists, politicians, lawyers, and businessmen.

Two concepts have guided our approaches to the problems of concentration and competition for many years: "concentration of manufacturing assets" and "concentration of market power." The measurements developed for these two aspects of economic concentration are widely accepted as giving us in conjunction both an X-ray photograph of the bony structure of our economy and reliable guides to diagnosis and treatment. But the first measurement is becoming unreliable, the second one misleading.

For a long time, from 1910 until 1960, "concentration of manufacturing assets" remained fairly constant. But according to the antitrusters it took a tremendous jump upward in the last twenty years. In 1950 the two hundred largest manufacturing companies controlled 40 percent of the country's manufacturing assets. In 1970, we are being told, the top two hundred manufacturing companies control 60 percent—the biggest increase in economic concentration ever recorded in this or any other country.

The funny thing, however, is that this tremendous concentration has not been accompanied by any increase in concentration in economic power in any single market for goods, that is, in any single market in which manufacturing companies operate. In most of these markets, concentration has probably gone down during the last twenty years. In market after market, new companies have challenged the big old companies and have taken away from them a piece here or a piece there of their traditional business. This is true whether we speak of book publishing or of pharmaceuticals, of building materials or of retail sales.

"Manufacturing assets" no longer define the concentration in the American producing economy. What is counted in this rubric includes assets shown in the balance sheets of American-domiciled businesses, wherever the assets may actually be, whether within or without the United States. In 1950 these assets were almost exclusively within the United States. Today, however, most major American companies are multinational, with at least 20 to 30 percent of their production and assets outside of the United States. One-quarter of these 60 percent, that is, 15 percentage points, should be subtracted right away from the official figure, which would bring the rate of concentration in United States manufacturing down to 45 percent.

At the same time, however, what counted as "manufacturing companies" in 1950 were largely companies that were actually manufacturing. To be sure, General Motors even then owned one of the largest finance companies, the General Motors Acceptance Corporation; but its assets were a very small fraction of total GM. Today, as a result of diversification mergers and takeover mergers, a very substantial number of companies which are still counted as "manufacturing" actually have large assets (some, the majority of their assets) outside of manufacturing, in service businesses and, above all, in finance. And in finance, "assets" are not really assets but essentially "liabilities," that is, money borrowed to be lent out immediately. Whenever a manufacturing company merged with a financial company, it acquired on its balance sheet very much larger financial assets than its own "manufacturing assets" had been, even though in terms of profitability, let alone of economic power, the manufacturing company may well have been the bigger one. From then on, however, these financial assets are considered "manufacturing assets" in the figures. When Control Data acquired Commercial Credit on December 31, 1967, it had manufacturing assets of $470 million. Commercial Credit had assets of $3 billion. The total of both, however, is now considered "manufacturing assets," since Control Data was legally the acquiring company. If the biggest of all attempted takeovers had gone through—that is, if Leasco, a computer service company, had succeeded in taking over Chemical Bank—New York Trust Company—Leasco assets of less than $800 million would have been augmented by Chemical Bank assets of $9 billion, with the combined total of almost $10 billion, however, all counted as manufacturing assets. We have, therefore, to deflate the official figure for "manufacturing assets" by at least another 10 percentage points to take out assets that should not have been counted as manufacturing assets at all. In other words, in terms of true manufacturing assets in the United States, the two hundred largest companies today almost certainly have a smaller share of manufacturing industry than they had twenty years ago.

This would bring the two sets of figures—manufacturing assets and concentration of market power—back into alignment. Yet, clearly, the conclusion that there has been no "concentration" is not plausible. For while there has been neither greater concentration of United States manufacturing assets nor greater market concentration, the diversification and takeover mergers—and the multinational expansion—have clearly produced a considerable concentration in decision-making power. They have led to the emergence of very large businesses, acting in many areas and countries, but nonetheless incorporated as one legal entity and directed by one top management.

The result, however, is often increased competition, even in the goods and services economy. And there is almost always increased competition—indeed, deconcentration—in the capital and investment economy and in the work and careers economy.

The Control Data—Commercial Credit merger increased concentration in neither the computer nor the installment-paper market. On the contrary, it made these markets more competitive by strengthening what had been the "underdogs" in both. An even more telling example is the acquisition a few years back of Folger, a rather small regional coffee blender, by Procter & Gamble. This clearly added to Procter & Gamble's bigness. Since P&G is also a leader in processed foods through its various brands of shortening, the new acquisition also added, albeit not greatly, to its market share in that industry and thereby to industrial concentration. But with the resources of Procter & Gamble behind it, Folger could reach out for national distribution. Since the national coffee market had been dominated for years by a very few brands in a typical "oligopoly" pattern, Folger's acquisition by Procter & Gamble therefore also meant significant deconcentration in one important market. What, then, were the "real" consequences: concentration or deconcentration?

We may well be drifting toward a situation in which leadership and concentration in one market—that of goods, of capital, or of careers—is the "countervailing force" for competition and deconcentration in one or both of the other markets. Surely, it is not without relevance that the most common criticism of multinationals, whether the Americans in Europe or the Europeans and Japanese in the United States, has been that their size enables them to indulge in "excessive competition."

The pressures toward this kind of concentration, which is so very different from what the term has implied traditionally, will increase rather than decrease. Technology is pushing in that direction, especially in the materials and chemicals industries. Technology is forcing Du Pont, traditionally primarily a producer of chemicals for the textile industry, e.g., synthetic fibers, to go into pharmaceuticals on the one hand and composite materials, including new combination metals, on the other hand. Technology has already forced the two big can companies, twenty years ago producers of a single product, the tin can, to become manufacturers of "packaging" which includes plastics, glass, paper products, and so on. And this, in turn, forced the largest manufacturer of paper-based packaging, Container Corporation of America, as said above, to merge with a retail and mail-order chain, Montgomery Ward, to obtain enough financial and management muscle to stand up to the new packaging giants. Another powerful force moving business toward concentration will be concern with the environment. Purity of heart by itself will not clean up the environment, whether we talk of air, water, the open spaces, or the city. It will require massive systems effort in every area, that is, companies that can mobilize major technological and economic resources across a variety of skills, disciplines, technologies, and markets.

But above all, the pressures of the new mass markets—the mass market for capital and investment and the mass market for jobs and careers—should push for continuous diversification in industry terms and diversification in geographic terms.

We will, therefore, have to think through what kind of diversification is desirable, productive, and rational and what is simply financial manipulation and empire building. What kind makes the economy more open, more flexible, more competitive, and what kind furthers concentration and monopoly? Which one creates enterprises that are more manageable and perform better, and which one creates managerial monstrosities?

What we should want is reasonably clear. We want diversification rather than diffusion. We want federalism rather than either centralized tyranny or dispersion. We want asset management rather than financial manipulation. But into which of these categories a given structure falls is by no means clear. Indeed, it is not even clear to the antitrusters, who are sharply split between those who accept and, indeed, welcome conglomerates as leading to increased competition, and those who bitterly oppose them as producing increased concentration. This issue predictably will be one of the main concerns of the next ten years, in the United States as well as abroad. That there is no "right" decision is not so important; there rarely is for problems of this kind. But that the old and accepted concepts and measurements are no longer appropriate is going to make the going rough. And that we will have to learn to "trade off," that is, to balance concentration in one economic dimension with competition in another, not only goes against the grain of decision makers, whether economists or politicians, businessmen or bureaucrats; they all, understandably, also resent and resist such complexity.

The economic developments of the last ten years signify more than a change in economic structure. They changed the structure of society. They changed economic reality. This will require new thinking and the sloughing off of a great many traditional concepts, ideas, and policies in respect to monopoly, concentration, and competition, for instance, and in respect to the relationship between world economy and nation-state. It will require the development both of new theoretical understanding and of new policy concepts. For so far we have no economic theory that embraces or even connects the three dimensions of the economy and thus integrates the new mass markets of capital and investment and of jobs and careers with the old mass market of goods and services, prices and productivity. The specific developments that characterized the sixties may well have been temporary phenomena, never to recur. The developments of which they were the first expression and the visible symptom have only begun.

CHAPTER TWO

The Unfashionable Kierkegaard

I

THE KIERKEGAARD BOOM of the last few years is showing the first signs of fatigue. For Kierkegaard's sake I hope it will burst soon. The Kierkegaard of the literary boom is a fellow wit and fellow modern, distinguished from the other members of the smart set mainly by his having lived a hundred years earlier. But this Kierkegaard of the psychologists, existentialists, and assorted ex-Marxists bears hardly any resemblance to the real Kierkegaard, who cared nothing for psychology or dialectics (save to show them to be inadequate and irrelevant), but concerned himself solely with religious experience. And it is this real Kierkegaard who is meaningful for the modern world in its agony. We have neither saint nor poet to make whole the shards of our experience; in Kierkegaard we have at least a prophet.

Like all religious thinkers, Kierkegaard places in the center the question, How is human existence possible?

First published in *Sewanee Review,* Autumn, 1949.

All through the nineteenth century this question—which before had been the core of Western thought—was not only highly unfashionable; it seemed senseless and irrelevant. The era was dominated by a radically different question, How is society possible? Rousseau asked it; Hegel asked it; the classical economists asked it. Marx answered it one way; liberal Protestantism another way. But in whatever form it is asked, it must always lead to an answer which denies that human existence is possible except in society.

Rousseau formulated this answer for the whole era of progress: whatever human existence there is; whatever freedom, rights, and duties the individual has; whatever meaning there is in individual life—all is determined by society according to society's objective need of survival. The individual, in other words, is not autonomous. He is determined by society. He is free only in matters that do not matter. He has rights only because society concedes them. He has a will only if he wills what society needs. His life has meaning only insofar as it relates to the social meaning and as it fulfills itself in fulfilling the objective goal of society. There is, in short, no human existence; there is only social existence. There is no individual; there is only the citizen.

It is hardly possible to exaggerate the differences between Rousseau's "General Will," Hegel's concept of history as the unfolding of ideas, and the Marxian theory of the individual's determination through his objectively given class situation. But they all gave the same answer to the question of human existence: there is no such thing, there is no such question! Ideas and citizens exist, but no human beings. What is possible is merely the realization of ideas in and through society.

For if you start with the question, How is society possible?, without asking at the same time, How is human existence possible?, you arrive inevitably at a negative concept of individual existence and of freedom: individual freedom is then what does not disturb society. Thus freedom becomes something that has no function and no autonomous existence of its own. It becomes a convenience, a matter of political strategy, or a demagogue's catch phrase. It is nothing vital.

To define freedom as that which has no function is, however, to deny the existence of freedom. For nothing survives in society save it have a function. But the nineteenth century believed itself far too secure in the possession of freedom to realize this. Prevailing opinion failed to see that to deny the relevance of the question, How is human existence possible?, is to deny the relevance of human freedom. It actually saw in the question, How is society possible?, a key to the gospel of freedom—largely because it aimed at social equality. And the break of the old fetters of inequality appeared equivalent to the establishment of freedom.

We now have learned that the nineteenth century was mistaken. Nazism and Communism are an expensive education—a more expensive education, perhaps, than we can afford; but at least we are learning that we cannot obtain freedom if we confine ourselves to the question, How is society possible? It may be true that human existence in freedom is not possible; which is, indeed, asserted by Hitler and the Communists as well as, less openly, by all those well-meaning "social engineers" who believe in social psychology, propaganda, re-education, or administration as a means of molding and forming the individual. But at least the question, How is human existence possible?, can no longer be regarded as irrelevant. For those who profess to believe in freedom, there is no more relevant inquiry.

I am not trying to say that Kierkegaard was the only thinker during the nineteenth century who saw the direction in which Rousseau was leading the Western world. There were the Romanticists, some of whom, especially in France, sensed what was coming. There was the futile and suicidal revolt of Nietzsche—a Samson whose gigantic power pulled down nothing but himself. There was, above all, Balzac, who analyzed a society in which human existence was no longer possible and drew an Inferno more terrible than Dante's in that there is not even a Purgatory above it. But although they all asked, How is human existence possible?, none but Kierkegaard answered.

II

Kierkegaard's answer is simple: human existence is possible only in tension—in tension between man's simultaneous life as an individual in the spirit and as a citizen in society. Kierkegaard expressed the fundamental tension in a good many ways throughout his writings—most clearly and centrally when he described the tension as the consequence of man's simultaneous existence in eternity and in time. He took his formulation from St. Augustine; it is the intellectual climax of the *Confessions.* But Kierkegaard gave to the antithesis a meaning that goes far beyond St. Augustine's speculation in dialectical logic.

Existence in time is existence as a citizen in this world. In time we eat and drink and sleep, fight for conquest or for our lives, raise children and societies, succeed or fail. But in time we also die. And in time there is nothing left of us after our death. In time we do not, therefore, exist as individuals. We are only members of a species, links in a chain of generations. The species has an autonomous life in time, specific characteristics, an autonomous goal; but the member has no life, no characteristics, no aim outside the species. He exists only in and through the species. The chain has a beginning and an end, but each link serves only to tie the links of the past to the links of the future; outside the chain it is scrap iron. The wheel of time keeps on turning, but the cogs are replaceable and interchangeable. The individual's death does not end the species or society, but it ends his life in time. Human existence is not possible in time; only society is possible in time.

In eternity, however, in the realm of the spirit, "in the sight of God," to use one of Kierkegaard's favorite terms, it is society which does not exist, which is not possible. In eternity only the individual does exist. In eternity each individual is unique; he alone, all alone, without neighbors and friends, without wife and children, faces the spirit in himself. In time, in the sphere of society, no man begins at the beginning and ends at the end; each of us receives from those before us the inheritance of the ages, carries it for a tiny instant, to hand it on to those after him. But in the spirit, each man is beginning and end. Nothing his fathers have experienced can be of any help to him. In awful loneliness, in complete, unique singleness, he faces himself as if there were nothing in the entire universe but him and the spirit in himself. Human existence is thus existence on two levels—existence in tension.

It is impossible even to approximate eternity by piling up time; mere time, even infinitely more time, will still only be time. And it is also impossible to reach time by subdividing eternity; eternity is inseparable and immeasurable. Yet it is only as simultaneous existence on both planes, existence in the spirit and existence in society, that human existence is possible. St. Augustine had said that time is within eternity, created by eternity, suspended in it. But Kierkegaard knew that the two are on different planes, antithetic and incompatible with each other. And he knew it not only by logic and by introspection but by looking at the realities of nineteenth-century life.

It is this answer that constitutes the essential paradox of religious experience. To say that human existence is possible only in the tension between existence in eternity and existence in time is to say that human existence is only possible if it is impossible: what existence requires on the one level is forbidden by existence on the other. For example, existence in society requires that the society's objective need for survival determine the functions and the actions of the citizen. But existence in the spirit is possible only if there is no law and no rule except that of the person, alone with himself and with his God. Because man must exist in society, there can be no freedom except in matters that do not matter; but because man must exist in the spirit, there can be no social rule, no social constraint in matters that do matter. In society, man can exist only as a social being—as husband, father, child, neighbor, fellow citizen. In the spirit, man can exist only personally—alone, isolated, completely walled in by his own consciousness.

Existence in society requires that man accept as real the sphere of social values and beliefs, rewards and punishments. But existence in the spirit, "in the sight of God," requires that man regard all social values and beliefs as pure deception, as vanity, as untrue, invalid, and unreal. Kierkegaard quotes from Luke 14:26, "If any man come to me, and hate not his father, and mother, and wife, and children, and brethren, and sisters, yea, and his own life also, he cannot be my disciple." The Gospel of Love does not say: *love* these *less* than you love me; it says *hate.*

To say that human existence is possible only as simultaneous existence in time and in eternity is thus to say that it is possible only as one crushed between two irreconcilable ethical absolutes. And that means (if it be more than the mockery of cruel gods): human existence is possible only as existence in tragedy. It is existence in fear and trembling; in dread and anxiety; and, above all, in despair.

III

This seems a very gloomy and pessimistic view of human existence and one hardly worth having. To the nineteenth century it appeared as a pathological aberration. But let us see where the optimism of the nineteenth century leads to. For it is the analysis of this optimism and the prediction of its ultimate outcome that gave Kierkegaard's work its vision.

It was the very essence of all nineteenth-century creeds that eternity can and will be reached in time; that truth can be established in society and through majority decision; that permanence can be obtained through change. This is the belief in inevitable progress, representative of the nineteenth century and its very own contribution to human thought. You may take the creed of progress in its most naïve and therefore most engaging form—the confidence that man automatically and through his very sojourn in time becomes better, more nearly perfect, more closely approaches the divine. You may take the creed in its more sophisticated form—the dialectic schemes of Hegel and Marx in which truth unfolds itself in the synthesis between thesis and antithesis, each synthesis becoming in turn the thesis of a new dialectical integration on a higher and more nearly perfect level. Or you may take the creed in the pseudo-scientific garb of the theory of evolution through natural selection. In each form it has the same substance: a fervent belief that by piling up time we shall attain eternity; by piling up matter we shall become spirit; by piling up change we shall become permanent; by piling up trial and error we shall find truth. For Kierkegaard, the problem of the final value was one of uncompromising conflict between contradictory qualities. For the nineteenth century, the problem was one of quantity.

Where Kierkegaard conceives the human situation as essentially tragic, the nineteenth century overflowed with optimism. Not since the year 1000, when all Europe expected the Second Coming, has there been a generation which saw itself so close to the fulfillment of time as did the men of the nineteenth century. Certainly there were impurities in the existing fabric of society. But the liberal confidently expected them to be burnt away within a generation or, at the most, within a century by the daily strengthening light of reason. Progress was automatic. And though the forces of darkness and superstition might seem to gain at times, that was only a momentary illusion. "It is always darkest just before the dawn" is a truly liberal maxim (and one, incidentally, as false in its literal as in its metaphorical sense). The apogee of this naïve optimism was the book which the famous German biologist Ernst Haeckel wrote just before the turn of the century—the one which predicted that all the remaining questions would be finally and decisively answered within a generation by Darwinian biology and Newtonian physics.

It is perhaps the best commentary on the fate of the nineteenth-century creed that Haeckel's *Weltraetsel* sold by the millions in the generation of our grandfathers (and still hides out on old bookshelves) at the very moment when the universe of Darwinian biology and Newtonian physics was completely disintegrating.

To those whom the optimism of liberalism or Darwinism failed to satisfy, Marx offered the more complicated but also infinitely more profound vision of a millennium that had to come precisely because the world was so corrupt and so imperfect. His was a truly apocalyptic message in which the impossible, the attainment of the permanent perfection of the classless society, is promised precisely because it is impossible. In Marx the nineteenth-century optimism admits defeat, only to use defeat as a proof of certain victory.

In this creed of imminent perfection, in which every progress in time meant progress toward eternity, permanence, and truth, there was no room for tragedy (the conflict of two absolute forces, of two absolute laws). There was not even room for catastrophe. Everywhere in the nineteenth-century tradition the tragic is exorcised, catastrophe suppressed. A good example is the attempt—quite popular these last few years—to explain so cataclysmic a phenomenon as Hitlerism in terms of "faulty psychological adjustment," that is, as something that has nothing to do with the spirit, but is exclusively a matter of techniques. Or, in a totally different sphere, compare Shakespeare's *Antony and Cleopatra* with Flaubert's *Madame Bovary* and see how the essentially tragic "eros" becomes pure "sex"—psychology, physiology, even passion, but no longer a tragic, i.e., an insoluble, conflict. Or one might, as one of the triumphs of the attempt to suppress catastrophe, take the early Communist explanation of Nazism as "just a necessary stage in the inevitable victory of the proletariat." There you have in purest form the official creed that whatever happens in time must be good, however evil it is. Neither catastrophe nor tragedy can exist.

There has never been a century of Western history so far removed from an awareness of the tragic as the one that bequeathed to us two world wars. Just over two hundred years ago—in 1755, to be exact—the death of 15,000 people in the Lisbon earthquake was enough to bring down the tottering structure of traditional Christian belief in Europe. The contemporaries could not make sense of it; they could not reconcile this horror with the concept of an all-merciful God; they could not see any answer to a paradox of catastrophe of such magnitude. For years now we have learned daily of vastly greater destruction, of whole peoples being starved or exterminated. And it is far more difficult to comprehend these man-made catastrophes in terms of our modern rationality than it was for the eighteenth century to comprehend the earthquake of Lisbon in the terms of traditional Christianity. Yet our own catastrophes make no impression on the optimism of those thousands of committees that are dedicated to the belief that permanent peace and prosperity will "inevitably" issue from today's horrors. To be sure, they are aware of the facts and duly outraged by them. But they refuse to see them as catastrophes. They have been trained to deny the existence of tragedy.

IV

Yet however successful the nineteenth century was in suppressing the tragic, there is one fact that could not be suppressed, one fact that remains outside of time: death. It is the one fact that cannot be made general, but remains unique; the one fact that cannot be socialized, but remains personal. The nineteenth century made every effort to strip death of its individual, unique, and qualitative aspect. It made death an incident in vital statistics, measurable quantitatively, predictable according to the actuarial laws of probability. It tried to get around death by organizing away its consequences. Life insurance is perhaps the most signficant institution of nineteenth-century metaphysics; its proposition "to spread the risks" shows most clearly the nature of the attempt to consider death an incident in human life rather than its termination. And the nineteenth century invented spiritualism—an attempt to control life after death by mechanical means.

Yet death persists. Society might make death taboo, might lay down the rule that it is bad manners to speak of death, might substitute "hygienic" cremation for those horribly public funerals, and might call gravediggers morticians. The learned Professor Haeckel might hint broadly that Darwinian biology is just about to make us live permanently; but he did not make good his promise. And so long as death persists, the individual remains with one pole of his existence outside of society and outside of time.

So long as death persists, the optimistic concept of life, the belief that eternity can be reached through time and that the individual can fulfill himself in society, must have only one outcome—despair. Suddenly every man finds himself facing death; and at this point he is all alone, all individual. If his existence is purely in society, he is lost—for now this existence becomes meaningless. Kierkegaard diagnosed the phenomenon and called it the "despair at not willing to be an individual." Superficially, the individual can recover from this encounter with the problem of existence in eternity; he may even forget it for a while. But he can never regain his confidence in his existence in society. Basically he remains in despair.

Society must make it possible for man to die without despair if it wants him to be able to live exclusively in society. And it can do so in only one way: by making individual life meaningless. If you are nothing but a leaf on the tree of the race, a cell in the body of society, then your death is not really death; you had better call it a process of collective regeneration. But then, of course, your life is not a real life either; it is just a functional process within the life of the whole, devoid of any meaning except in terms of the whole. Thus, as Kierkegaard foresaw a hundred years ago, an optimism that proclaims human existence as existence in society leads straight to despair. And this despair can lead only to totalitarianism. For totalitarianism—and that is the trait that distinguishes it so sharply from the tyrannies of the past—is based on the affirmation of the meaninglessness of life and of the nonexistence of the person. Hence the emphasis in the totalitarian creed is not on how to live, but on how to die; to make death bearable, individual life had to be made worthless and meaningless. The optimistic creed, that started out by making life in this world mean everything, led straight to the Nazi glorification of self-immolation as the only act in which man can meaningfully exist. Despair becomes the essence of life itself.

V

The nineteenth century arrived at the very point the pagan world had reached in the late Roman Empire. And like antiquity, it tried to find a way out by escaping into the purely ethical—by basing virtue on man's reason. The great philosophical systems of German idealism—above all Kant's, but also Hegel's—dominated the age because they identified reason with virtue and the good life. Ethical culture and that brand of liberal Protestantism that sees in Jesus the "best man that ever lived," with its slogans of the Golden Rule, of the "categorical imperative," and of the satisfaction of service—these and related ethical formulas became as familiar in the nineteenth century as most of them had been in antiquity. And they failed to provide a basis for human existence in modernity, just as they had failed two thousand years before.

In its best representatives, the ethical concept leads, indeed, to moral integrity and moral greatness. Nineteenth-century humanism, based half on Plutarch, half on Newton, could be a noble thing. (We have only to remember the great men of the last nineteenth-century generation, such as Woodrow Wilson, Masaryk, Jaurès, or Mommsen.) Kierkegaard himself was more attracted by it than he realized. Though fighting every inch of the way, he could never quite free himself from the influence of Hegel; and Socrates, symbol of the ethical life, remained to him the apogee of man's natural history.

But Kierkegaard also saw that the ethical concept, while it may give integrity, courage, and steadfastness, cannot give meaning—neither to life nor to death. All it can give is stoic resignation. Kierkegaard considered this position to be one of even greater despair than the optimistic one; he calls it "the despair at willing to be an individual." And only too often the ethical position does not lead to anything as noble and as consistent as the Stoic philosophy, but turns into sugar coating on the pill of totalitarianism. This is, I feel, the position of many an apologist for Soviet Russia; he hopes that man will find individual fulfillment in the ethical attempt at making his neighbor happy and that this will suffice to offset the reality of totalitarianism. Or the ethical position becomes pure sentimentalism—the position of those who believe that evil can be abolished and harmony established by good intentions.

And in all cases the ethical position is bound to degenerate into relativism. For if virtue is to be found in man, everything that is accepted by man must be virtue. Thus a position that starts out—as did Rousseau and Kant some two hundred years ago—to establish man-made ethical absolutes must end in the complete denial of absolutes and, with it, in the complete denial of the possibility of a truly ethical position. This way there is no escape from despair.

Is then the only conclusion that human existence can be only existence in tragedy and despair? Are the sages of the East right who see the only answer in the destruction of self, in the submersion of man into the Nirvana, the nothingness?

Kierkegaard has another answer: human existence is possible as existence not in despair, as existence not in tragedy; it is possible as existence in faith. The opposite of Sin (to use the traditional term for existence purely in society) is not Virtue; it is Faith.

Faith is the belief that in God the impossible is possible, that in Him time and eternity are one, that both life and death are meaningful. Faith is the knowledge that man is creature—not autonomous, not the master, not the end, not the center—and yet responsible and free. It is the acceptance of man's essential loneliness, to be overcome by the certainty that God is always with man, even "unto the hour of our death."

In my favorite among Kierkegaard's books, a little volume called *Fear and Trembling,* he raises the question: What distinguished Abraham's willingness to sacrifice his son, Isaac, from ordinary murder? If Abraham had never intended to go through with the sacrifice, but had intended all the time only to make a show of his obedience to God, then Abraham, indeed, would not have been a murderer, but he would have been something more despicable: a fraud and a cheat. If he had not loved Isaac but had been indifferent, he would have been willing to be a murderer. Yet Abraham was a holy man; God's command was for him an absolute command to be executed without reservation; and we are told that he loved Isaac more than himself. The answer is that Abraham had faith. He believed that in God the impossible would become possible—that he could carry out God's command and yet retain Isaac.

Abraham was the symbol for Kierkegaard himself, and the sacrifice of Isaac the symbol for his own innermost secret, his great and tragic love—a love he had slaughtered although he loved it more than he loved himself. But the autobiographical allusion is only incidental. The story of Abraham is a universal symbol of human existence which is possible only in faith. In faith the individual becomes the universal, ceases to be isolated, becomes meaningful and absolute; hence in faith there is a true ethic. And in faith existence in society becomes meaningful, too, as existence in true charity.

The faith is not what today is so often glibly called a "mystical experience"—something that can apparently be induced by the proper breathing exercises or by prolonged exposure to Bach. It can be attained only through despair, through suffering, through painful and ceaseless struggle. It is not irrational, sentimental, emotional, or spontaneous. It comes as the result of serious thinking and learning, of rigid discipline, of complete sobriety, of humbleness, and of the self's subordination to a higher, an absolute will. The inner knowledge of one's own unification in God—what

St. Paul called hope and we call saintliness—only a few can attain. But every man is capable of attaining faith. For every man knows despair.

Kierkegaard stands squarely in the great Western tradition of religious experience, the tradition of St. Augustine and St. Bonaventura, of Luther, St. John of the Cross, and Pascal. What sets him apart, and gives him this special urgency today, is his emphasis on the meaning of life in time and society for the man of faith, the Christian. Kierkegaard is "modern," not because he employs the modern vocabulary of psychology, aesthetics, and dialectics—the ephemeral traits which the Kierkegaard boom ballyhoos—but because he concerns himself with the specific disease of the modern West: the falling apart of human existence, the denial of the simultaneity of life in the spirit and life in the flesh, the denial of the meaningfulness of each for the other.

Instead, we have today a complete divorce, the juxtaposition of "Yogi" and "Commissar"—the terms are, of course, Arthur Koestler's—as mutually exclusive possibilities: an either-or between time and eternity, charity and faith, in which one pole of man's dual existence is made the absolute. This amounts to a complete abdication of faith: the "Commissar" gives up the entire realm of the spirit for the sake of power and effectiveness; the "Yogi" assigns human existence in time (that is, social life) to the devil and is willing to see millions lose their lives and their souls if only his own "I" be saved. Both are impossible positions for any religious man to take, but especially for a Christian who must live in the spirit and yet must maintain that true faith is effective in and through charity (i.e., in and through social responsibility).

But at least both are honest positions, honestly admitting their bankruptcy—in contrast to the attempt at evading the problem by way of the various "Christian" political parties in Europe, Protestant and Catholic, or the movement for "Social Christianity" still powerful in this country. For these attempts substitute morality and good intentions for faith and religious experience as mainsprings of action. While sincere and earnest, while supported and sometimes led by good, even by saintly men, they must not only be as ineffectual in politics as the "Yogi" but must also fail, like the "Commissar," to give spiritual life; for they compromise both life in time and life in eternity. That Austrian cleric and Catholic party leader who, in the thirties, came out for Hitler with the argument, "At least he is opposed to mixed bathing," was a ghastly caricature of the Christian moralist in politics; but he caricatured something that is ever present where morality is confused with faith.

Kierkegaard offers no easy way out. Indeed, it could be said of him, as of all religious thinkers who focus on experience rather than on reason and dogma, that he greatly overemphasizes life in the spirit, thus failing to integrate the two poles of human existence into one whole. But he not only saw the task; he also showed in his own life and in his works that there is no escape from the reality of human existence, which is one in tension. It is no accident that the only part of Kierkegaard's tremendous literary output that did not originally appear under a pseudonym but under his own name was the *Edifying Discourses.* Not that he wanted to conceal his authorship of the other works—the pseudonyms could not have fooled anybody; but the "edifying" books alone translate faith into social effectiveness and are thus truly religious and not just "Yogi." It is also not an accident that Kierkegaard's whole work, his twenty years of seclusion, of writing, thinking, praying, and suffering, were but the preparation for the violent political action to which he dedicated the last months of his life—a furious one-man war on the established church of Denmark and its high clergy for confusing morality and tradition with charity and faith.

Though Kierkegaard's faith cannot overcome the awful loneliness, the isolation and dissonance of human existence, it can make it bearable by making it meaningful. The philosophy of the totalitarian creeds enables man to die. It is dangerous to underestimate the strength of such a philosophy; for, in a time of sorrow and suffering, of catastrophe and horror (that is, in our time), it is a great thing to be able to die. Yet it is not enough. Kierkegaard's faith, too, enables man to die; but it also enables him to live.

CHAPTER THREE

Notes on the New Politics

THE OBJECTIVE REALITIES to which American politics must address itself have been changing drastically in the last fifteen years or so:

- in population structure;
- in social and political structure;
- in respect to the power centers in American society;
- and in the international environment.

As a result, fundamental assumptions accepted as near axioms in both our domestic and our foreign policies are becoming increasingly untenable.

The issues around which American politics is tending to organize itself will increasingly be both new and different from those of the last half-century. Long-accepted issues, or at least their traditional formulations, will increasingly come to appear unreal, if not meaningless.

First published in *The Public Interest,* Summer, 1966.

Above all, the new realities are rapidly obsoleting traditional political alignments.

Alignments that have molded the American political process for most of the last hundred years—the "bridge" role of the "Solid South" and its political power, the strategic role of economic blocs, and so on—are likely to lose their significance. This process is just beginning to be visible, above all in the turmoil and agony of the Republican party. It is likely to change both parties, however, if not to revise the accepted polarization of American politics around "nonideological" interests and around domestic affairs. It is also quite unlikely that foreign policies can continue to be "bipartisan"; they are more likely to become the center of major political controversy.

President Johnson's "Great Society" represents a first response to some of the new issues, both at home and abroad. But it approaches these new issues largely within the old framework. It appeals primarily to the old values, and it employs mostly the traditional rhetoric. It is thus essentially a transitional phase; and one would guess that the President is highly conscious of this. The emphasis on "consensus" is, above all, an attempt, both highly constructive and politically very dangerous, to accomplish some of the most important of the new tasks *before* they have become political issues. Even at its most successful, the era of "consensus," like any earlier "Era of Good Feeling," can therefore only be a prelude to a (probably prolonged) period of vocal dissent, violent political ferment, and sudden political landslides.

New Domestic Realities

The recent past—the two decades since the end of World War II, or the fifteen years since the Korean War—has produced clearly visible shifts in the political, social, and economic realities at home and abroad.

In bald statement, the changes that appear most significant to me are:

(1) Within the last fifteen to twenty years, the United States has

become a *Metropolitan Society* in which the great majority of the people live in a fairly small number of large, densely populated metropolitan areas, dependent on common services, each an intricate system of great technical and political complexity.

(2) The center of gravity of the American work force has been shifting from manual worker—skilled or unskilled, on the farm or in workshop or factory—to the *Knowledge Worker* with a very high degree of formal schooling. For the knowledge worker, and for an economy based on knowledge work, poverty ceases to be the general condition of mankind. Not that the knowledge worker is "rich," but his income tends to be so high as to remove the constant anxiety about the next meal in which mankind as a whole has always lived. Above all, the knowledge worker enjoys a job security unknown to history.

As a further result of this shift to knowledge work, there is in process a radical change in the position of the manual worker. Neither his job security nor his income deteriorates. But he tends to be seen as economically "nonproductive" and as socially "marginal." He is no longer seen as essential. In his stead the employed, educated middle class is increasingly becoming the *New Majority.*

(3) Within these last fifteen years, the United States has become a society of big, semiautonomous, and tightly organized institutions. There is not only "big government"—federal as well as state and municipal (within which the civil services and the armed forces represent large, tightly organized power centers of their own, semiautonomous and with their own rules and their own leaders); there are also the big university, the big hospital, the big labor union, and many others.

Business was only the first sphere in American society in which the large organization appeared—which explains in part why we tend to think of "business" whenever we say "bigness." American society, as, indeed, every modern industrial society, has become a *Pluralist Society* of big organizations, each serving one, but only one, of the purposes and needs of society.

The decisive interactions in American society today, and

increasingly in American politics, are therefore interactions between highly organized, large, powerful, and professionalized institutions, each concerned with its own specific task.

(4) Traditional federalism sees relationships of coexistence and competition between the federal government and the various states. But in the *New Federalism* other political units in addition to the states (especially the metropolitan areas) are directly in relation with the federal government and work directly with it. More important, perhaps, institutions that are not "government" but "private" increasingly become the agents of government in the fulfillment of public functions and even in the formulation of public policy: the universities, the big corporations, the large teaching hospitals.

(5) There is an emergence of new power centers in our society, rivaling if not already overshadowing the traditional power centers of American politics, such as the traditional economic interests. These new power centers are: the *Military, Education,* and *Big Science.* True, education, while rapidly becoming the largest single employer and investor of capital in this country, is not yet organized as a power center. Yet surely the emphasis on the diploma as a condition of employment represents a tremendous social victory for the educator and puts him in a position of social control such as this country never before granted to any single group.

Military strength and educational strength are now seen as the twin pillars of national strength in the modern world and as the two attributes of great power status.

These two power centers, the military and education, come together in the commitment of government to the promotion of *Scientific and Technological Thrust* as a major new national responsibility and a major new national purpose.

New Domestic Issues

(1) In domestic politics we have already *shifted from economically centered issues to issues that are basically political: constitutional, moral,*

and aesthetic. The outstanding example is, of course, civil rights. Indeed, civil rights is a major issue only because it became apparent that economics alone cannot provide citizenship to the American Negro.

The "War on Poverty," too, though it uses economic terminology, is a shift away from the economic and toward the political. It was imposed by an affluent society on itself by its own bad conscience—and, in large measure, by an aesthetic concern with the squalor and ugliness in which so many live in an economy of abundance.

The educated professional employee, on the other hand, is altogether

- prone to alienation rather than to poverty;
- beset by the fear of futility rather than by lack of income.

What he lacks is not a job but the satisfaction of achievement and a sense of function. The creation of such satisfaction will be a basic purpose of American politics.

(2) *Congress* and its function may well become an issue by itself. The developments of the last two decades have largely pushed Congress out of being a partner in political decisions. It is being reduced, instead, in a good many areas to being a critic and commentator. The complex arrangements of the New Federalism are largely beyond the power of Congress, if not altogether beyond its purview.

Issues in International Politics

The central reality which is likely to generate, or at least to shape, the issues in American international politics is the fading away of the two axioms on which American foreign policy hase been based since World War II: the axiom that the international economy was dependent on the United States economy, rather than that there was interdependency; and the much more important axiom that

"Communism" and "Russia" were synonymous, and both words for "the enemy."

As the result of the erosion of these axioms, it is no longer possible to assume that any action taken by the United States in its capacity of leader of the Free World community is automatically in the interest of the United States as a nation, and vice versa. The national-interest approach might, for instance, give us a "soft" policy in respect to China where the world-leadership approach might lead to a very "hard" one, i.e., containing Chinese aggression anywhere and everywhere.

Bipartisanship in foreign affairs cannot last. "Pragmatism" has had its day; we now need policy again.

I. Political Alignments

The most important decisions of the last fifteen years in American politics were made essentially outside of the political process proper. They could have hardly been made within it: they concerned issues on which no decision is possible within the traditional alignments.

The two crucial decisions in domestic politics during the last decade or so were probably School Segregation and Re-apportionment. Both were reached, without any political discussion to speak of, by the Supreme Court, that is by an organ outside of party politics.

Similarly in foreign affairs: the most important decision was surely the one that committed us to a major war in Vietnam. This decision was reached without any "decision" whatever and certainly without any public debate. What is amazing is not that there has been criticism of our involvement in Vietnam, but that there was so little discussion and so little dissent until we were irrevocably committed.

Indeed, the most important among the traditional alignments of American policy are in the process of disappearing altogether.

The South Loses Its Casting Vote

During the last few years, one of the two main bases of the traditional alignments, the "Compromise of 1876," has in effect been repealed.

The history books tell us little of this Compromise other than that it seated a Republican Presidential candidate (Rutherford Hayes) who had actually been outpolled by his Democratic opponent, in exchange for which the federal government withdrew the troops that had kept the "carpetbagger" administrations in power in the states of the former Confederacy. But implicit in this deal, as was clearly understood by all concerned, was a far-reaching compact between North and South. It guaranteed the South noninterference in its "domestic institution," that is, the unchallenged maintenance of white supremacy. In exchange the South promised tacitly to accept and not to challenge the leadership of the North in all areas excepting only race relations. This was expressed in the common saying that no southerner could become President.

The Compromise gave the South power in American politics, and especially in Congress, way beyond its population strength, way beyond even the quality of southern leadership. One reason for this was the control by the southerners of the chairmanship of important congressional committees as a combined result of the congressional seniority system and the unchallenged one-party structure of the South.

More important, perhaps, though much less visible, was the function of the South as the *bridge* between the major parties and major factions; this guaranteed almost every President a workable majority in Congress, but also made the South indispensable. It was obviously to the interest of the South not to have any one party predominate in Congress: the southerners in Congress, therefore, always tended to make common cause with the minority—except in times of great emergency, such as the outbreak of war or the first hundred days of Roosevelt's New Deal.

For ninety years, practically every administration has faced a coalition in Congress in which the South, though the junior partner, essentially dictated the terms.

The proximate cause for the "repeal" of the Compromise of 1876 was the northward migration of the Negro which began after World War I. With the Negro in the North having formal political equality, deprivation of the same rights in the South could no longer be considered a "domestic affair." As soon as—following the Supreme Court school decision of 1954—the federal government attacked white supremacy in the South, the southerners ceased, therefore, to honor their part of the bargain. This in large part explains the frustration of President Kennedy's domestic policies.

But the ultimate cause of the sharp change in the position of the South in American politics is the shift in the white population and its distribution. Because the Old South has tended to stay heavily rural and small-town, it no longer has the numbers to support a bridge role and to cast the deciding vote. Or, rather, a South that stays rural and small-town cannot have enough population to matter; while a South that becomes metropolitan ceases to be the "Solid South," as Atlanta and Miami have demonstrated.

That both Mr. Truman and Mr. Johnson were not supported by the South amounted to a renunciation of the traditional alliance. But that both could be elected without the votes of the South was much more important: it proved that the South no longer held the balance of power. Even Mr. Kennedy would still have been elected, despite the hairline margin in his popular vote, if most of the states of the Old Confederacy had given their electoral votes to a states-rights southerner. That, as a by-product, a southerner has been shown to be capable of winning both nomination and election to the Presidency is a rather meager consolation.

The price in civil rights that the nation paid for the bridge role of the South was, of course, exorbitant. But in terms of contemporary American politics, during these ninety years, the peculiar role of the South has on the whole been healthy and productive.

There is a belief abroad that the southerners in Congress tended to be "reactionaries." But this holds true only for their position on race relations, which did not become an issue in American politics until the Depression and perhaps not until World War II. Otherwise, the southerner in Congress was more often than not a populist radical. But above all, to preserve the power position of the South, the southerner in Congress had no choice but to seek a consensus. National policy did not shift to the left or to the right because the South shifted: the South shifted because the national center shifted first. In effect, the southerners always had to make it possible for "liberals" and "conservatives" to agree at least sufficiently to permit the business of government to go on.

The long-serving committee chairmen, while often autocratic and immovable, also usually did their homework and thoroughly knew their area. They endowed Congress with a solid backbone of expertise such as no other parliamentary body in the world possesses. One would be hard-pressed to find men who worked harder or who knew their area better than the two men from Georgia, Senator Russell and Congressman Vinson, who for so many years headed the Armed Services Committees in their branches of Congress. It is this expert knowledge that makes Congress still capable of dealing with the federal bureaucracy and gives us a degree of political and policy control over the civil service such as is unknown in any other modern nation.

In foreign affairs, the absence of major manufacturing and labor union interests in the South enabled the southerner often to regard the national interest and to take a much larger view than the Midwesterner or New Englander, swayed as he so often has been by the immediate, shortsighted interests of this or that company or industry.

Finally, "that no southerner could become President" meant that the senior southerners in Congress had no further ambition and knew that they had to make their mark in history through their performance as legislators.

For better or worse, this position of the South is gone.

It is no accident that for the first time in the history of the Senate a civil-rights filibuster could be broken so decisively (in the fight over President Kennedy's Civil Rights bill) that, two years later, the South did not even try to filibuster against Mr. Johnson's much more sweeping bill of 1965. It is no accident, either, that, for the first time since the present system of committee chairmen was introduced around the turn of the century, committee members have successfully revolted against their chairmen (against Representative Smith of Virginia, the Chairman of the House Rules Committee, and Representative Patman of Texas of the House Banking Committee).

I am by no means convinced that the South will abandon the one-party system. It is conceivable that, for many years to come, the pressures toward conformity, and for resistance to an alien and critical outside world, may enforce strict voting discipline, to the point where opposition candidates have no chance at all in large areas.

But even if nothing changes in the South, it would not matter greatly one way or another. For almost a century, the arrival of a two-party system in the South has been looked forward to by "liberals," inside and outside the South, as the hour of deliverance, if not as the panacea for all the ills of the South. It is ironic that, just when the two-party system has a real chance to establish itself in the South, it has also become quite unimportant. In national affairs the South must increasingly cease to be something separate, indeed, something unique. Whatever is left of the "Old South" is rapidly becoming just another sparsely settled and relatively poor section of the country—and, as such, a fairly unimportant one.

The Erosion of the Economic Blocs

The second major shift in the structure of alignments in American politics is the steady erosion of the traditional economic blocs. These blocs, whether "labor" or "farmer" or "business," *can no longer be carriers of policies.* They can only, increasingly, become *obstacles* to any policy whatever; for any change is, in effect, a threat to them.

The three agencies of the federal government which reached Cabinet status between the Civil War and World War II were Agriculture, Commerce, and Labor. Each was created to represent a major economic estate of the realm and to make sure that its interests were protected. The particular interest group which any one of these bureaucracies represented had a virtual veto power over the appointment of the secretary. Indeed, the secretaries often behaved like ambassadors of a powerful foreign sovereign rather than as members of the President's Cabinet.

By sharp contrast, the two new Cabinet posts created since World War II (leaving out Defense as a special case in which formerly separate agencies of Cabinet rank were consolidated) were Health, Education, and Welfare, and Housing and Urban Affairs—both established not to represent economic interests but *to remove major areas of policy from the control of, and domination by, economic interests.* And the proposal to make Transportation a Cabinet department serves the same purpose.

Of all the traditional groups, only one has an opportunity to remain influential and a carrier of policy: the "managers." For managing is a function that is essential in all the new big organizations; indeed, managing is the specific function of big complex organizations—whether business or armed service, university or government agency, or hospital. But, of course, the only reason why this group might survive as a distinct and organized power center is that the "capitalist" of yesterday had been replaced by the "professional manager" of today who is not confined to one economic interest but pervades the entire society and who is not exclusively economically oriented. The extent to which managers have succeeded in the much-publicized attempt to make themselves "trustees" for all the interests in the organization—employees, investors, customers, and so on—is a moot point. That they are trying is the important thing. This explains why President Johnson has been wooing them: they are a bridge between yesterday's alignments and tomorrow's alignments and, as such, essential to Mr. Johnson's "consensus."

Labor, by contrast, has not even begun such a transformation. Except in the event of a major economic crisis, it seems rather unlikely that a sufficiently large part of the "employed professional middle class" will unionize itself, not only to restore labor's vitality and growth potential, but also to change the characteristics of labor even more drastically than the change from capitalist to manager has transformed the characteristics of the business interest. The aims of a unionized professional middle class are, in any case, likely to be social rather than economic. And insofar as they are economic, they are likely to be in direct conflict with the economic aims of the rank-and-file blue-collar worker of the traditional unions.

The traditional economic blocs no longer represent the dynamics of American society, if only because the big tasks and the big problems are not economic but political, social, moral, or aesthetic. This does not mean that the economic blocs will become unimportant or powerless. The farmer, for instance, has long ceased to have the key position he had up until World War I; but the farm lobby is losing its importance only very slowly.

What does happen, however, is that such groups become purely negative. Any change is a threat to them. The aims of policy are not their aims. They therefore become increasingly "vested interests," concerned with the maintenance of a privileged status. Extortion, rather than policy, becomes their business.

The Changing Role of Ethnic Blocs

The most confusing area is that of ethnic and religious blocs, such as the Irish Catholics, the Jews, the Italians, and so on.

In different parts of the metropolis, their importance will change in different directions.

In the core city, the old "downtown"—the five boroughs of New

York, for instance—such blocs should become much more important. The Negro clearly is just now emerging as an organized and powerful ethnic bloc in the core city. His tendency to act as a bloc in city politics must increase; for the individual Negro can achieve advancement and access to opportunities only through organized use of his political power, that is, as a bloc and through "patronage." The same applies to the Puerto Rican and to the Mexican-American.

This, in turn, is likely to force other groups in the core city to organize themselves and act as blocs. The way in which Irish Catholics in Boston, for instance, have again coalesced as a bloc to beat off a Negro attack on the "neighborhood school" is only an example. And the same holds true of other ethnic groups largely composed of industrial workers or lower-grade service employees, such as the Czechs in Chicago, the Poles in Cleveland, and the Hungarians in Pittsburgh.

Outside the core city, however, in the suburban areas of the metropolis, ethnic blocs are likely to become very much less important. Regardless of his origin (unless he should be a Negro), the suburbanite sees himself characterized by his education—which tends to be advanced—and by his cultural level, rather than by his origin. In fact, he is likely to resent too blatant an appeal to his origin, as questioning his status in the American community.

Ethnic or religious blocs are, therefore, likely to become complicated, with both appeal to them and nonappeal equally unpredictable. Inside the core city, the blocs can be expected to become far more important, and with this advent would come the strong "boss" and the appeal to "solidarity" instead of issues, ideas, or men. Outside the core city, ethnic origin is likely to mean less and less, though religious affiliation may still play an important role in a number of areas.

Core City and Suburb

The different appeal of ethnic and religious blocs in core city and suburb, respectively, is only one of the differences that are likely to characterize these two elements of the metropolis and that eventually might divide them sharply in national politics.

Altogether, *the core city is increasingly likely to present yesterday's politics, yesterday's issues, and yesterday's alignment.* The very fact that bloc voting is likely to be such a factor will make the core city look to the past rather than to the future—plus the fact, of course, that the core city is likely to be the least affluent part of the "affluent society." The suburbs, representing the young people and therefore the more highly educated and more prosperous citizens, are likely to be looking, increasingly, toward tomorrow's problems, especially toward the problems of the metropolitan area.

Also, the core city will increasingly have to bear the burden of the metropolitan services while having fewer and fewer tax resources. These latter will be in the suburbs; indeed, it is conceivable that deterioration of the core city will bring a mass exodus of business headquarters to the suburbs. Some of the biggest companies have already moved out. This will create increasing demands on the part of the core city that the suburbs become part of its tax domain—and increasing resistance to the core city on the part of the suburbanites.

But more important than these tangible factors are probably the intangible ones. Increasingly, these two parts of the metropolis will represent two facets of metropolitan culture. It is not only the man from Iowa who says, "New York is a nice place to visit, but I wouldn't want to live there." The man from Westchester County feels this even more strongly.

It is, therefore, conceivable that the geographic alignments in this country—between North and South; between country and town; between agrarian and industrial society—may be gradually replaced by *a split between the core city and the suburbs throughout all regions and all areas of the country.* It is conceivable that tomorrow the job of building a national party will, in effect, mean bringing together enough groups from those two constituent parts of the metropolis behind one program and one candidate.

It is also conceivable that tomorrow's political parties will primarily be characterized by having a "core city" or a "suburban" temperament.

The Impact on the Parties

The change in alignments which is already in full swing is likely to present serious problems to both parties.

(1) The Struggle for a Republican Future

In terms of its traditional vote base, the Republican party has become *the permanent minority party*—and becoming the majority in the Old South would not in any way change this; it would rather accentuate the isolation of the Republican party. The reason for this is that the Republican party today is "white protestant" by temperament, no matter how many Jews, Catholics, or Negroes vote the Republican ticket. And the white Protestant is no longer the political majority.

Statistically, of course, white Protestants do constitute two-thirds of the population. Culturally, also, this is, and will remain, a white Protestant country (despite the prevalence of Jewish jokes and Italian pizzas). But, politically, a white Protestant party is no longer capable of organizing majority support. Almost half of the white Protestants in the country are rural and small-town and as such are not an adequate foundation for national power any more. In the metropolis, the white Protestant group is just about half or less, but does not see itself as a coherent group and does not vote as such—precisely because it does not see itself as the minority. And minorities, that is, groups that otherwise would have little influence and little voice, are the ones that see the need for organizing themselves for the fight for power.

What the strategies are that are available to the permanent minority party we know. For this was the position of the Democrats for sixty long years, from the Civil War until Franklin D. Roosevelt's election in 1932. In fact, there are only two strategies available; and the party is likely to be torn internally by the fight between the adherents of either.

There is, first, the *"moderate"* strategy—the strategy of those who essentially say "me too." They expect to come to power precisely because it is not easy to tell them apart from the majority party, except that they are "out" and therefore not responsible for a catastrophe, a scandal, or whatever accident befalls the majority party in power. In such a situation, the "moderates" hope to be able to attract enough protest votes from the majority party to get into power and to start working on making themselves in turn the permanent majority.

The second strategy is the *radical* one which aims to recreate a new party "dedicated to principles." In tune with the ancestor worship that characterizes the rhetoric of American politics, this strategy is likely to present itself as aiming at the restoration of the ideals of the past. William Jennings Bryan was a "Fundamentalist" and Goldwater a "Conservative." Actually, the strategy aims at creating a major crisis and hopes to capitalize on it.

Both strategies have rather stringent prerequisites, none of which is likely to be satisfied for the Republicans in the present situation. The moderates can operate only if they control some important power centers, such as the Democrats' control of the Solid South and of the big cities of the North in the long years of their exile after the Civil War. Specifically, the Republican moderates would have to gain control of major metropolitan areas. This would probably require the consolidation of core city and suburbs into one political unit. The voting strength of the Republicans in the suburbs, however, rests squarely on their promise not to let the core city "gobble up" the suburbs.

For the radical strategy to work—short of a catastrophe such as this country has so far been spared—requires a candidate who has shown ability for political leadership and enough maturity not to frighten off potential recruits from the moderate ranks of his own party as well as from the opposition. If all he does is to attract the radicals of the other party (as Bryan and Goldwater did), he almost insures defeat through distrust on the part of the great majority which fears (and rightly) political adventurers.

This, however, only means that the *Republican party is unlikely to make up its mind for either strategy*—just as Democrats did not decide, before the New Deal. This would guarantee long years of internal turmoil for the Republican party, in the course of which the first aim of each Republican politician is likely to be to prevent the victory of another Republican rather than to defeat a Democrat. As John Lindsay's campaign in New York City showed, the only way for a Republican to win in such a situation is to be as little of a Republican as possible and to try to be accepted as a genuine "Independent."

The Republicans will, therefore, be forced to look for issues that can unite them and to shun issues that must divide them. Because of the shift in alignments in the country, domestic issues are almost certain to divide the Republicans—save only in the event of international catastrophe, serious depression, or truly sensational scandal. The Republicans may, therefore, attempt to make foreign policy into the platform that unites them; and it is possible that, for the first time since the very early days of the Republic, a major party will organize itself on a foreign affairs platform rather than on a domestic platform.

(2) The Dilemma of the Democrats

The Democratic party, too, will be seriously affected by the shifting alignments. It has to gain the allegiance of the "new majority," the educated, employed middle class. But it must at the same time hold the allegiance of the old power groups, the economic blocs and the ethnic blocs. The attempt to hold the one is likely to alienate the other. It may alienate both, as did the Democratic strategy in the 1965 New York City elections, in which the patent attempt to have the "right" old-fashioned ticket—one Jew, one Irish Catholic, one Italian, and so on—only made the younger and better-educated members of these groups cross over and go Republican in large numbers.

In this dilemma, the Democratic party will try to focus on the issues likely to unify these two groups—and these are the *urban issues:* the metropolis, health care, and, above all, education. By the same token it is likely to play down what will divide these two groups: the old-style economic issues and foreign affairs.

(3) Creating a New Majority

Victory, in the long run, will not go to the party that does the best job gluing together the shards of yesterday. Victory will go to whoever creates a new national alignment and a new power base, resting not on economic interests but on the "new majority" of the educated professional middle class and capable of crystallizing the issues that are meaningful to them. (The last time a similar job was done in American politics was after the election of 1896, when Mark Hanna used the economic blocs to erect the structure that is still housing American politics, even though the tenant has changed.) Today one can barely even speculate what these alignments might be and on what they might rest.

Thus there is great opportunity for creative party politics—and great need for it. Politicians are needed who can establish the new alignments—politicians who can dramatize the new issues and mobilize the new power centers.

II. Politics for a New Generation

So far I have given an inventory rather than an analysis. Even if correct in every detail, it would still not enable us to anticipate

American politics in the years ahead. What matters in politics is far less the specific problems and the answers found to them than the pattern, the configuration. It is not what issues are debated, but what emphasis is given to issues in relation to each other and in a scale of political values. It is not so much what laws are being written as what kind of personality can exercise leadership. Measures and policy matter less than the mood and the basic assumptions.

The most important fact with respect to this configuration of tomorrow may well be that the United States—indeed, the whole world—is in the midst of a major generational shift.

The outward sign of this is, of course, that so many of the world's political leaders, from President Johnson to Chairman Mao, are so clearly the last of their line, by age alone. Their formative years were the twenties and thirties; but even the postwar era of the forties and fifties is rapidly becoming history.

In terms of age structure of the population, the United States is not a particularly young country today, compared with underdeveloped Latin America, India, or China, for instance, where the "population explosion," propelled by drastic cuts in infant mortality, is pushing the average age of population down to fifteen or so. But compared to its own history and recent experience, *the United States is becoming a very young country, indeed,* with half the population already less than twenty-six years old, and most of them highly educated and with experiences and expectations that differ markedly from those that still underlie our social, political, and economic policies. The middle generation (ages thirty to fifty), by contrast, is very thin in this country today and bound to get thinner for another decade—the result, of course, of the lean birth years of the thirties. By 1972, more than half of all Americans old enough to vote will be under thirty-two (a fact which, however, no politician, except Senator Robert Kennedy, seems to have found out).

Power and position are therefore likely to pass fast from people whose working life began before or during the Great Depression to people to whom the Depression is, at the very best, a dim childhood memory—if not to people to whom even World War II is something they heard about in their high-school courses. President Johnson's young men—his assistants in their early thirties—are only the advance guard of the generation that must get to the top in all important areas of American life very soon—in business and in government, in the universities and in the armed services, and perhaps even in the labor unions.

But this, even more than a shift in chronological age, is a shift in outlook, perception, and formative experience. The world this new generation of Americans considers as "normal" is one of long years of advanced education, of very high job security, of affluence—a world dominated by science and technology. It is also a world of international turmoil and dangers such as would have been unimaginable to their parents at the same age.

Even greater, perhaps, is the jump in perception. What the new generation takes for granted, the older one has not really learned to see. For the new generation takes for granted

- the "global village": that is, the integration of the entire earth through communications into one locus of immediate experience;
- "man in space": that is, the reaching out beyond what were considered the human limits of existence;
- technology, both in respect to doing physical tasks and in respect to making economic problems amenable to systematic, organized, and essentially technical solutions.

This new perception may not at all have the results most people envisage. But it will have very significant results.

The perception of the global village may not make us more "internationalist." Indeed, it may considerably discourage the old American missionary impulse to do things *for* others without necessarily increasing the desire (also an old American tradition) to do things *with* others. The perception of the global village is, however, likely to make us stop seeing the outside world through European glasses (whether that of the German savant or the English Fabian), which is the way the American "liberal" has always seen the world.

There are even strong indications that the new generation will turn away from the "secularism" of their parents—not to organized religion but to a new "inner-directedness" with stress on personal values and personal commitment. Most of the "crazy mixed-up kids" on the campuses today will, of course, grow up into depressingly sane adult conformists, and they are a tiny minority, in any case. But they might signal a shift ahead in values and concerns—a shift toward moral and aesthetic values and toward a concern with the person.

This is, however, mere speculation. What one can say with a good deal of assurance is that the generation shift ahead is likely to be also a political shift—a shift in the climate, the mood, the values, the alignments, and the issues of American politics.

Such a shift is bound to be disorderly. It implies a *time of transition* likely to be characterized by vocal dissent, by sudden sharp landslides burying long-familiar landmarks, by partisanship, and by political passion. It is not likely to be a time of "consensus"; it is exceedingly unlikely to be a time of political apathy; and foreign affairs is likely to be one of the political storm centers.

The election of 1964 clearly marked a watershed in American politics. We now face a period rather similar to that after 1896, if not after 1822—periods that ended an "Era of Good Feeling" and brought long-lasting realignment to American politics.

The Great Society—Substance and Rhetoric

In its concerns, President Johnson's Great Society clearly addresses itself to the new realities and to tomorrow's issues. Its main domestic themes are the metropolis, education, health care, and the aesthetics of an industrial society, not to mention its basic morality.

In his most significant speech to date, the speech on the Negro in America given at Howard University in 1965, the President clearly put ethics into the center of his politics.

The Johnson administration, also, has begun work on some of the *constitutional* problems. (This, by the way, is one area where it continues what President Kennedy began.) The "White House Conferences"—on education, for instance, or on the natural environment—at least remove the planning of the "New Federalism" from the inner office and subject it to public exposure. And the new subordination of the military to civilian control, however much it may be due to the personality and forcefulness of one particular Secretary of Defense, was clearly, from the beginning, Presidential policy as well.

Even in international affairs, where both the Kennedy and the Johnson administrations have been neither "bold" nor "innovators," new thinking may have begun, if only because of the realities of Southeast Asia.

But in its rhetoric, the Great Society is old and addresses itself to yesterday.

"Consensus," as President Johnson uses that term, means in effect bringing *all* of yesterday's power groups (and especially all economic interests) together behind one policy for today's problems. In particular, of course, it means bringing in the one economic interest that has hitherto not joined up with the other economic interests in a common economic policy: the business interest.

In practical politics, "consensus" unites all who accept the accomplished facts of yesterday and excludes only the irreconcilables who still want to repeal history.

The effectiveness of this approach, at least so far, cannot be denied. It has enabled the Johnson administration to get more done than any administration in living memory. Above all it has enabled the Johnson administration to get more of the *new* tasks done. I doubt that this country, or any other, has ever seen greater skill or more purpose than the President exhibits when he uses the near unanimity of the country on the problems of yesterday to advance new solutions to the problems of today. Perhaps the one thing wrong with the President's effective use of "consensus" to solve problems and respond to challenges, *before* they can become issues, is that it is done so skillfully that many do not fully appreciate an extraordinary performance.

There probably is no other way to get done what Mr. Johnson gets done; the experience of his predecessor would indicate this. Mr. Kennedy, too, was a man of the transition period. But he reversed the balance between substance and rhetoric. In his actions he was primarily concerned with clearing up and finishing the tasks of yesterday; and his politics was clearly based on the old New Deal alignments. But his rhetoric—his "style," if you please—was that of a new generation. Yet he had to fight every inch of the way and accomplished, essentially, very little. This cannot be blamed on Congress: President Johnson had the same Congress during his first year and got out of it all the actions it had refused President Kennedy. President Johnson, in other words, may have had to smother dissent to get any action whatever.

There are great dangers, however, in the politics of "consensus," and they are likely to grow with time.

The first danger is clearly that of *losing the young*—the "new majority" of the educated professional middle class.

There is little doubt, I believe, that the President is no hero to this group. Indeed, there is little doubt that this is the one group in which Mr. Goldwater in 1964 found a great deal of response. This is, in terms of the *old* issues, a very conservative group; yesterday's "liberal" rhetoric is bound to bore them. That they have much interest in the program of the extreme right is very doubtful. But at least the Gold-waterites talked "principles."

Quite apart from personality—and Mr. Johnson is so clearly, unlike his predecessor, not one of the "new generation" and not really "sophisticated"—Mr. Johnson is in danger of being totally misunderstood by the "new majority." They are likely to miss the policy in his actions altogether and to mistake it for a clever publicity gimmick. Altogether they are likely to hear cleverness where they expect conviction.

How long it will remain prudent, therefore, to risk losing the young by not talking policy (even though talking policy will certainly alienate the old power groups) is a fundamental question for Mr. Johnson. Will he still be able to get through to the young if he waits? Does he, indeed, even understand, after all these years in the Congress, that it is conflict that creates political excitement, generates support, and mobilizes hitherto uncommitted political energies?

Another real danger is that "consensus" which smothers dissent *also smothers discussion and understanding.* This is particularly dangerous in foreign policy today, precisely because we may have to execute rather startling shifts fast. The public is totally unprepared. And the public has been kept intentionally in the dark—whether the reason for this be Mr. Johnson's dislike of criticism, or his fear that discussion of his policies might restrict his freedom of movement. Very few people in this country even understand that we have committed ourselves to a major new task: that of the containment of China. Fewer still realize the great challenges to our traditional military, diplomatic, and economic policy that lie ahead in Europe. The reason why this is so dangerous is, of course, that there is grave risk of a violent and irrational reaction should anything go wrong—and something surely will, in so complex and precarious a world.

But the greatest weaknesses of the politics of "consensus" are in their *restrictions on Presidential leadership,* both in respect to formulating policy and in respect to building the new political alignments.

The new thinking is not being done. Mr. Johnson may expect new policies to grow out of his actions. He could be right. *But, in politics, deeds do not necessarily speak louder than words.* And the words are not being said. That Mr. Johnson is capable of saying them—forcefully, indeed movingly—he showed in his Howard

University speech. But despite (perhaps because of?) his constant public exposure, Mr. Johnson clearly refrains from formulating a new political point of view, a new political idea, a new political direction. And he may, thereby, misjudge the country and the times. There seems to me to be an expectation in the land, a sense of foreboding beneath all the prosperity, a receptivity for seriousness that is not being satisfied.

The politics of consensus also makes it difficult, if not impossible, for the President to be the *political master builder,* the designer of the new alignments and the modeler of the new—or at least the changed—configuration of forces, perceptions, and ideas which the new realities at home and abroad demand. He is, perforce, so busy making the old configuration serve a little longer that he does not seem to have any time left over to work on creating a new one.

This is not said in criticism. In fact, it would be hard to imagine what else President Johnson could have done—and there is no doubt that what he is doing, he is doing with consummate skill. But it nevertheless seems likely that the question whether the Great Society is, indeed, a destination for the American people, or a mere whistle stop which later generations will pass by, will be decided by Mr. Johnson's ability to become the master builder of tomorrow—despite the need to preserve, indeed to perpetuate, yesterday.

That the Johnson administration is one of transition is clear. But is the future going to see it as a transition *from* the Old, or as a transition *to* the New?

CHAPTER FOUR

This Romantic Generation

"I AM MOTHER O'Rourke," the voice on the telephone said. "I am Dean of Students at a large Catholic women's college. Mother President and all our faculty very much hope that you will accept our invitation to talk to our girls on social issues and their importance. Ten years ago our students were deeply interested in labor relations, international relations, and in other major social and political problems. Now they care only for matters of conscience and personal behavior, such as civil rights, a 'personal philosophy of life,' or the size of their own future family and how to raise it. That's wonderful, of course, and we are all for it. But economic and political questions still exist and are far from solved. The girls surely ought to know something about them and not just concern themselves all the time with their little selves and their own conscience."

A dean trying to con a prospective speaker (especially if there is no fee) has no more truth in him than a Texas wildcatter raising sucker money. Yet Mother O'Rourke's call pulled together for

---

First published in *Harper's Magazine,* May, 1966.

me a lot of observations that have made me question the accepted picture of an important group of today's young adults—the men and women between twenty and twenty-five who are in college or graduate school. This picture, it seems to me, does not fit at all the influential, though not very large, group which sets the intellectual fashions on campuses from San Diego State to the Harvard Yard.

"Everybody knows" for instance that these educated young adults have discarded the Protestant Ethic of their forefathers. And ever since David Riesman's brilliant book *The Lonely Crowd* in 1950, it has been almost an axiom that the young American is increasingly outer-directed. But when I hung up after extricating myself from Mother O'Rourke's invitation, it suddenly dawned on me that many of the young Americans now in college and graduate school are searching for an ethic based on personal (if not spiritual) values, rather than on social utility or community mores—what one might call an Ecumenical Ethic. The old ideologies and slogans leave these young adults cold—as does President Johnson's Great Society. But there is a passionate groping for personal commitment to a philosophy of life. Above all, a new inner-directedness is all the rage in this group.

The clearest symptom of this is, perhaps, the books that are the fashion on campus. Undergraduates and graduate students alike read a great deal of what one of them—a teaching assistant in history—aptly calls "Instant Zen." They read Erich Fromm. They devour those two apparently incompatible but actually complementary pamphleteers: (1) Paul Goodman (*Growing Up Absurd, Utopian Essays*), a latter-day Thoreau opposed to society and all its work whose Walden Pond is the graduate psychology department; and (2) Ayn Rand (*Fountainhead, Atlas Shrugged,* and a new book, *The Virtue of Selfishness*), a Nietzsche of the NAM, preaching the organization superman. And they read Sartre. (Despite their professed interest in Existentialism, they tend to consign Camus to the limbo of "required reading"; his very compassion, generosity, and concern for his fellowman make him suspect as a "classic.")

Ever since adolescence was invented two hundred years ago, in Goethe's *Young Werther* (incidentally the first international best seller), it has always had a literature it claimed for its very own. Salinger's *Catcher in the Rye*—another *Young Werther,* though one living in an affluent society which can afford salvation by psychoanalysis, instead of by suicide as in Goethe's book—was the "in" book of the young adults ten years ago. Our grandmothers hid in their bosoms tear-stained albums of Swinburne's slightly rancid sensuality. Generations of level-headed, no-nonsense New England girls have got drunk on the low-calorie carbonated syrup of Kahlil Gibran's *The Prophet.* Generations of equally level-headed European boys, diligently preparing to be German engineers or French customs inspectors, have swooned over Stendhal's passionately passionless male Lolitas. When my own generation reached young adulthood around 1930, T. S. Eliot's *The Waste Land* and the early Donne were our Bibles; we missed the H. L. Mencken and Nietzsche fashions by only a few years.

The specific authors and books of the campus fashion thus vary greatly from one generation to the other—and not only in their literary merits. But the whole genre has common characteristics. It is naïvely sentimental, for instance, or saturated with the bittersweet sadness the Germans call *Weltschmerz* (and which only the very healthy, vigorous, and hopeful—that is the young—can afford). It tends to wallow in self-pity (in which department *The Sorrows of Young Werther* still holds the unchallenged world record). The idols of every campus generation have always been against everything and *for* nothing. The twenty-year-olds, after all, while mature in body and mind, are still exempted from responsibility—are, indeed, being encouraged in the pleasant delusion that Daddy will take care of everything, whether they smash an automobile fender or an institution.

This literature always reflects the mood of its generation. It is the young adult's own, precisely because it says what he feels but is unable to express himself. These books do not talk *to* their reader; they talk *for* him. Even though ephemeral—and, often enough, trash—the books faithfully mirror how the campus generation of the moment sees itself, or at the least how it wants to see itself.

The books of this kind in fashion today are contemptuous of, if not hostile to, society and its demands, values, and rewards. They proclaim that truth can be found only in one's own inner experience and that the demands of one's own personal conscience are a trustworthy guide to behavior and action. Sartre is "in"—as Camus is not—because only the cocoon of his own words and thoughts exists for him.

The "moderate" among these authors today is clearly Erich Fromm, the neo-Freudian psychoanalyst. He plays in today's campus culture the role that Reinhold Niebuhr played thirty years ago. Niebuhr even then warned against forgetting the person and his spiritual needs. But he was the idol of the young because in those days he preached the "social gospel" of public responsibility and liberal reform. Fromm today, by contrast, warns against forgetting community and society; but he is accepted because his main stress is on the person and his relationship to himself. Niebuhr asked, What society do you, as a moral man, want? Fromm asks, What kind of person do you want to be? Like the other writers who speak for the young adults—from "Instant Zen" to Paul Goodman and Ayn Rand—Fromm is self-centered.

There are a good many other symptoms of the new "inner-directedness." The vogue of the word "sincerity" is one. To the older generation this is an embarrassing word; we remember the appeasers and quislings of thirty years ago saying, "At least Hitler is *sincere.*" But to today's young adult "sincerity" is again a valid, if not the ultimate, test of behavior, especially in public life. I listened a year ago to some graduate students, bright and well informed, discussing an all-night teach-in at Columbia University. They were not a bit interested in logic or in the arguments, let alone in the factual assertions of the various speakers. All they wanted to know was, "Do you think he was sincere?"

A related phenomenon is the current interest in the "mind drugs" such as LSD. Whatever else they do, the hallucinations they produce are entirely self-centered inner experiences of one's own consciousness, with no outside world, no other person, no relationships in them.

On a mountain hike last summer, a few weeks after Mother O'Rourke's telephone call, a psychologist friend began to talk about the "management problems" of a midwestern mental-health center which trains postgraduate students in sizable numbers to become psychiatrists, psychologists, and social workers.

"To what do you attribute these management problems," I interrupted; "your growth?"

"We have grown of course very rapidly—fourfold since 1950," he answered. "But this is a minor factor. Our big problem is the radical shift in student attitude. The men who came to us ten or fifteen years ago wanted to be scientists. They were research-oriented. They got upset when they found out that in psychology or psychiatry empirical data and scientific theory are not enough. We had to hammer home day after day that the practitioner always deals with a unique human being, his emotions, aspirations, experiences, values—and that the practitioner himself is a human being, too.

"The men we get today are scientifically much better trained as a rule. But they tend to be frustrated clergymen who only come to us because there is no ecumenical, non-denominational seminary around. We have to tell them every day that fulfilling oneself, compassion, and love for one's neighbor aren't enough—indeed, will do damage unless supported by empirical facts and buttressed by sound theory. The men we got ten or fifteen years ago were out to find the facts; the men we get today are out to find themselves."

What explains such a shift from the outer-directed student of the 1950's to the inner-directed student of today?

One cause is certainly the disenchantment of this particular group of young people with the traditional social issues. However important they may be, such issues are not very exciting in the 1960's. It is hard for anybody to get up much emotional steam about the pension demands of the newspaper unions. And who is the "wicked imperialist" in the conflict between India and Pakistan? Indeed, most social problems have ceased to be "issues" and have become "fields of study." Where they used to call for passion leading to commitment and action, they now call for hard, plodding work leading to a Ph.D. thesis. And very few Ph.D. theses have ever fired the imagination and engrossed the emotions even of the men who wrote them, let alone of a generation of young people.

A second factor is that there are so many more graduate students in pursuit of a higher degree. The emergence and rapid growth of a distinct graduate-student community fosters emphasis on "inner experience," on "sincerity," and on the search for a "personal philosophy." Many graduate students have an outsized guilt feeling and therefore need an inner-directed ethic to justify themselves to themselves.

In part, they need a rationalization for their economic status. Most graduate students, while far from rich, live well above the poverty line. Their income, however, comes from fellowships or grants rather than from wages. If there is a wage earner in the family it is the wife rather than the husband. As consumers they are part of the affluent society. But as producers they are outside of it. Some graduate students are so self-conscious about this that they seriously advocate the payment of regular wages for going to graduate school. But many more search for an ethic which would base economic reward on what work means to a man and contributes to his self-development, rather than on its social utility and its value to others.

Above all, however, the graduate student needs such an inner-directed ethic to rationalize his own motives. To be sure, love of scholarship is the main motivation for some; others are attracted by the rewards which our economy offers the man with advanced specialized training. But a good many graduate students know perfectly well that they decided to stay in school in large part because grants and fellowships made it easy. Often they secretly suspect that they use graduate school as a pleasant way to postpone growing up, with its many commitments and decisions. Others are in graduate school for the sake of the draft exemption—and they cannot help knowing it. When they talk about their reasons for staying on in school—and they talk about them on and on and on—they therefore tend to stress "self-fulfillment," "sincerity," "basic values," and "personal philosophy of life."

Though going on to graduate school is fast becoming the correct thing to do in the better colleges, the graduate-school community is quite small—maybe half a million people at any one time, counting the students, their wives, and children. This group, however, has influence out of all proportion to its size. It is highly concentrated in a very few large universities, such as the University of California at Berkeley, Harvard, MIT, Cal Tech, New York University, Chicago, and Stanford. As a result it tends to dominate the prestige schools, which are, of course, the pacesetters and fashion makers for the entire academic world, faculty as well as students. Indeed, for the first time—in the Berkeley riots and in a good many of the teach-ins—graduates rather than undergraduate students took the lead.

The great catalyst of the new mood has, of course, been the civil-rights campaign. It gave the campus generation the Cause it had been waiting for: a cause of conscience. The young people are much closer in their views on civil rights to the abolitionists of a century ago than they are to yesterday's liberals. The oppression of the Negro is to them a sin rather than a wrong. "We Shall Overcome" has the ring of a gospel hymn rather than that of a *New Republic* editorial. This explains in large part the tremendous impact the civil-rights movement has had on the mood, vision, and world view of the campus generation. In addition, civil rights has offered scope for individual initiative and effectiveness, something our society otherwise does not readily grant to men or women in their early twenties. There are the students, white and colored, who have gone South to teach in the Freedom Schools. There are the white college girls up North who in considerable numbers venture into the meanest Negro ghettos of the big cities to tutor or counsel, often entirely on their own.

Yet developments in this country alone cannot explain the shift in mood. It is by no means an American phenomenon. It is, indeed, going on in all industrially developed countries, regardless of race or political and economical systems. In both Western and Eastern Europe those apostles of inner-directedness, the American Beat poets such as Allen Ginsberg, are extraordinarily popular. The idol of Russia's university students is Yevgeni Yevtushenko—a poet of the individual conscience, before which society is all but irrelevant. And the one mass movement in any industrial country today that has attracted large numbers of the college generation is the Japanese Soka Gakkai—half religious fundamentalism preaching the absolute primacy of inner experiences, half political fanaticism with "sincerity" its only slogan.

Fashions—especially adolescent fashions—do not as a rule outlast their generation. There is just a slim chance, however, that the mood of this campus generation will prove to be one of the rare exceptions: a first premonition of a change in the consciousness and vision of modern man.

The present lack of interest on campus in social problems may possibly—just barely possibly—be a first hint that the conventional social issues are increasingly becoming red herrings. Terms such as "management and labor," the "concentration of economic power," or "big government" all assume that there are a few big organizations in a society which is otherwise relatively power-free. But actually in our society all social tasks tend to ball together into large and complex organizations of tremendous power.

The institution that has grown the most in this century is not in the economic or political sphere at all. It is the university. There is actually more concentration of brain power in the twenty largest universities than there ever was a concentration of economic power in the heyday of the Morgans and the Rockefellers, before the passage of the antitrust laws. The hospital has also become big and complex—and so has the Catholic Diocese in the modern metropolis, the American Medical Association, the armed forces, the civil service, and so on. The fact of big, complex organization rather than this or that embodiment of it is now the matter of central significance. To single out any one institution as *the* organization is to make impossible an understanding of the issue, let alone a solution.

This, I think, is beginning to be felt. Or is it pure coincidence that we recently had two totally unconnected revolts against organizational power structures which were never before seen as problem areas: the Berkeley student riot and the attack on the Roman bureaucracy of the Catholic Church at the Vatican Council, especially in its first two sessions before Pope John's death?

The big complex modern organization does, indeed, present a number of strange problems. In the first place, there is plenty of evidence that we do not yet really know how to make it work or how to control it. It tends to be overadministered but undermanaged, tends to mistake procedures and "proper channels" for direction and energy. The student riots at Berkeley were greatly aggravated by management malfunctioning and by a ludicrous failure of communication within a very small top-management group sitting in adjoining offices. Yet Clark Kerr, the university's president, is one of the most accomplished professional managers in the country. Similarly, management malfunctioning and communications failure seem to have greatly aggravated the grievances of the Catholic bishops against the Roman Curia.

Even more important, of course, is the new set of problems which confronts a society of big organizations: their relationship to each other and to the common good; their effective control by government; the effective control of government by the public and its representatives; and the power, authority, and responsibility of these institutional monsters.

Despite everything Paul Goodman—one of the heroes of the campus—has been saying in his all-out attacks on the very idea of organization, we will not do away with it. On the contrary, we clearly need more large organizations—for the task of running the modern metropolis, for instance, and for a good many new jobs in the international community such as the policing and traffic control of outer space. But despite everything Miss Ayn Rand—another hero of the campus—has been saying, the problems of the big organization will not disappear if only we give free rein to the superman executive. McNamaras and Hammarskjolds (not to mention the executive-suite Genghis Khans of Miss Rand's *Atlas Shrugged*) are in very short supply.

The problems of the big organization demand new political theory and new social policy. At the moment, indeed, both politics and society require greater skill and greater responsibility precisely because no generally accepted and understood theory is available to statesmen and politicians. The example of Sartre and of some of the more extreme splinter groups of the student leftists shows clearly, I submit, how fast in such a situation inner-directedness degenerates into irresponsibility. Yet one can also understand why the young might conclude that the major tasks in society are jobs for the professional, the political philosopher, and the social innovator, for which amateurs, such as they are, need not apply.

But a society of big organizations also raises in new and acute form the question of the person. What is his relationship to these new leviathans which are at one and the same time his servants and his master, his opportunity and his restraint, his tool and his environment? How can the individual maintain his integrity and privacy in such a society? Is individual freedom necessarily limited to whatever small air space will be left between the towering organizational skyscrapers? In such a society of big organizations, the need becomes more urgent for new answers to the old questions, Who am I? What am I? What should I be? These are questions the West has tended to consider either as solved or as unimportant, for the last few hundred years, while it put its main emphasis on the nature of matter rather than on the nature of man. But now these questions, the young may rightly feel, cannot be ignored. They are their own direct, personal concerns.

The current mood of the present campus generation is not without serious dangers. It is being exploited by some dubious people—on the right and the left—for political purposes of their own; but this, while undoubtedly a threat, may not be the major danger. For the present mood encourages irresponsibility. And the emphasis on "sincerity" might only too easily degenerate into adulation of that professional specialist in sincerity, the demagogue, or of the synthetic TV personality. Is it pure accident that California, the state most strongly influenced by the young adults and their fashions, is also the one state where TV or movie success seems increasingly to be accepted as adequate preparation for the job of Governor or United States Senator?

The present campus mood is, above all, drearily futile. Most of the rebels against big organization will end up—and very soon—as well-paid and fairly successful members of big organizations, whether big university, big government, or big business. They will then predictably impose their own emotional need for security and conformity on their organization, despite all their fine contempt for the Organization Man. The odds are astronomical against Instant Zen's fathering anything but another bull session.

Yet in its return to "inner-directedness," today's college crowd may, just may, play-act in their school years their homework as tomorrow's adults. The bull session may, for once, be awareness rather than echo. For once today's young-adult fashions may foretell the concerns, and prefigure the intellectual landscape, of tomorrow.

CHAPTER FIVE

Calhoun's Pluralism

THE AMERICAN PARTY system has been under attack almost continuously since it took definite form in the time of Andrew Jackson. The criticism has always been directed at the same point: America's political pluralism, the distinctively American organization of government by compromise of interests, pressure groups, and sections. And the aim of the critics, from Thaddeus Stevens to Henry Wallace, has always been to substitute for this "unprincipled" pluralism a government based, as in Europe, on "ideologies" and "principles." But never before—at least not since the Civil War years—has the crisis been as acute as in this last decade; for the political problems which dominate our national life today—foreign policy and industrial policy—are precisely the problems which interest and pressure-group compromise is least equipped to handle. And while the crisis symptoms—a left-wing third party and the threatened split-off of the southern wing—are more alarming in the Democratic party, the Republicans are hardly much better off.

First published in *The Review of Politics*, October, 1948.

The 1940 boom for the "idealist" Willkie and the continued inability to attract a substantial portion of the labor vote are definite signs that the Republican party, too, is under severe *ideological* pressure.

Yet, there is almost no understanding of the problem—precisely because there is so little understanding of the basic principles of American pluralism. Of course, every politician in this country must be able instinctively to work in terms of sectional and interest compromise; and the voter takes it for granted. But there is practically no awareness of the fact that organization on the basis of sectional and interest compromise is both the distinctly American form of political organization and the cornerstone of practically all major political institutions of the modern United States. As acute an observer as Winston Churchill apparently did not understand that Congress works on a basis entirely different from that of Britain's Parliament; neither do nine out of ten Americans and 999 out of 1,000 teachers of those courses in "Civics." There is even less understanding that sectional and interest-group pluralism is not just the venal expediency of that stock villain of American folklore, the "politician," but that it in itself is a basic ideology, a basic principle—and the one which is the very foundation of our free society and government.

I

To find an adequate analysis of the principle of government by sectional and interest compromise, we have to go back more than a hundred years to John C. Calhoun and to his two political treatises* published after his death in 1852. Absurd, you will say, for it is practically an axiom of American history that Calhoun's political theories, subtle, even profound though they may have been, were

*A *Disquisition on Government* and A *Discourse on the Constitution and Government of the United States.*

reduced to absurdity and irrelevance by the Civil War. Yet, this "axiom" is nothing but a partisan vote of the Reconstruction Period. Of course, the specific occasion for which Calhoun formulated his theories, the slavery issue, has been decided; and for the constitutional veto power of the states over national legislation, by means of which Calhoun proposed to formalize the principle of sectional and interest compromise, was substituted in actual practice the much more powerful and much more elastic but extraconstitutional and extralegal veto power of sections, interests, and pressure groups in Congress and within the parties.* But *his basic principle itself: that every major interest in the country, whether regional, economic, or religious, is to possess a veto power on political decisions directly affecting it,* the principle which Calhoun called, rather obscurely, *"the rule of concurrent majority,"* has become the organizing principle of American politics. And it is precisely this principle that is under fire today.

What makes Calhoun so important as the major key to the understanding of American politics is not just that he saw the importance in American political life of sectional and interest pluralism; other major analysts of our government, de Tocqueville, for instance, or Bryce or Wilson, saw that, too. But Calhoun, perhaps alone, saw in it more than a rule of expediency, imposed by the country's size and justifiable by results, if at all. He saw in it a basic principle of free government.

Without this (*the rule of concurrent majority based on interests rather than on principles*) there can be . . . no constitution. The assertion is true in reference to all constitutional governments, be their forms

---

*Calhoun's extreme legalism, his belief that everything had to be spelled out in the written Constitution—a belief he shared with his generation—is one of the major reasons why the importance of his thesis has not been generally recognized. Indeed, it is of the very essence of the concept of "concurrent majority" that it cannot be made official and legal in an effective government—the express veto such as the UN Charter gives to the Great Powers makes government impossible.

what they may: It is, indeed, the negative power which makes the constitution,—and the positive which makes the government. The one is the power of acting;—and the other the power of preventing or arresting action. The two, combined, make constitutional government.

. . . it follows, necessarily, that where the numerical majority has the sole control of the government, there can be no constitution . . . and hence, the numerical, unmixed with the concurrent majority, necessarily forms, in all cases, absolute government.

. . . The principle by which they (governments) are upheld and preserved . . . in constitutional governments is *compromise;*—and in absolute governments is *force.* . . .*

And however much the American people may complain in words about the "unprincipled" nature of their political system, by their actions they have always shown that they, too, believe that without sectional and interest compromises there can be no constitutional government. If this is not grasped, American government and politics must appear not only as cheap to the point of venality; they must appear as utterly irrational and unpredictable.

II

Sectional and interest pluralism has molded all American political institutions. It is the method—entirely unofficial and extra-constitutional—through which the organs of government are made to function, through which leaders are selected, policies developed, men and groups organized for the conquest and management of political power. In particular it is the explanation for the most distinctive features of the American political system: the way in which Congress operates, the way in which major government depart-

*Quotations from *A Disquisition on Government* (Columbia, S.C., 1852), pp. 35–37.

ments are set up and run, the qualifications for "eligibility" as a candidate for elective office, and the American party structure.

To all foreign observers of Congress two things have always remained mysterious: the distinction between the official party label and the "blocs" which cut across party lines; and the power and function of the congressional committees. And most Americans, though less amazed by the phenomena, are equally baffled.

The "blocs"—the "Farm Bloc," the "Friends of Labor in the Senate," the "Business Groups," and so on—are simply the expression of the basic tenet of sectional and interest pluralism that major interests have a veto power on legislation directly affecting them. For this reason they must cut across party lines—that is, lines expressing the numerical rather than the "concurrent" majority. And because these blocs have (*a*) only a negative veto and (*b*) that only on measures directly affecting them, they cannot in themselves be permanent groupings replacing the parties. They must be loosely organized; and one and the same member of Congress must at different times vote with different blocs. The strength of the blocs does not rest on their numbers, but on the basic mores of American politics which grant every major interest group a limited self-determination—as expressed graphically in the near sanctity of a senatorial filibuster. The power of the Farm Bloc, for instance, does not rest on the numerical strength of the rural vote—a minority vote even in the Senate with its disproportionate representation of the thinly populated agricultural states—but on its "strategic" strength, that is, on its being the spokesman for a recognized major interest.

Subordination of a major interest is possible, but only in a "temporary emergency." Most of the New Deal measures were, palpably, neither temporary nor emergency measures; yet their sponsors had to present them, and convincingly, as "temporary emergency measures" because they could be enacted only by overriding the extraconstitutional veto of the business interest.

Once the excuse of the "temporary emergency" had fully lost

its plausibility, that major interest could no longer be voted down; and the policy collapsed. By 1946, for instance, labor troubles could be resolved only on a basis acceptable to both labor and employer: higher wages *and* higher prices. (Even if a numerical majority had been available to legislate against either party—and the business group could probably still have been voted down in the late forties—the solution had to be acceptable to both parties.)

The principle of sectional and interest compromise leads directly to the congressional committee system—a system to which there is no parallel anywhere in the world. Congress, especially the House, has largely abdicated to its committees because only in the quiet and secrecy of a committee room can sectional compromise be worked out. The discussion on the floor as well as the recorded vote is far too public and therefore largely for the folks back home. But a committee's business is to arrive at an agreement between all major sectional interests affected; which explains the importance of getting a bill before the "right" committee. In any but an American legislature the position of each member, once a bill is introduced, is fixed by the stand of his party, which, in turn, is decided on grounds that have little to do with the measure itself, but are rather dictated by the balance of power in the government and by party programs. Hence it makes usually little difference which committee discusses a bill or whether it goes before a committee at all. In the United States, however, a bill's assignment to a specific committee decides which interest groups are to be recognized as affected by the measure and therefore entitled to a part in writing it ("who is to have standing before the committee"), for each committee represents a specific constellation of interests. In many cases this first decision therefore decides the fate of a proposed measure, especially as the compromise worked out by the committee is generally accepted once it reaches the floor, especially in the House.

It is not only Congress but every individual member of Congress himself who is expected to operate according to the "rule of concurrent majority." He is considered both a representative of the

American people and responsible to the national interest and a delegate of his constituents and responsible to their particular interests. Wherever the immediate interests of his constituents are not in question, he is to be a statesman; wherever their conscience or their pocket-books are affected, he is to be a business agent. This is in sharp contrast to the theory on which any parliamentary government is based—a theory developed a full two hundred years ago in Edmund Burke's famous speech to the voters at Bristol—according to which a member of Parliament represents the commonweal rather than his constituents. Hence in all parliamentary countries, the representative can be a stranger to his constituency—in the extreme, as it was practiced in Weimar Germany, there is one long national list of candidates who run in all constituencies—whereas the Congressman in this country must be a resident of his constituency. And while an American Senator considers it a compliment and an asset to be called "Cotton Ed Smith," the Speaker of the House of Commons not so long ago severely reprimanded a member for calling another member—an official of the miners' union—a "representative of the coal miners."

The principle of sectional and interest pluralism also explains why this is the only nation where Cabinet members are charged by law with the representation of special interests—labor, agriculture, commerce. In every other country an agency of the government—any agency of the government—is solemnly sworn to guard the public interest against "the interests." In this country the concept of a government department as the representative of a special interest group is carried down to smaller agencies and even to divisions and branches of a department. This showed itself, for example, during World War II in such fights as that between OPA, representing the consumer, and the War Production Board, representing the producer; or within WPB between the Procurement branches, speaking for the war industries, and the Civilian Requirements Branch, speaking for the industries producing for the "home front."

The mystery of "eligibility"—the criterion which decides who will make a promising candidate for public office—which has baffled so many foreign and American observers, Bryce, for instance—also traces back to the "rule of the concurrent majority." Eligibility simply means that a candidate must not be unacceptable to any major interest, religious, or regional group in the electorate; it is primarily a negative qualification. Eligibility operates on all levels and applies to all elective offices. It has been brilliantly analyzed in "Boss" Flynn's *You're the Boss.* His classical example is the selection of Harry Truman as Democratic Vice-Presidential candidate in 1944. Truman was "eligible" rather than Wallace, Byrnes, or Douglas precisely because he was unknown; because he was neither easterner nor westerner nor southerner, because he was neither New Deal nor Conservative, and so on; in short, because he had no one trait strong enough to offend anybody anywhere.

But the central institution based on sectional pluralism is the American party. Completely extraconstitutional, the wonder and the despair of every foreign observer who cannot fit it into any of his concepts of political life, the American party (rather than the states) has become the instrument to realize Calhoun's "rule of the concurrent majority."

In stark contrast to the parties of Europe, the American party has no program and no purpose except to organize divergent groups for the common pursuit and conquest of power. Its unity is one of action, not of beliefs. Its only rule is to attract—or at least not to repel—the largest possible number of groups. It must, by definition, be acceptable equally to the right and the left, the rich and the poor, the farmer and the worker, the Protestant and the Catholic, the native and the foreign-born. It must be able to rally Mr. Rankin of Mississippi and Mr. Marcantonio of New York—or Senator Flanders and Colonel McCormick—behind the same Presidential candidate and the same "platform."

As soon as it cannot appeal at least to a minority in every major group (as soon, in other words, as it provokes the veto of one section, interest, or class) a party is in danger of disintegration.

Whenever a party loses its ability to fuse sectional pressures and class interests into one national policy—both parties just before the Civil War, the Republican party before its reorganization by Mark Hanna, both parties again today—the party system (and with it the American political system altogether) is in crisis.

Consequently, it is not that Calhoun was repudiated by the Civil War which is the key to the understanding of American politics, but that he has become triumphant since.

The apparent victors, the "Radical Republicans," Thaddeus Stevens, Seward, Chief Justice Chase, were out to destroy not only slavery and states rights but the "rule of the concurrent majority" itself. And the early Republican party—before the Civil War and in the Reconstruction Period—was, indeed, determined to substitute principle for interest as the lodestar of American political life. But in the end it was the political thought of convinced pluralists such as Abraham Lincoln and Andrew Johnson, rather than the ideologies of the Free Soilers and Abolitionists, which molded the Republican party. And ever since, the major developments of American politics have been based on Calhoun's principle. To this the United States owes the strength as well as the weaknesses of its political system.

III

The weaknesses of sectional and interest compromise are far more obvious than its virtues; they have been hammered home for a hundred years. Francis Lieber, who brought the dominant German political theories of the early nineteenth century to this country, attacked pluralism in Calhoun's own state of South Carolina a century ago. Twenty years later Walter Bagehot contrasted, impressively, General Grant's impotent administration with those of Gladstone and Disraeli to show the superiority of ideological party organization. The most thorough and most uncompromising criticism came from Woodrow Wilson; and every single one of the Professor's points was amply borne out by his later experience as President. Time has not made these weaknesses any less dangerous.

There is, first of all, the inability of a political system based on the "rule of the concurrent majority" to resolve conflicts of principles. All a pluralist system can do is to deny that "ideological" conflicts (as they are called nowadays) do exist. Those conflicts, a pluralist must assert, are fundamentally either struggles for naked power or friction between interest groups which could be solved if only the quarreling parties sat down around a conference table. Perhaps, the most perfect, because most naïve, expression of this belief remains the late General Patton's remark that the Nazis were, after all, not so very different from Republicans or Democrats. (Calhoun, while less naïve, was as unable to understand the reality of "ideological" conflict in and around the slavery problem.)

In nine cases out of ten the refusal to acknowledge the existence of ideological conflict is beneficial. It prevents fights for power, or clashes of interests, from flaring into religious wars where irreconcilable principles collide (a catastrophe against which Europe's ideological politics have almost no defense). It promotes compromise where compromise is possible. But in a genuine clash of principles—and, whatever the pluralists say, there *are* such clashes—the "rule of concurrent majority" breaks down; it did, in Calhoun's generation, before the profound reality of the slavery issue. A legitimate ideological conflict is actually aggravated by the pluralists' refusal to accept its reality: the compromisers who thought the slavery issue could be settled by the meeting of good intentions, or by the payment of money, may have done more than the Abolitionists to make the Civil War inevitable.

A weakness of sectional and interest pluralism just as serious is that it amounts to a principle of inaction. The popular assertion, "It's better to make the wrong decision than to do nothing at all," is, of course, fallacious; but no nation, however unlimited its resources, can have a very effective policy if its government is based on a principle that orders it to do nothing important except unanimously. Moreover, pluralism increases exorbitantly the weight of well-organized small interest groups, especially when they lobby *against* a decision. Congress can far too easily be high-pressured into emasculating a bill by the expedient of omitting its pertinent provisions; only with much greater difficulty can Congress be moved to positive action. This explains, to a large extent, the eclipse of Congress during the last hundred years, both in popular respect and in its actual momentum as policy-making organ of government. Congress, which the founding fathers had intended to be the central organ of government—a role which it fulfilled up to Andrew Jackson—became the compound representative of sections and interests and, consequently, progressively incapable of national leadership.

Pluralism gives full weight—more than full weight—to sections and interests; but who is to represent the national welfare? Ever since the days of Calhoun, the advocates of pluralism have tried to dodge this question by contending that the national interest is equal to the sum of all particular interests and that it therefore does not need a special organ of representation. But this most specious argument is contradicted by the most elementary observation. In practice, pluralism tends to resolve sectional and class conflicts at the expense of the national interest which is represented by nobody in particular, by no section and no organization.

These weaknesses had already become painfully obvious while Calhoun was alive and active—during the decade after Andrew Jackson, the first President of pluralism. Within a few years after Calhoun's death, the inability of the new system to comprehend and to resolve an ideological conflict—ultimately its inability to represent and to guard the national interest—had brought catastrophe. For a hundred years and more, American political thought has therefore revolved around attempts to counteract if not to overcome these weaknesses. Three major developments of American constitutional life were the result: the growth of the functions and powers of the President and his emergence as a "leader" rather than as the executive agent of the Congress; the rise of the Supreme Court, with its "rule of law," to the position of arbiter of policy; the development of a unifying ideology—the "American Creed."

Of these the most important—and the least noticed—is the American Creed. In fact, I know of no writer of major importance since de Tocqueville who has given much attention to it. Yet even the term "un-American" cannot be translated successfully into any other language, least of all into "English" English. In no other country could the identity of the nation with a certain set of ideas be assumed—at least not under a free government. This unique cohesion on principles shows, for instance, in the refusal of the American voter to accept Socialists and Communists as "normal" parties, simply because both groups refuse to accept the assumption of a common American ideology. It shows, for another example, in the indigenous structure of the American labor movement with its emphasis on interest pressure rather than on a political philososphy. And this is also the only Western country where "Civics" are taught in schools—the only democratic country which believes that a correct social philosophy could or should be part of public education.

In Europe, a universal creed would be considered incompatible with a free society. Before the advent of totalitarianism, no European country had ever known anything comparable to the flag salute of the American school child.* For in Europe all political activity is based on ideological factions; consequently, to introduce a uniform ideology in a European country is to stamp out *all* opposition. In the United States ideological homogeneity is the very basis of political diversity. It makes possible the almost unlimited freedom of interest groups, religious groups, pressure groups, and the

* The perhaps most profound discussion of the American ideological cohesion can be found in the two decisions of the Supreme Court on the compulsory flag salute, and in the two dissents therefrom, which deserve high rating among American state papers.

like; and in this way it is the very fundament of free government. (It also explains why the preservation of civil liberties has been so much more important a problem in this country—as compared to England or France, for instance.) The assumption of ideological unity gives the United States the minimum of cohesion without which its political system simply could not have worked.

IV

But is even the "American dream" enough to make a system based on the "rule of the concurrent majority" work today? Can pluralism handle the two major problems of American politics—the formulation of a foreign policy, and the political organization of an industrial society—any more successfully than it could handle the slavery issue? Or is the American political system as much in crisis as it was in the last years of Calhoun's life, and for pretty much the same reasons?

A foreign policy can never be evolved by adding particular interests—regional, economic, or racial—or by compromising among them; it must supersede them. If Calhoun's contention that the national interest will automatically be served by serving the interests of the parts is wrong anywhere, it is provably wrong in the field of foreign affairs.

A foreign policy and a party system seem to be compatible only if the parties are organized on programmatic grounds, that is, on principles. For if not based on general principles, a foreign policy will become a series of improvisations without rhyme or reason. In a free society, in which parties compete for votes and power, the formulation of a foreign policy may thus force the parties into ideological attitudes which will sooner or later be reflected in their domestic policies, too.

This was clearly realized in the early years of the Republic, when foreign policy was vital to a new nation, clinging precariously to a long seaboard without hinterland, engaged in a radical experiment with new political institutions, surrounded by the Great Powers of that time, England, France, and Spain, all of them actually or potentially hostile. This awareness of foreign policy largely explains why the party system of the founding fathers—especially of Hamilton—was an ideological one; it also explains why the one positive foreign-policy concept this country developed during the nineteenth century, the Monroe Doctrine, was formulated by the last two politically active survivors of the founding generation, Monroe and John Quincy Adams. No matter how little Calhoun himself realized it, his doctrine would have been impossible without the French Revolution and the Napoleonic Wars which, during the most critical period of American integration, kept our potential European enemies busy. By 1820, the country had become too strong, had taken in too much territory, to be easily attacked; and it was still not strong enough, and far too much absorbed in the development of its own interior, to play a part in international affairs. Hence Calhoun, and all America with him, could push foreign policy out of their minds—so much so that this is the only country in which it is possible to write a comprehensive work on an important historical period without as much as a mention of foreign affairs, as Arthur M. Schlesinger, Jr., managed to do in his *Age of Jackson.*

But today foreign policy is again as vital for the survival of the nation as it ever was during the administrations of Washington and Jefferson. And it has to be a foreign *policy,* that is, a making of decisions; hence neither "isolationism" nor "internationalism" will do. (For "internationalism"—the search for formulas which will provide automatic decisions, even in advance—is also a refusal to have a foreign policy; it may well have done this country, and the world, as much harm as "isolationism"—perhaps more.) To survive as the strongest of the Great Powers, the United States might even have to accept permanently the supremacy of foreign policies over domestic affairs, however much this may go against basic American convictions, and indeed against the American grain. But no foreign policy can be evolved by the compromise of sectional interests or economic pressures; yet neither party, as today constituted, could develop a foreign policy based on definite principles.

The other great national need is to resolve the political problems of an industrial society. An industrial society is by nature ultrapluralistic, because it develops class and interest groups that are far stronger, and far more tightly organized, than any interest group in a preindustrial age. A few big corporations, a few big unions, may be the actually decisive forces in an industrial society. And these groups can put decisive pressure on society: they can throttle social and economic life.

The problem does not lie in "asocial behavior" of this or that group, but in the nature of industrial society, which bears much closer resemblance to feudalism than to the trading nineteenth century. Its political problems are very similar to those which feudalism had to solve—and failed to solve. It is in perpetual danger of disintegration into virtually autonomous fiefs, principalities, "free cities," "robber baronies," and "exempt bishoprics"—the authority and the interest of the nation trampled underfoot, autonomous groups uniting to control the central power in their own interest or disregarding government in fighting each other in the civil conflict of class warfare. And the alternative to such a collapse into anarchy or civil war—the suppression of classes and interest groups by an all-powerful government—is hardly more attractive.

An industrial society cannot function without an organ able to superimpose the national interest on economic or class interests. More than a mere arbiter is needed. The establishment of the "rules of civilized industrial warfare," as was done by both the Wagner Act and the Taft-Hartley Act, tries to avoid the need for policies by equalizing the strength of the conflicting sections; but that can lead only to deadlock, to collusion against the national interest, or, worse still, to the attempt to make the national authority serve the interest of one side against the other. In other words, an industrial society cannot fully accept Calhoun's assumption that the national good will evolve from the satisfaction of particular interests. An industrial society without national policy will become both anarchic and despotic.

Small wonder that there has been increasing demand for a radical change which would substitute ideological parties and programmatic policies for the pluralist parties and the "rule of the concurrent majority" of the American tradition. Henry Wallace's Third Party Movement, while the most publicized, may well be the least significant development; for third parties are, after all, nothing new in our political history. But for the first time in a hundred years there is a flood of books—and by serious students of American government—advocating radical constitutional reform. However much Senator Fulbright, Henry Hazlitt, and Thomas Finletter disagree on details, they are one in demanding the elimination—or at least the limitation—of the "rule of the concurrent majority" and its replacement by an ideological system functioning along parliamentary lines. More significant even may be Walter Reuther's new unionism with its blend of traditional pressure tactics and working-class, that is, ideological, programs and aims.

V

Yet all these critics and reformers not only fail to ask themselves whether an ideological system of politics would really be any better equipped to cope with the great problems of today—and neither the foreign nor the industrial policy of England, that most successful of all ideologically organized countries, looks any too successful right now; the critics also never stop to consider the unique strength of our traditional system.

Our traditional system makes sure that there is always a legitimate government in the country; and to provide such a government is the first job of any political system—a duty which a great many of the political systems known to man have never discharged.

It minimizes conflicts by utilizing, rather than suppressing, conflicting forces. It makes it almost impossible for the major parties to become entirely irresponsible: neither party can afford to draw strength from the kind of demagogic opposition, without governmental responsibility, which perpetually nurtures fascist and communist parties abroad. Hence, while the two national parties are willing to embrace any movement or any group in the country that commands sufficient following, they in turn force every group to bring its demands and programs into agreement with the beliefs, traditions, and prejudices of the people.

Above all, our system of sectional and interest compromise is one of the only two ways known to man in which a free government and a free society can survive—and the only one at all adapted to the conditions of American life and acceptable to the American people.

The central problem in a free government is that of factions, as we have known since Plato and Aristotle. Logically, a free government and factions are incompatible. But whatever the cause—vanity and pride, lust for power, virtue or wickedness, greed or the desire to help others—factionalism is inherent in human nature and in human society. For two thousand years the best minds in politics have tried to devise a factionless society—through education (Plato), through elimination of property (Thomas More), through concentration on the life of the spirit outside of worldly ambition (the political tradition of Lutheranism). The last great attempt to save freedom by abolishing faction was Rousseau's. But to create the factionless free society is as hopeless as to set up perpetual motion. From Plato to Rousseau, political thought has ended up by demanding that factions be suppressed, that is, that freedom, to be preserved, be abolished.

The Anglo-American political tradition alone has succeeded in breaking out of this vicious circle. Going back to Hooker and Locke, building on the rich tradition of free government in the cities of the late Middle Ages, Anglo-American political realism discovered that if factions cannot be suppressed, they must be utilized to make a free government both freer and stronger. This one basic concept distinguishes Anglo-American political theory and practice from continental European politics and accounts for the singular success of free and popular governments in both countries. Elsewhere in the Western world the choice has always been between extreme factionalism, which makes government impotent if not impossible and inevitably leads to civil war, and autocracy, which justifies the suppression of liberty with the need for effective and orderly government. Nineteenth-century France with its six revolutions, or near revolutions, stands for one, the totalitarian governments of our time for the other alternative of continental politics.

But—and this is the real discovery on which the Anglo-American achievement rests—factions can be used constructively only if they are encompassed in a frame of unity. A free government on the basis of sectional interest groups is possible only when there is no ideological split in the country. This is the American solution. Another conceivable solution is to channel the driving forces, the vectors of society, into ideological factions which obtain their cohesion from a program for the whole of society and from a creed. But that presupposes an unquestioned ruling class with a common outlook on life, with uniform mores and traditional, if not inherent, economic security. Given that sort of ruling class, the antagonist in an ideological system can be expected to be a "loyal opposition," that is, to accept the rules of the game and to see himself as a partner rather than as a potential challenger to civil war. But a ruling class accepted by the people as a whole, and feeling itself responsible to the people as a whole, cannot be created by fiat or overnight. In antiquity only Rome, in modern times only England, achieved it. On the Continent, all attempts to create a genuine ruling class have failed dismally.

In this country, the ruling-class solution was envisaged by Alexander Hamilton and seemed close to realization under the Presidents of the "Virginia Dynasty." Hamilton arrived at his concept with inescapable consistency; for he was absorbed by the search for a foreign policy and for the proper organization of an industrial society—precisely the two problems which, as we have seen, pluralism is least equipped to resolve. But even if Hamilton had not made the fatal mistake of identifying wealth with rulership, the American people could not have accepted his thesis. A ruling class was incompatible with mass immigration and with the explosive territorial expansion of nineteenth-century America. It was even more incompatible with the American concept of equality. And there is no reason to believe that contemporary America is any more willing to accept Hamilton's concept, Mr. James Burnham's idea of the managerial elite notwithstanding. This country as a free country has no alternative, it seems, to the "rule of the concurrent majority," no alternative to sectional pluralism as the device through which factions can be made politically effective.

It will be very difficult, indeed, to resolve the problems of foreign and of industrial policy on the pluralist basis and within the interest-group system, though not provably more difficult than these problems would be on another, ideological, basis. It will be all the harder as the two problems are closely interrelated; for the effectiveness of any American foreign policy depends, in the last analysis, on our ability to show the world a successful and working model of an industrial society. But if we succeed at all, it will be with the traditional system, horse trading, logrolling, and politicking all included. An old saying has it that this country lives simultaneously in a world of Jeffersonian beliefs and in one of Hamiltonian realities. Out of these two, Calhoun's concept of "the rule of the concurrent majority" alone can make one viable whole. The need for a formulated foreign policy and for a national policy of industrial order is real, but not more so than the need for a real understanding of this fundamental American fact: the pluralism of sectional and interest compromise is the warp of America's political fabric; it cannot be plucked out without unraveling the whole.

CHAPTER SIX

American Directions

PRESIDENT JOHNSON CLEARLY hopes, and probably expects, that his administration will become another "Era of Good Feeling." In his first major speech after the 1964 election he claimed that the country had reached a new "consensus on national purpose and policy," and he forecast "a long age of constructiveness" in which all segments of the public would work together for the common good. What he hopes to get, obviously, is a modern counterpart of the original Era of Good Feeling that started in 1817 when President Monroe came into office (like LBJ) with overwhelming public support and a splintered, ineffectual opposition.

He is not likely to get it. On the contrary, the United States almost certainly is entering a period of political turbulence unlike anything we have known for at least a generation. In the decades just ahead, our domestic politics will be dominated by unfamiliar issues—not only new, but different in kind from the things we have been arguing about since 1932. They will be concerned, not

---

First published in *Harper's Magazine*, February, 1965.

primarily with economic matters, but with basic values—moral, aesthetic, and philosophical. Moreover, the center of our political stage is now being taken over by a new power group: a professional, technical, and managerial middle class—very young, affluent, used to great job security, and highly educated. It will soon displace the old power centers—labor, the Farm Bloc, Big Business in the old-fashioned sense of that term. Around this new power center tomorrow's majority and tomorrow's consensus about the new issues will have to be built.

But the process will be accomplished only after eye-gouging struggles and bitter disagreement over the way to tackle our new set of national problems. For traditional power groups never give up their dominion gracefully; nor is it easy for any of us to turn our eyes away from the old, familiar issues which have preoccupied us for so long. Witness how the Goldwater people, during the 1964 campaign, were obsessed almost exclusively with their yearning to repeal history.

The old questions—mostly economic—of course will not go away. Debate over the role and limitations of the unions surely will be with us for a good long time. So will our worry about intractable poverty in the midst of affluence . . . about the impact of automation . . . about tax policy, conservation, and many another ancient staple.

Different in Quality

But the focus of domestic politics is likely to shift to two new areas: *the metropolis and the school.*

The major new issue of the last few years has been the Negro's integration into American society. It became a political issue precisely because economics alone could not solve the race problem. A good many civil-rights problems, of course, look as if they were primarily economic—access of the Negro to membership in craft unions, for instance. But at bottom we all know that it is our hearts, and not just our pocketbooks, that we are asked to open.

Similarly the central problem of the metropolis is not an economic one. It is concerned with political structure; indeed, with political constitution. In the coming debate over the schools, educational policy and purpose will clearly be the focal points. In both cases, the ultimate issue is the quality of life in America.

That our big cities are hell-bent on committing suicide is hardly news. They are rapidly becoming unlivable. Attempts to assuage the disease seem to aggravate it. New freeways create more traffic jams and more air pollution; urban renewal dispossesses the poor or moves them from the jungle of the slum into the desert of the housing development; zoning for "racial balance" ends up by creating another Black Belt or Bronzeville.

A real solution, if one can be found, will have to be primarily aesthetic (or, if you prefer the word, moral). At stake is the environment of modern man, rather than administration. We need a city that enriches and ennobles rather than degrades the individual, and not one that most efficiently fits him into well-planned public services. But long before we can hope to come to grips with the city as a human environment we will have to come to grips with the city as a government.

And the need is desperate. Within a few years three-quarters of the American people will live in a fairly small number of metropolitan areas, fewer than two hundred. Nearly two-fifths of the population will live in or close by the three monster supercities—one spreading from Boston to Norfolk, another from Milwaukee to Detroit (if not to Cleveland), and a third from San Francisco to San Diego. We will have to be able to supply people in the metropolis with water, sewers, and clean air. We will have to provide decent housing and schools for them, plus easy mobility for people, things, and ideas—which is the very reason for the existence of a city.

And for all this we shall need governmental institutions that will, of necessity, cut across or replace a whole host of local governments in existence today.

The Government We Lack

The metropolis is the decisive community today. But it does not exist as a government at all. Instead our system is built on the old preindustrial units of town, county, and state. No attack on the problems of the metropolis is possible without attacking at the same time these most deeply entrenched political bodies of our tradition and laws.

The tax issue alone will make sure of that. During the sixties, local government expenses will double—from fifty billion to one hundred billion, very largely for education. But most of the big cities have already drained their tax reservoirs. We might tackle the financial problem of the big city by bringing the suburbs into the metropolitan tax system, by using the taxing powers of the states to finance the cities, or through large-scale grants from the federal government. My guess is that we will use all three methods. And each of them is sure to touch off a major political fight.

Similarly the "war on poverty" will raise the issue of metropolitan government. For the hard core of present-day poverty consists of city people who dwell outside our affluent, high-education society. Compared to them, the unemployed coal miners in the hollows of West Virginia or the submarginal farmers of Appalachia are a mopping-up operation.

The battle over the city's place in American government has already been joined. The 1964 Supreme Court decision on reapportionment decreed that state legislatures must give equal representation to all voters, regardless of their residence. It was fully as revolutionary as was that other Supreme Court decision, ten years earlier, that decreed racial integration for the public schools. And like the school decision, reapportionment clearly was just the first skirmish in what will be a long and bitter fight. Lieutenant Governor Malcolm Wilson of New York was not exaggerating when he warned (in a 1964 speech to the County Officers Association of New York) that reapportionment eventually might lead to the end of counties as units of government. Connecticut has already abolished them. And when New Jersey celebrated its Tercentenary in 1964, quite a few of its inhabitants must have wondered whether their state now serves any real purpose—with a population divided between residents of Metropolitan New York and residents of Metropolitan Philadelphia, separated rather than held together by Princeton Junction.

Of course, the issue will be fought out on specifics. It will be fought out as an issue of power balances within the nation, over tax sources and their division, and over the by-passing of states and counties by a federal government which increasingly works directly in cooperation with the cities.

Mass transportation in and out of our big cities is, for instance, likely to be entrusted to a new federal agency before very long. In our largest cities (New York, Philadelphia, and Chicago) it requires planning beyond the boundaries of one state and money beyond the capacity of any local government. And the same holds true for intercity rail traffic.

But such specifics are only symptoms of a great constitutional crisis of our political institutions and structure.

The Schools Move into Politics

Education has been our chief "growth industry" in the last twenty years. If the economists considered schooling part of the national product (as they should), our economic growth rate would have looked pretty good all through the postwar period.

But an even greater expansion is just ahead. It will catapult the American school into national politics. The colleges during the next few years—as by now everybody must have heard—will be hit by the wave of youngsters born during the "baby boom" following World War II. Five to eight years from now, around 50 percent more students should be in American colleges than are there today. The greatest growth will be in an entirely new and largely untried institution, the two-year "community college," which, unlike any earlier college in American history, is usually run by the same local school board that administers the public schools. Meanwhile, the private college, at least as far as undergraduate education goes, will become quantitatively an almost negligible factor.

The first consequence will be a drastic increase in the costs of education. And to make this increase even more drastic, salaries will certainly go up again, since the supply of qualified teachers cannot possibly keep up with this sudden jump in demand. It is hard to see how we can avoid large-scale federal support for education on all levels. In the poorer areas, in particular, the schools already cost more than the local population can afford. It is sheer hypocrisy to pretend that federal support of education is possible without some considerable measure of national control. Will we support, for instance, schools that practice racial segregation? Or schools with curricula and standards below a national minimum, or with a short school year?

At the same time a technological revolution will hit American education. "Programmed learning" is the first major technological change in teaching and learning since the printed book, and likely to have equal impact.

The teacher shortage alone will hurry new methods of teaching and learning, no matter how sturdily the teaching profession resists. However, only skills and knowledge can be transmitted through a program. Everything else—character, values, behavior, and above all the use of imagination and the discovery of the new and exciting—requires a teacher. Programmed instruction, therefore, predictably will unleash a debate over the function and methods of the American school such as we have not seen for a very long time. Opponents will argue that it undermines the basic educational values and underfeeds the growing child. On the other side will be the fanatics who see in programmed instruction a panacea—which it surely will not be—and the doctrinaires who want to eliminate as "unscientific" whatever in the school curriculum cannot be programmed.

Altogether our society will be school-centered. At least one-third of the American people will be in school a few years hence. (Only one-fourth is there now.) Preschool children, ready for nursery school or kindergarten, will make up another tenth of the population. Teachers are already the largest occupational group in the country. Total school expenditures, a few years from now, will exceed our present defense budget by a substantial amount. At the same time, the structure of American education, its purposes, values, content, and direction, will all become hot issues.

Education is about to take over from the Welfare State as a basic commitment of the American people. One might call this new phenomenon the Knowledge State. Education is bound to become a focus of political life and political conflicts. So far, however, we have not even begun to think through national policies on education, let alone a national commitment to educational values and purposes. All we have so far—and it is a great deal—is a national commitment to education in quantity, and for everyone.

The Young Take Over

President Johnson may be tempted to maintain a little longer the cozy illusion of an Era of Good Feeling. But it can't last—partly because the new issues already are exploding, partly because a new power center is about to emerge on the American scene. Whatever the President may want, the educated young people who make up the professional, technical, and managerial middle classes will force on us new political alignments.

In 1960, when Kennedy was elected, the average American was about thirty-three years old. By 1968 the mid-age will have dropped to twenty-five or lower. This age drop—eight years within the span of eight years—is the biggest ever recorded in American history. It must also be one of the biggest any country ever went through. The reason is, of course, that because of the lean birth years of the thirties, relatively few Americans are now reaching middle age; while those born in the bumper years right after the war are now coming to maturity. (The over-sixty-five group, which has grown so rapidly in these past decades, will definitely become a static proportion of the population after 1970.) For the next fifteen years, then, the most rapidly expanding age group will be young adults reaching voting age. By 1970 ours will be the youngest country in the Free World. And the center of political gravity will soon lie with a generation that will know the New Deal and even World War II only out of history books and as events that happened mostly before it was born.

In "psychological age" we will be even younger, and the jump between generations will be greater still. One out of every three Americans alive in the early 1970's is likely to be in school—a bigger percentage than in any other country. In their outlook on life and politics, students are "young," even if they are in graduate school and twenty-five years old, for they still consider themselves outside the labor force.

More important than the age shift itself is the shift in expectations from the New Deal and World War II generations to that now coming of age. Fully one-half of the young men now reaching adulthood have education beyond high school. Consequently, most of them join the professional, technical, and managerial class, expecting high opportunities for themselves and even greater ones for their children. But work as a machine operator or as a salesgirl was the normal expectation for the last large wave of young people to become voters—the generation that reached adulthood in the late twenties and the thirties; in education they had gone no further, by and large, than a year or two in high school.

The initiative in American politics has already shifted to this new group. Boys still in college or just out of it discovered Barry Goldwater ("invented him" might be a more appropriate term), made him their hero, and furnished the fanatical following which bludgeoned a reluctant Republican party into accepting him as its candidate. It was the educated young Negro who overthrew his old "moderate" leadership and forced the pace of civil rights. Both the Civil Rights Act and the forcing of school integration even in rural Mississippi are due largely to the explosive response of white youths in college and high school to the cry for racial justice. And the one innovation in American political institutions since President Truman has been the college students' very own Peace Corps.

The educated and affluent managerial, professional, and technical people are, of course, only one half—perhaps a little more—of the young adults. In the other half is a small but highly visible group: the "problems" (largely members of the minority groups in big cities) who become school dropouts, narcotics addicts, and unemployables. The more affluent our society becomes, the greater will be our concern with them, especially as we are unlikely to find a cure fast.

The Politics of Youth

But political and social power will not be where the "problems" are. It will lie increasingly with the successful, well-adjusted young people who are the beneficiaries of this high-pressure and high-education society of ours. Their buying will largely shape the economy. Economic policies will inevitably be tailored to their needs and aspirations. They are the community leaders of tomorrow. Above all, they will have the voting power. They are not only the largest but the only homogeneous group among the new voters—and different from any earlier group. They already dominate the suburbs, which increasingly hold the decisive vote in the big states. Before long, no party and no major candidate will be able to win unless they carry at least a large minority of the affluent, young, educated middle class. And no national consensus will be possible which does not in large measure reflect their beliefs, attitudes, and values. *Here is the center around which the New Majority will have to be built and which will determine the direction and the character of American politics for the next generation.*

Yet this group, so far, is politically faceless. It has not aligned itself. Indeed, it does not fit into the present structure of American politics. To ask, say, whether these educated young people are "conservatives" or "liberals" makes practically no sense.

By the traditional yardsticks of American politics, they would appear to be highly conservative. They are the first "haves" in a long time to become a major new power center. Their incomes are well above average. Their jobs are as secure as jobs can be—or at least look to them secure enough—and their opportunities are great. They do not identify themselves with the traditional liberal groups. They are certainly not prolabor. A proposal to do away with restrictive practices of the labor unions—for instance, by bringing labor under the antitrust laws—would probably be supported by most of them. If they identify themselves at all, in terms of economic interests or social position, it is with management. Even the young teachers are likely to think and speak of themselves as professional people.

Yet they also do not answer the traditional definition of the conservative in American politics. They are hired hands. Most of them have never met a payroll and do not expect ever to have to meet one. They surely have little in common with the small businessman. And even among the young engineers or market researchers in the big companies, who clearly identify themselves with management—indeed, even among the young owner-managers and entrepreneurs who form the membership of the Young Presidents Organization—John F. Kennedy, despite his much-publicized "hostility to business," would (according to all reports) have polled a larger vote than did Lyndon Johnson, whose "understanding of business" had potent appeal to so many of the older big-business executives. A good many of the issues which traditionally marked the boundary line between "conservative" and "liberal" can hardly be explained to them.

I found this out in the 1964 campaign in a meeting with an extremely bright group of graduate students and young instructors at a large midwestern university. Senator Goldwater had just proposed turning over the Tennessee Valley Authority to private enterprise. The proposal seemed quite reasonable to most of the young men, few of whom, otherwise, had much use for Goldwater. After all, they argued, why should the government do a better job than private enterprise as manager of power stations and fertilizer plants? "To plan and to build a TVA required government, of course; but in running it, is government likely to contribute much?" What puzzled them, however, was the reason for making an issue out of this. "Why not call in competent economists and management engineers and have them find out what would be most efficient?" Most of the men were political scientists or economists and had heard, if only vaguely, of yesterday's great private-versus-public-power controversy. But, in their own words, it seemed to them as irrelevant and as quaint as the debate over free silver.

A few years ago it was fashionable to explain this detachment from the burning issues of yesterday as "apathy." But the events of the last few years—the Goldwater movement, for instance, or the civil-rights explosion—have clearly shown that the educated young people of the new power center are passionate in their politics to the point of violence.

The true explanation may well be that these young people will not define themselves politically in the terms in which American political alignments have been couched for seventy years—since Mark Hanna created the modern Republican party after 1896—that is, in terms of economic issues and interests. Feeling secure in their jobs, they are free from the driving fear of yesterday's "have-nots." Being employees, they lack any grim determination to defend property rights. But they care deeply for education—for themselves and their children—and for their community. They are passionate about matters that directly touch them and have a direct impact on their security, opportunities, and place in society. They will, therefore, be highly susceptible to such new issues as metropolitan structure and educational purpose.

Economics Becomes a Bore

For the last seventy years, at least, economic issues have defined the political position of an individual or of a group in the American spectrum. Noneconomic issues were largely treated as adjuncts; the position of a man on economic issues determined, by and large, where he stood on all others. Where a noneconomic issue could not be folded into an economic framework—for example, a good many foreign-policy issues—we tried, on the whole with success, to treat it as "bipartisan."

But for the new power center, these noneconomic issues may well become the core of political belief and action. Consequently, the attempt to build a new majority around this center—that is, the attempt to find a community of interests and viewpoints between the new group and the older national groups, such as labor and agriculture—must center on noneconomic issues. It must focus on the quality of life, rather than on the division of the economic product.

Whenever a decisive new power center has appeared in our history—the New West of the 1820's, the skilled worker around 1890, or the machine operator in mass-production industry between 1910 and 1930—the political map of the country was overturned as if by an earthquake. Such changes are always dangerous. The general confusion over issues and alignments opens the door wide to the demagogue and the rabble-rouser. But such an earthquake change also makes possible the creative leadership of an Andrew Jackson, a Teddy Roosevelt, or a Franklin Roosevelt. Each of these managed to forge a new majority in which the needs of the new power center of his time became the foundation for effective national policy and constructive political achievements.

Lyndon Johnson's Dilemma

Lyndon Johnson made his way to the top as a superb tactician of the American political process, with a rare instinct for the timing needed to make effective an already formulated idea and to push forward an already accepted policy. He has been field commander rather than strategist. Now he must demonstrate, if he has it, a different kind of talent: the art of political innovation, of leadership in formulating new issues and in designing new policies.

In years of political service, Lyndon Johnson (who first went to Washington as a congressional assistant just before Hoover left the White House) is the most senior leader of the Free World. Yet his Presidency will see a generation jump which will shift the center of political gravity to an age group so young that it can barely remember World War II, let alone the Depression.

Johnson is the one original New Dealer still prominent in American political life; yet his success as President will largely depend on his attracting and inspiring a host of middle-class young people who have traditionally been somewhat right of center and barely understand the New Deal issues, emotions, and experiences. In this tension between what he has been and what he will have to be lies Lyndon Johnson's dilemma.

There is only one precedent in American history for the 1964 election, only one parallel to this President's situation. That is the 1896 election and the position of the victorious Republicans afterward. There may be a powerful lesson for today in this parallel. In both elections the spotlight of the campaign was not on the winner: McKinley aroused as little popular enthusiasm as did Lyndon Johnson. The loser was the focal point.

There are striking similarities between Barry Goldwater and William Jennings Bryan, their respective campaigns and their defeats. Both men aimed at a coalition of the disaffected. Both embodied, in their righteous confusion, the frustration and bafflement of a great many Americans at the speed and ruthlessness with which change had plowed under all the landmarks of their accustomed world. Both, while publicly disavowing bigotry, exploited it. Both represented fundamentalism—that is, the refusal to think—as a considered political philosophy. Both hinged their strategy on the rural South and its revolt. Both thereby alienated large numbers of the one group they absolutely needed to win: the new power center. In 1896 this was the skilled industrial workers—foundrymen, printers, crane operators in the steel mills; in 1964 it was the young technical, professional, and managerial middle class.

But the winners, too, found themselves in very similar positions. In choosing Lyndon Johnson, as in choosing McKinley, the American people voted *against* irresponsibility, unreason, dissension, and bigotry. They did not vote *for* a man and even less *for* issues, programs, and policies. In both elections the victor was the last of his line. As Mr. Johnson is the last New Dealer, so McKinley was the last Civil War veteran to attain political prominence. Like Mr. Johnson today, McKinley in 1896 found himself in a new and alien world—with a new power center and with no fresh issues to take the place of the old slogans of Reconstruction.

The Opportunity

The comparison with 1896 also suggests that such an election creates a tremendous opportunity. It is a great emotional trauma, which tears people off their old political moorings and sets them adrift—ready to be caught by new currents. It forces people who normally react to politics in terms of simple clichés—the great majority for whom politics is only of peripheral importance—to reexamine their stand. Altogether the year from President Kennedy's assassination to President Johnson's election was a year of shock, of self-questioning, of self-doubt such as must leave lasting effects. And it demonstrated that there is no going back to yesterday, even for the most nostalgic. As a result there is wide awareness of the need for something new, and receptivity to it.

The emotional shock of 1896 was used by Mark Hanna to forge a new and lasting majority, built around the skilled industrial worker in alliance with business and with the successful commercial farmer. By designing this alignment around the "full dinner pail," that is, around strictly economic issues, Mark Hanna determined the character of American politics for the next sixty-five years.* Shortly after Hanna, Teddy Roosevelt grasped the opportunity for political innovation. He came out with an altogether new political program—one which created a strong, positive Presidential government to tackle the new issues of the Welfare State and of the social control of economic activity.

In retrospect these achievements may seem easy, if not inevitable. But, at the time, they were inconceivable to most Americans. And the world of 1896, which to us seems so simple, appeared to the men of that time (as any reader of *The Education of Henry Adams* may remember) complex beyond human understanding.

A similar opportunity awaits today. The man to seize it could well be Lyndon Johnson. In the first year he succeeded to the

* Hanna is remembered (if at all) as the villain in a political morality play and as the prototype of all the top-hatted, cigar-smoking, evil "capitalists" who ever attempted to dispossess a poor widow and seduce her daughter. But he was one of the most effective organizers of political power in our history, second perhaps only to Jefferson. He refashioned a Republican party that had become totally flabby and lifeless, after living for thirty years off the memory of the Civil War and the spoils of Reconstruction, into the new majority party of an industrialized America. He was probably the first politician to realize that America had become an industrial society, and certainly the first to understand the tremendous wealth-creating potential of an industrial economy. This led him into becoming founder of the National Association of Manufacturers (NAM) but also godfather of the infant American Federation of Labor and sponsor of young Sam Gompers. Hanna (an honest and an honorable man, by the way) is probably the least known and most underrated figure in American political history.

Presidency, Mr. Johnson proved himself effective, shrewd, energetic, and self-confident.

Still, will Mr. Johnson have the courage, the vision—above all, the self-discipline—to tackle the new, the difficult, the controversial? Or will his very virtuosity at managing the old alignments and the old issues keep him busy doing yesterday's jobs for yesterday's national consensus? If Lyndon Johnson misses his chance in that fashion, then the yet unknown men who will rebuild a second party from the shambles of the GOP will have a unique opportunity to forge a new majority to cope with the new issues. For no one—neither Johnson nor Goldwater nor anyone else—will be able to push this country back onto the old slope of the political watershed we crossed in the 1964 election.

CHAPTER SEVEN

The Secret Art of Being an Effective President

ACCORDING TO THE campaign orators, our next President will be a wondrous man. Above all, he will be a statesman. He will also be a first-class administrator, dedicated to efficient government. His political philosophy will be sound. (Either soundly liberal or soundly conservative, but in any case sound.) To hear them tell it, he may even be suffused with that elusive quality, "greatness."

These are the terms in which we always discuss our candidates—and, indeed, it will be nice for all of us if November's winner actually proves to be endowed with these blessings. But they are not the things which will decide whether he is going to be a success or a failure. That will depend on something else, seldom mentioned during any campaign: his effectiveness.

All our experience tells us that a President needs, above all else, to be effective. No effective President in our history has been a failure, whatever his convictions or his personal stature. No ineffectual one has ever succeeded, no matter how great a man or how right his policies.

First published in *Harper's Magazine*, August 1960.

Polk and McKinley, for example, were hardly great men, but they made fairly effective Presidents. Herbert Hoover, a much bigger man, did not. Neither did John Adams, though he was a truly great man and a statesman to boot. Mr. Truman, on the other hand, never considered himself a great man; but he learned to be a highly effective President.

This is something that any reasonably intelligent man can hope to learn, for it is about 80 percent system. Our history indicates that an effective President always does three things. First, he organizes his work so that he can concentrate on his decisive job—which is not administration, but political leadership. Second, he focuses American politics on the issues that are relevant to the situation—not on those which fit his program or his political convictions. Finally, he takes such a big view of his own office and of the American people that he never tries to "sell" anything; he demands.

The Eisenhower administration tried one major political innovation: a new organization of the President's job and work. It did not work out. Eisenhower, the man, enjoyed from the first tremendous popularity. Eisenhower, the President, did not really become effective until he had lost Sherman Adams and John Foster Dulles, his two "theater commanders" or "general managers." Their loss forced him to become a political leader instead of the nonpolitical administrator he had tried to be. The man didn't change, but his role and impact did, thus proving again that Presidential effectiveness depends on system rather than personality.

There is nothing mysterious about this kind of system. All our effective administrations have organized their work pretty much the same way, from that miracle that built a nation, George Washington's first term, to the first "New Deal" term of Franklin D. Roosevelt.

As far as the office of the President goes—his role as chief of state, head of government, and commander in chief—the requirements for effectiveness are well known.

First of all, there can be no substitute for the President in the American system, no "deputy," no "general manager," no "chief of staff." Every one of our effective Presidents has always made the big decisions himself; he did not just say "yes" or "no" to a staff recommendation. Each of them has in one way or another brought about what George Washington accomplished when he asked Hamilton and Jefferson for their separate recommendations on the same topic: a full presentation of all alternatives, rather than a joint recommendation of an innocuous but ineffective compromise.

Aside from making decisions, an effective President, however, does not *do* anything. He delegates all work. And he delegates only to individuals. He is not one bit interested in having a "harmonious team"; he wants strong, independent, ambitious men who can get their jobs done. He entrusts decision or action to a committee only if he really wants neither.

The next President will badly need to restore individual responsibility throughout the government. It is paralyzed today by the fatty degeneration of committees, co-ordinators, special assistants, and advisers, all busily "making one more study," yet powerless to act. We have split responsibility for an area—for example, Brazil—so many ways that no one can do anything. In the end the President has to go in person to settle matters that a State Department section head used to dispose of adequately in earlier, less "efficient," but more effective days.

Even the strongest and most influential Cabinet member or adviser is neither the President's "colleague" nor his "friend." A President has only subordinates. They are his tools. They are also expendable. The only "indispensable man" is the President himself.

But the President's job goes way beyond the formal duties of his office. And effectiveness in this other, extraconstitutional part of his work may matter even more. The President must be able to escape the strait jacket of official channels. He must be able to bring the world into his vision and imagination. For this he needs a corps of unofficial, volunteer eyes and ears outside and independent of both government and party. Every effective President has had someone to do the indispensable chores that Mrs. Roosevelt handled for FDR.

Every one of them could keep his Secretary of State waiting for hours in the outer office while listening to some unimportant missionary from the Congo or (as Lincoln did, to the great scandal of the righteous) to his wife's rebel relatives from the Confederacy. Every one of them also knew that it is hard work to build this eyes-and-ears network—especially as it had better consist of people who see things differently from the President and have minds of their own.

An effective President is always an active politician. "The President is the head of his party," says every textbook. But it forgets to add that an effective President must create the political alignments that make a "party" out of the mad swirl of groups, interests, national antecedents and religious ties, traditions, personal loyalties and convictions, which—to the despair of the orderly political scientist—is the stuff of American politics.

To say that a President should be "above politics" is as silly as to say that a violinist should be above tuning his strings and rosining his bow. No effective President, to be sure, is ever a "good party man." He doesn't aim to please his party; he tries to give it new shape, new leaders, new direction, and new alignments. But all this requires shrewd, aggressive politicking.

A "nonpolitical" President—a Grant or a Hoover—simply hands things over to the party hacks. Eisenhower's failure to create the "modern Republican party" that he once proclaimed was the inevitable result of his being, for most of his eight years, "not a politician." For there is no conflict between being a politician and being a statesman in the American system. To become a statesman, a President must first be a truly competent politician.

How to Use Experts

Finally the President, to be effective, needs "idea men" in his government—for himself first of all.

Few even of our greatest Presidents have been original thinkers. Admiral Rickover would hardly have considered Abe Lincoln "promising college material." What a President needs is an active mind—a mind interested in other people and their ideas; able to find the kernel of sense in a farrago of abstract theorizing; quick to see where imagination turns into riot, but also where logic turns into absurdity. Such a mind needs constant nourishment and stimulation through the ideas of others.

This the experts usually cannot provide. They know how to do better what is already being done. But they rarely ask: What should we do? What might we stop doing?

The idea man in government is needed even more to create public interest in politics, public excitement over issues, public imagination that new things can be done.

The American "ruler" who used the most such men was not a President, but General MacArthur as Supreme Commander in occupied Japan. But MacArthur often let them make policy, which was not their proper job. Franklin D. Roosevelt was much closer to the tradition. His idea men had little influence on New Deal measures and were dropped as soon as they asserted any. They spouted ideas and proposals, thus creating controversy, excitement, and interest.

Government, in other words, cannot be left entirely to the experts, whether administrators or politicians. It needs the idea man who is neither. Today, however, such men are not to be found in the government. They have been stifled by the blanket of "no controversy"—a legacy of wartime security and McCarthyism. They are not even wanted. They are certainly not "efficient." They are a menace to orderly administration and a scandal to the administrator who seldom remembers that today's well-oiled procedure was yesterday's harebrained and impractical idea.

But the idea men, and they alone, can make politics become a human drama. Thus they arouse public opinion, creating understanding and public commitment. And no President can be effective unless he makes politics—his politics—grip us as high drama of men and ideas.

Putting Together a New Party

The demands on the next President's effectiveness as a politician and a political leader will be extraordinary. Whether Republican or Democrat, he may have to redesign and rebuild the very foundations of party cohesion and political alignments. He will have to bring into public life a new generation that has grown to manhood since the Depression and World War II. And he will have to tackle the new job of the American President: to win acceptance as a leader by the people of the non-Communist world.

Whether the New Deal coalition of farmers, workers, and urban minority groups can still be glued together may well still decide a presidential election. By itself, however, this coalition no longer represents even a decisive minority; farmers and manual workers each are a much smaller percentage of the population than they were only a few years ago. And as soon as the next administration gets under way, new alignments will be forged and old ones will be cut asunder.

For the new issues of American politics do not fit the established political boundaries. Neither do the realities of American social structure. Within the next few years, the farmer as a major interest group may fade from the American political scene. Labor and management may band together as the "producer interest," on basic economic policies. "Spenders" may learn also to be "economizers" and vice versa. The fight over tax sources that is likely to break out might even produce a new states-rights alliance. Southerners, afraid of federal control in race matters, may get unexpected support from the powerful northern liberals who run the growing programs of states, cities, and regions. These men like federal grants; but they will fight tooth and claw for the fiscal autonomy of local governments.

Our existing political alignments go back much further than 1932. Franklin D. Roosevelt remodeled extensively; but the basic structure was designed a generation earlier by that political master builder, Mark Hanna—who was, ironically, a Republican. By 1965, however, basic political terms such as "labor," "business," "South," or "farmer" may begin to change—if not to lose—their political meaning. They may increasingly become irrelevant. A new central question of domestic politics will emerge: the allegiance of the as yet uncommitted, as yet politically amorphous, new majority—the educated middle class of employed technicians, professionals, managers, and teachers.

These political miracles may take a long time, if they happen at all. But their very possibility is enough to make both existing parties shaky. This means that the next administration will be highly political. Our next President will have to choose between being the impotent victim of the politicians' maneuvers and being himself the master politician who will create tomorrow's political alignments.

And this, of course, ties in with the "generation jump" that lies ahead. By the end of his first term, our next President will appoint as generals and admirals men who were too young to serve in World War II. Half of our present top-management people will have been replaced; the average age of this group is fifty-nine now. And half of our present union leaders, too, are already at (or past) normal retirement age. Searching for "nationally known" women to put on a public-affairs panel, one of the radio networks last spring could not find a single name that would not have been on such a list in the late thirties.

The successors are likely to be men and women twenty or thirty years younger—new leaders rather than the lieutenants of the outgoing old ones. Meteoric careers like those of Richard Nixon and John Kennedy will become commonplace in politics as well as in business and labor unions.

It is pretty obvious that the common slogans and issues of today will make very little sense to this next generation. "Liberals" and "conservatives" alike still invoke the rhetoric of the thirties—the "rights of labor" or the "virtues of free enterprise." But for the people under thirty-five—and they are a full third of all voters—such slogans are as topical as "Remember the Maine!" Even the distinction between the two Roosevelts, Teddy and Franklin, must be as blurred for them as are most things one had to learn for a high-school test.

But no one—not even its own members—seems to know what the new generation stands for, believes in, wants. It has no spokesman so far—no one who does what Reinhold Niebuhr, Norman Thomas, or Walter Lippmann did for their fathers. The new generation has not even rebelled. It is silent, if not uninterested.

To be effective, our next President must, however, kindle in this generation—which will supply both tomorrow's majority and its leaders—the excitement of politics. He must convince it that politics deals with great issues, that it is concerned with right and wrong rather than with procedures, with the nature and destiny of man rather than with "who gets what."

Finally, the next President will have to gain acceptance as the leader of the Grand Alliance. Unlike his predecessor, he will come into office unknown to most of our friends abroad. Yet trust in the American President is the invisible bond which alone can hold together the non-Communist world. Take that away, and our power becomes a threat to other countries, rather than their common shield and buckler. Our friends in other countries are not constituents of the American President, but they must be his "followers"—in our own national self-interest and theirs.

And abroad, too, a generation jump is close at hand. The Macmillans, Nehrus, de Gaulles, Khrushchevs, and Adenauers are all men who reached manhood in those faraway days before World War I, and little is known about their successors except that they will be much younger and quite different.

Leadership of the peoples beyond our shores cannot be gained in popularity contests. It must rest on clear understanding of American policy and position. To achieve this, however, requires a President organized for political leadership of unusually high effectiveness.

These new demands also heighten the need for relevant issues. If our next President clings to the old familiar issues—the ones all our political campaigns still chew over—he cannot expect to be effective as a leader either of his party or of the new "publics" at home or abroad. For these issues have become irrelevant.

A List of Priorities

"I would rather be relevant than right" should be the motto of the effective President. The right answer to the irrelevant question misdirects. But the wrong answer to a relevant issue still puts the spotlight where it belongs. And only by raising the relevant issues can a President hope to accomplish anything.

For example, Andrew Johnson held nothing of the Presidency but the empty title—and even that he came within one vote of losing by impeachment. Yet he, rather than the seemingly all-powerful Radical Republicans, set the course of Reconstruction. His definition of the issue was relevant to the national goal and the need of restoring the Union; the Radicals' view of the issue as punishment and revenge was irrelevant.

Herbert Hoover was completely right in his two basic beliefs: that the American economy and society were at bottom strong and sound and that the real dangers were the international demonic forces beneath the surface. But Hoover's definition of the issue as preservation of the international gold standard was irrelevant. What was relevant, domestically and internationally, was preservation of the human values. Because FDR saw that clearly, he was effective, as Hoover was not.

What a President deems right is determined by his convictions. What is relevant, however, is decided objectively, by the logic of the situation.

What, then, are the relevant issues today?

"Isolationism" and "internationalism" have become as irrelevant for 1960 as the maintenance of the international gold standard was in 1932. So has "foreign aid." "Interdependence" is now the relevant fact—interdependence between our strength and that of the rest of the Free World; interdependence between our economic growth and rapid economic development elsewhere; but also interdependence between foreign and domestic policy, in defense, economic management, education, and many other fields.

"Capitalism versus Communism," as the issue has been posed these last twenty-five years, is no longer relevant. Almost any "ism" can now produce material goods and technical knowledge. And no "ism" by producing these things alone can insure its own victory.

"Freedom versus tyranny" is now the relevant issue. The basic fact is not the economic success, but the human failure, of Communism. Mr. Khrushchev is right in considering all his steel mills and missile pads no offset to West Berlin. It is our job to make the world see that the steel mills are secondary. What is really relevant is the stampede of broken human beings through the smallest pinhole in the Iron Curtain.

"Peace versus war" also has become a phony issue, and a very dangerous one. As John Fischer has pointed out,* it can easily slide into an argument for surrender: war means destruction of the human race and is unbearable; we must therefore have peace even at the price of submitting to Communist tyranny for a few centuries. That, of course, is not the real issue. What is relevant is how to make bearable a prolonged period of strain which is neither peace nor war. For the foreseeable future the man in the White House will be neither a "war President" nor a "peacetime President," but both at the same time. Our ability to maintain our freedom, our ideals, and our sanity during this period will be the acid test of our character and institutions. To make such a period livable for the world—both through control of the absolute weapons and through the common constructive tasks that engender hope—has to be the

*John Fischer, in *Harper's* (March 1960).

goal of our foreign policy. Above all, we have to understand ourselves, and make others understand as well, that the present kind of truce is the true alternative to war and that it is the only path that might lead eventually to genuine peace.

In domestic affairs the Welfare State is a fact, and the New Deal history. Today's relevant issues are the shape and values of the new society that is being created rapidly all over the world by what might be called the Second Industrial Revolution. The sweep of this revolution is much broader, its impact heavier, its spread much faster than that of the first Industrial Revolution two hundred years ago—which was, by and large, confined to the Western world.

Our role in this second revolution is completely different. The first affected us very late. The second one is "made in the U.S.A." and has grown largely out of our success in solving the problems of the first. Now we will have to find the answer to many unfamiliar problems.

Our next President does not need a quiverful of specific proposals. He needs big new goals and compass bearings to show us how to move toward them. His job is not to "solve" the new issues. It is to make us start work on them. Above all, he has to create understanding, and this requires dissent and controversy as much as it requires support and approval. It requires our accepting his priorities and his definition of what issues matter. The next President need not be right; indeed, nobody can as yet say what is "right" for these new tremendous tasks. But he very much needs to be relevant.

The Unhidden Persuader

There is one more ingredient in Presidential effectiveness: an effective President always demands more from the American people than they think themselves capable of.

Roosevelt acted on this precept when, in early 1942, he asked for the production of 40,000 planes. His closest advisers thought him both mad and irresponsible. They knew that even half that figure was "absolutely impossible." But FDR was right, and he got a great many more planes than he asked for. Lincoln, Wilson, Theodore Roosevelt, all in their different ways, were equally demanding; and the country always responded.

All our effective Presidents were expert at public relations, untiring propagandists for themselves and their ideas. The slickest Madison Avenue outfit is bush-league compared to Thomas Jefferson.

But they also knew that leadership is not just getting one's measures through Congress or one's proposals accepted by foreign governments. It means making the American people see that new tasks have to be tackled, that old issues had better be forgotten, and that cherished habits have to be broken to preserve basic values.

And our effective Presidents never "sold."

They all knew instinctively what the last few years have proven: The Hidden Persuaders do not really persuade. Since the great propaganda binge of World War II, all the black and white arts of "creative selling" have been employed to get the American people excited about politics. Yet we have never been so bored, so uninterested, so stubborn in our sales resistance. (When Mr. Eisenhower crusaded against "inflation" in 1959, he did stir up some public interest—but on that occasion he addressed us as adults.) The methods which sell lipstick to the twelve-year-old mentality have been found wanting in politics; effective leadership is not the merchandising of a brand image.

"The President of the United States does not sell anything," could be blazoned on the President's crest. Effective Presidents have been demagogic; but no effective President has ever been ingratiating. Every effective President knew that his job was not to reach the "mass mind," but to stir up the bright boys and girls in the class. Every one knew that the President leads through vision and not through cajolery, through courage and not through popularity.

The American people may be readier for such leadership than their TV programs indicate—and so might be the peoples throughout the Free World and the secret listeners behind the Iron Curtain. Reluctant as we may be to admit it, we all know that there is no "return to normalcy," whether that of Franklin D. Roosevelt or of Herbert Hoover, of the Americans for Democratic Action or of the Daughters of the American Revolution. We prefer to read forecasts about the glittering future ahead; but actually for the first time since Lincoln came in as an untried and unknown President, even the stoutest heart may tremble in the night for the future of the Union.

We are, I suspect, ready for effective leadership from the next President. We know by now that we have to be both a "superpower," to survive, and "the last best hope on earth," to prevail. The whole moral and intellectual climate of the country may change overnight, if only we get soon a President who takes a big view of his function, who takes pride rather than fright from the challenges that lie ahead—a President who demands much of us.

CHAPTER EIGHT

Henry Ford

I

HENRY FORD'S HOLD on America's imagination—indeed, on the imagination of the world's masses—was not due to his fabulous financial success. And it can only partly be explained by the overwhelming impact of the automobile on our way of life. For Henry Ford was less the symbol and embodiment of new wealth and of the automobile age than the symbol and embodiment of our new industrial mass-production civilization.

He perfectly represented its success in technology and economics; he also perfectly represented its political failure so far—its failure to build an industrial order, an industrial society. The central problem of our age is defined in the contrast between the functional grandeur of the River Rouge plant, with its spotless mechanical perfection, and the formlessness and tension of the social jungle that is Detroit. And the two together comprise Henry Ford's legacy.

First published in *Harper's Magazine,* July, 1947.

Both his success and his failure can be traced to his being thoroughly representative of that most native and most dominant of all American traditions, the one which in Populism found its major political expression. Indeed, Henry Ford was both the last Populist and perhaps the greatest one. He owed all his basic convictions to Bryan: pacifism, isolationism, hatred of monopoly and of "Wall Street" and of "international bankers," firm belief in a sinister international conspiracy, and so forth. He also made true the great dream of the political crusaders of 1896: that industrial production might be made to serve the common man. This dream had obsessed the American people since Brook Farm and Robert Owen's New Harmony, half a century before Bryan.

The Populists had believed that a Jeffersonian millennium would result automatically from eliminating "monopoly" and the "money power" and the "satanic mills" of crude industrialism—as these terms were understood in the nineteenth century. Ford fulfilled the dream. He succeeded without benefit of monopoly; he defied the big bankers; he gave his factories a clean and airy efficiency which would have delighted nineteenth-century reformers. But in fulfilling the dream he dispelled it. And in the place of the old enemies which he vanquished, we have today, in the industrial system which Ford did so much to develop, new problems to face: the long-term depression, and the political and social problems of industrial citizenship in the big plant. Henry Ford's solution of the industrial problems with which the nineteenth century had wrestled unsuccessfully constituted his success, his achievement. His inability to solve the problems of the new industrial system, his inability to see even that there were such problems, was the measure of his final and tragic failure.

It may seem paradoxical to interpret Henry Ford's importance in terms of a concept—especially a political concept such as Populism. He himself had nothing but contempt for concepts and ideas and prided himself on being neither a theoretician nor a politician, but a "practical man." And the main criticism which has been leveled against him and against everything he stood for—the criticism embodied in, for instance, Charlie Chaplin's *Modern Times*—has been that he made mechanical perfection an end in itself. But even his contribution to technology was not really a technical but a conceptual one—superb production man and engineer though he was. For he invented nothing, no new technique, no new machine, not even a new gadget. What he supplied was *the idea of mass production itself:* organization of men, machines, and materials into one productive whole.

In economics, too, Ford discovered no new facts; the data showing the effect of volume production on costs had all been collected and analyzed. But Ford was the first manufacturer to understand that these data disproved the traditional theory that restricted production and a high profit margin—that is, monopoly—provided the most profitable form of industrial production. He demonstrated that one could raise wages, cut prices, produce in tremendous volume, and still make millions.

Above all, Ford himself regarded his technical and economic achievements primarily as means to a social end. He had a definite political and social philosophy to which he adhered to the point of doctrinaire absurdity. Concern with the social effects of his actions determined every one of his steps and decisions throughout his entire life. It underlay the break with his early partners who wanted to produce a luxury car for the rich rather than follow Ford's harebrained idea of a cheap utility car for the masses. It motivated the radical wage policy of the early Ford who in 1914 fixed his minimum wage at the then utopian figure of $5.00 a day for unskilled labor. It showed in Ford's lifelong militant pacifism, of which the tragicomic Peace Ship episode of 1915–1916 was only one manifestation. It showed in his isolationism, in his hostility to Wall Street, and in the raucous pamphleteering of the Dearborn *Independent* in the twenties. This social philosophy explains the millions he poured into "chemurgy" or into utopian village communities of self-sufficient, sturdy, yeoman farmers. It was responsible for his belief in decentralization and for his nostalgic attempt to recreate the atmosphere of an earlier and simpler America in a museum community—right next door to the River Rouge plant.

It might almost be said that Henry Ford's lifework, despite these moves of his, brought about the opposite kind of world from the one he hoped for and believed in. Thus Ford, the pacifist, built up one of the world's greatest armament plants and helped to make possible the mechanized warfare of our age. Ford, the isolationist, more than any other man has made it impossible for this country to stay out of international politics and international wars: for he made this country the most powerful industrial nation on earth. Ford, the agrarian decentralist, left as his life's work the River Rouge plant, the most highly centralized and most completely mechanized concentration of industrial power in the world. The enemy of finance capital and bank credit, he made installment buying a national habit. An orthodox Jeffersonian, he has come to stand for the extreme application of the assembly-line principle, with its subordination of the individual to the machine. And the very workers at the Ford Motor Company, whose mass production was to give economic security and full industrial citizenship to all, organized before his death the most class-conscious union in America—and a Communist-dominated local at that.

Yet it would be wrong to argue from the failure of Ford's social ideas that they never were anything but "eccentric hobbies," as the obituaries rather condescendingly called them. The tragic irony with which his every move turned against him in the end does not alter the fact that his was the first, and so far the only, systematic attempt to solve the social and political problems of an industrial civilization. There is also little doubt that Ford himself believed—certainly until 1941 when the Ford workers voted for the CIO, and perhaps even afterward—that he had actually found the answer for which the American people had been searching for almost a century: the realization of the Jeffersonian society of independent equals through industrial technology and economic abundance.

Nor was he alone in this appraisal of the meaning of his work. It was shared by the American people as a whole in the years immediately following World War I; witness Wilson's urging in 1918 that Ford run for the Senate and the powerful "Ford for President" boom of 1923. The view was also held abroad, especially in the Europe of the early twenties and in Lenin's Russia—perhaps even more generally there than here. Indeed, it was the performance of Henry Ford's America which in 1918 and 1919 gave substance to Wilson's promise of the millennium of peace, democracy, and abundance and which established America's moral and political authority in those years. And the Ford spell remained potent long after Wilson's promise had faded under the cold light of the international realities of the 1920's.

The world of Ford's death, the world after World War II, was at least as much under the spell of Franklin D. Roosevelt's name as an earlier generation had been under that of Wilson. But Henry Ford in 1946 no longer symbolized an America that had successfully solved the basic social problems of an industrial world. He stood instead for the lack of a solution. And that surely accounted in large measure for the difference between 1919 and 1947 in the acceptance and the effectiveness of America's moral and economic leadership.

II

Henry Ford took the conveyor belt and the assembly line from the meat-packing industry, where they had been in general use as early as 1880. The interchangeability of precision-made parts was an even older principle; it went back to the rifle plant which Eli Whitney built in Bridgeport for the War of 1812. The idea of breaking down a skilled job into the constituent elementary motions, so that it could be performed by unskilled men working in series, had been thoroughly explored—by Taylor among others—and had been widely used in American industry twenty years before Ford came on the scene, as, for example, by Singer Sewing Machine and National Cash Register. Yet we associate all these principles with Henry Ford, and rightly so. For each of them had been employed only as an auxiliary to the traditional manufacturing process. It was Ford who first combined them and evolved out of them consciously and deliberately a new concept of industrial production, a new technology. It is this new concept of mass production which in scarcely more than one generation gave us a new industrial civilization.

To Ford the importance of this new principle lay in its impact on society as the means for producing an abundance of cheap goods with the minimum of human effort and toil. Mass production itself, however, he considered as something purely technical, as simply a new method of organizing *mechanical* forces. Ford disciples, heirs, and imitators, the engineers and production men who still run our big industries, are certainly as convinced as their master that mass production is a mechanical technique; many use it as if it were a mere gadget. And Charlie Chaplin took the same view when, in *Modern Times,* he caricatured our modern industrial civilization.

But if mass production were, indeed, only a technique, and primarily mechanical—if it were different in degree but not in kind from pulley, lever, or wheel—it could be applied only to mechanical tasks similar to the ones for which it was first developed. But long before the World War II, mass production principles were used for such jobs as the sorting and filling of orders in a mail-order house and the diagnosis of patients in the Mayo Clinic. Henry Luce even used it successfully to organize writers—traditionally regarded as extreme individualists—for the mass production of interchangeable "formula-writing." During World War II we applied mass-production principles to thousands of new products and processes and to such problems as the selection and training of men in the armed services. In all these uses the mechanisms of the assembly line are purely subordinate, if, indeed, applied at all. In other words, mass production is not fundamentally a mechanical principle, but *a principle of social organization*. It does not co-ordinate machines or the flow of parts; it organizes men and their work.

Ford's importance lies precisely in the fact that his principle of mass production substitutes the co-ordination of human beings for the co-ordination of inanimate parts and of mechanical forces on which industry was originally based. When we talk of the Industrial Revolution, we think at once of Watt's steam engine. It is true that there was a lot more to the Industrial Revolution than new machines; but the steam engine is a good symbol for it because the essence of early industry was the new organization of mechanical forces. Mass production is based, however, on the organization of human beings and of human work—something radically different from anything that was developed in the early days of industry. Indeed, it has brought about a new Industrial Revolution. The assembly line is a symbol for a new principle of social organization, a new relationship between men who work together in a common task, if not for a common purpose.

On what basis does this mass-production principle organize men? What kind of society does it either assume or create? It assumes or creates a society in which things are produced by the co-operation of individuals, not by a single individual. By himself the individual in modern mass-production industry is completely unproductive and ineffectual. But the organized group produces more, better, and more effectively than any individual or any number of individuals working by themselves ever could. In this society the whole—the organized group—is clearly not only more than, but different from, the sum of its parts.

Proof of this is what happens when a man loses his place in the organized group or his access to the productive organism; when, in other words, he becomes unemployed. Under modern mass-production conditions, the man who has lost his job is not just out of luck economically; in fact, in a rich country such as ours, the direct economic consequences of unemployment can be minimized almost to the vanishing point. But he is incapable of producing anything, of being effective in society; in short, he is incapable of being a citizen; he is cast out. For he derives his productiveness, his function in the community, his citizenship—at least his effective rather than purely formal citizenship—from his position in the group effort in the team, in the productive organism.

It is this social effect of unemployment, incidentally, rather than the economic effect, that makes it the major catastrophe it is. That unemployment endangers people's standards of living is, of course, bad enough; but that it endangers their citizenship and self-respect is its real threat and explains our panicky fear of the "next depression."

In the society of the modern mass-production plant everyone derives his effectiveness from his position in an organized group effort. From this follow some important consequences. One is that such a society needs a government, a direction, a management responsible to no one special-interest group, to no one individual, but to the over-all purpose, the over-all maintenance and strengthening of the whole without which no individual, no special-interest group, could be effective. It also follows that in such a society there must be rank: a difference of authority and prestige based on the differentiation of functions. But at the same time, in such a society no one individual is less important or more important than another. For while no one individual is irreplaceable—only the organized relationship between individuals is irreplaceable and essential—every single operation, every single function, is equally necessary; the whole order would collapse, the entire productive machine would come to a stop, were one to take out one function, one job—just as the whole chain becomes useless if one takes out one link. That is why, in such a society, there should be simultaneously an inequality of subordination and command, based on the differentiation of functions, and a basic equality, based on membership and citizenship.

This is by no means a new type of social organization; on the contrary, it is a very old one. It was described in the old Roman fable retold in Shakespeare's *Coriolanus* which likened society to the human body, none of whose organs—neither feet, nor hands, nor heart, nor stomach—could exist or work by itself, while yet the body could not properly work without any of them. It was expressed in the medieval metaphors of the order of the spheres and of the chain of being. And even as a practical way of organizing men for economic production, the mass-production principle is not new. Indeed, the first thorough applications of mass production and the assembly line were not in the Ford plant in Detroit, but hundreds of years earlier and thousands of miles away, in the workshops of the medieval stonemasons who built the great cathedrals. In short, mass-production society, of which the assembly line is the symbol, is a hierarchical one.

This shows clearly when we analyze what popularly passes for a clear explanation of the essence of mass production: the saying that it replaces skilled by unskilled labor. That is pure nonsense, if taken literally. Of course, in mass production manual skill is eliminated by breaking up each operation into the component simple operations, with each worker performing only one unskilled operation or a series of such. But this presupposes a fantastic skill in analyzing and breaking up the operation. The skill that is taken out of the manual operation has to be put back again further up the line, in the form of much greater knowledge, much more careful planning for the job; for there is such a thing as a law of the preservation of skill. And in addition mass production needs a new skill: that of organizing and leading the human team. Actually "unskilled" mass production needs proportionately more and more highly skilled men than "skilled" production. The skills themselves have changed from those of the craftsman to those of engineer, draftsman, and foreman; but the number of trained and skilled men in American industry has been growing twice as fast since 1910 as that of unskilled and semiskilled men.

Above all, the co-operation and co-ordination which are needed to make possible the elimination of manual skill presuppose an extraordinarily high level of social skill and social understanding, of experience in working together. The difficulties that our war plants had with new labor showed that very graphically. And, contrary to popular belief, it is no more difficult to export the old methods of industrial production to a new industrial country, even though those methods require considerable manual skill on the part of the worker, than it is to export mass-production techniques where no manual but a great deal of social skill is required.

What we mean when we say that mass production is based on unskilled labor is simply that the individual becomes effective and productive only through his contribution to the whole, and not if viewed separately. While no individual does the job, each one is necessary to get the job done. And the job, the end product of co-operative effort, is more skilled than anything the most skilled person could have produced by himself. As in every hierarchical society, there is no answer in the mass-production plant to the question of who does the job; but there is also no answer to the question of who does not do the job. For everybody has a part in it.

There were a good many industries even in the forties which did not use the mass-production principle. Among them are some of the most efficient ones, for instance, the modern cotton mills (in which one worker may manage a great many looms) and a good many of our chemical industries (in which one worker may perform a number of different functions). Nevertheless, the mass-production industries were representative of American industry as a whole because they expressed in the purest form the essence of industrial production, i.e., a principle of social organization. The real Industrial Revolution of our day—the one which Henry Ford led and symbolized—was not a technological one, was not based on this or that machine, this or that technique, but on the hierarchical co-ordination of human efforts which mass production realizes in its purest form.

III

It is understandable that Henry Ford's disciples and imitators failed to see the political and social implications of mass production until they were confronted by them in the form of an aggressive union movement, and very often not even then. For most of these men were really concerned with technical problems only and really believed in mechanical efficiency as an end in itself. But Henry Ford's own blindness cannot be so simply explained as due to a lack of social or political concern—not even as due to a lack of social or political imagination. The real explanation is that Ford was concerned exclusively with the solution of the *social and political problems of the pre-Ford, the pre-mass-production industrial civilization.* And because his answers really did solve these problems, or at least the more important of them, it never entered his mind to subject this answer of his in turn to a social and political analysis. His gaze was firmly fixed on the industrial reality of his own youth—the industrial reality against which Populism had revolted in vain. He never even saw what he himself had called into being. As a high official of his own company once said, "What Mr. Ford really sees when he looks at River Rouge is the machine shop in which he started in 1879."

Though Henry Ford may never have heard of Brook Farm, of Robert Owen's New Harmony, or of any of the scores of utopian communities that had dotted the Midwest not so many years before his birth in 1863, they were his intellectual ancestors. He took up where they had left off; and he succeeded where they had failed. Colonel McCormick's Chicago *Tribune* called him an "anarchist" in the red-hunting days of 1919 when the term meant more or less what "Communist" would mean today in the same paper. But in spite of the obvious absurdity of the charge, the jury awarded Ford only six cents in damages when he sued for libel; for he was undeniably a radical. He turned into a stand-patter after 1932, when his life's work had shown itself a failure in its inability to produce the stable and happy society of which he had dreamed. But the Henry Ford of the earlier Model T days was an iconoclast attacking in the name of morality and science the established order of J. P. Morgan and of Mark Hanna's Republican party.

The utopias of the 1830's and 1840's were in themselves the reaction to a failure: the abortive attempt during Jackson's administration to bring back to America the lost innocence of the Jeffersonian society of self-sufficient independent farmers. The utopians no longer hoped to be able to do away with the modern division of labor or even with industry. On the contrary, they promised to obtain for mankind the full benefits of industrial productivity, but without its having to pay the price of subjecting itself to the "money power" or to "monopoly" or of having to work in the "satanic mills" of Blake's great and bitter poem. These were to be eliminated by a blend of pious sentiment, community regulations, and social science.

Of all the utopians only the Mormons survived—and they only by flight from the land of the Gentiles. But though they failed, Brook Farm, New Zion, New Harmony, and all the other attempts at the American industrial Jerusalem left a very deep imprint on the consciousness of the American people. Neither Fourier, whose ideas fathered Brook Farm, nor Robert Owen was an American. Yet it is possible, indeed probable, that the mixture of earnest, semireligious sentiment and trust in a "scientific" principle which is so typical of the American "reformer" or "radical" has its roots in much older and deeper layers in our history than the utopias. But it is certain that the utopias determined the specific form which American radicalism was to take for a whole century. They provided the targets, the battle cries, and the weapons for Populism, for Wilson's New Freedom, and even for much of the early New Deal (such as the "scientific" gold magic of 1933). They fathered

Henry George, Bellamy, and the anti-trust laws. They molded the beliefs and the hopes of America's inland empire in the Midwest. But they remained a futile gesture of revolt until Henry Ford came along.

Today we know that in depression and unemployment we have as serious an economic problem as "monopoly" and the "money power" ever were. We see very clearly that mass production creates as many new social and political questions as it answers. Today we realize that as a *final* solution to the problems of an industrial civilization, Henry Ford's solution is a failure.

But Ford's mass production was not aimed at these new dangers, but at the traditional devils of American radicalism. And these it actually did exorcise. Ford succeeded in showing that industrial production can be production *for* the masses—instead of production for the benefit of monopolist or banker. Indeed, he showed that the most profitable production is production for the masses. He proved that industrial production could give the workers increasing purchasing power to buy industrial products and to live on a middle-class standard; that was the meaning of his revolutionary $5.00-a-day minimum wage.

Finally—and to him most importantly—he proved that, properly analyzed and handled, industrial production would free the workers from arduous toil. Under modern mass-production conditions, the worker is confined to one routine operation requiring neither skill nor brawn nor mental effort. This fact would not have appeared to Henry Ford as a fatal defect, but as a supreme achievement; for it meant that—in contrast to the tradition of the "satanic mills"—the worker's skill, intelligence, and strength would be fully available for his community life as an independent Jeffersonian citizen outside of the plant and after working hours.

At Brook Farm, too, the "real life" was supposed to come in the "communion of the spirits" in the evening after the day's work had been done; but the day's work took so much time and effort that the "real life" could be lived only by neglecting the work. Mass production cuts both time and energy required for the day's work so as to give the worker plenty of scope for this "real life." No wonder that Ford—the Ford of 1919—thought he had built the "New Jerusalem" on a permanent foundation of steel, concrete, and four-lane highways.

IV

It was Ford's personal tragedy to live long enough to see his utopia crumble. He was forced to abandon his basic economic principle—the principle of the cheapest possible production of the most utilitarian commodity. First he scrapped the Model T. That was in 1927. Then, five years later, he abandoned the Model A and adopted the annual model change which substitutes the appeal of prestige and fashion for the appeal of cheapness and utility. When he did this he became just another automobile manufacturer. Even so, his share in the market dropped from nearly half in 1925 to less than 20 percent in 1940. Even more decisively proven was his failure to give the worker industrial citizenship; in 1941 the Ford workers voted to join the CIO almost three to one.

Up to the hour when the results were announced, the old man is said to have firmly believed that "his" workers would never vote for a union. All along he had fought off realization of his defeat by pretending to himself that his downfall was being caused by sinister conspiracies rather than by faults in the structure of the community which he had built. This tendency to look for personal devils—itself a legacy from the utopians—had shown itself quite early in the tirades of the Dearborn *Independent* against international bankers, Wall Street, and the Jews during the 1920's. It became the basis on which he fought the unions all through the thirties. It also probably explains why Harry Bennett, starting as the plant's chief cop, rose to be the most powerful individual in the Ford organization of the thirties and the only one who really seemed to enjoy the old man's confidence. But the union victory, followed shortly by the unionization of the foremen, must have hit Henry Ford as a repudiation of all he had thought he had achieved, and had achieved primarily for the workers. The last years of the old man must have been very bitter ones, indeed.

The lesson of Ford's ultimate failure is that we cannot hope to solve the problems of the mass-production society by technological devices or by changing the economics of distribution. These were the two approaches on which all nineteenth-century thought had relied, whether orthodox or rebel. Henry Ford went as far along these lines as it is possible to go.

For the time being, the political results of Ford's achievement were extraordinary. It took the wind out of the sails of the socialist critique of capitalist society. In this country it brought about the change from the fiery political action of Eugene Debs to the politically impotent moralism of Norman Thomas; in continental Europe it converted social democracy from a millennial fighting creed into a respectable but timid bureaucracy. Even more telling was the reaction of Communist Russia to Ford. In the twenties the Russians had to add to the messianic hopes of Karl Marx the promise of achieving eventually in a socialist society what Ford had already achieved in a capitalist one: a chance for the worker to drive to the plant in his own car and to work in collar and tie, and without getting calluses on his hands. And until 1929, as every meeting of the Third International affirmed, the Communists were completely convinced that Ford's America had actually solved the basic problems of capitalism and had restored it to ascendancy all the world over. Not until the Great Depression were the Communist leaders able to revitalize their creed by making it appear to do what it cannot do: to solve, by the sheer force of the police state, the new, the post-Ford problems of industrial society as they appeared after 1929.

As we in America confront these problems, the economic ones will not be the most difficult. Indeed, the chief economic problem of our time—the prevention of depressions—should be solvable by basically mechanical means: by adapting our employment, fiscal, and budgeting practices to the time span of industrial production—that is, to the business cycle. Much more baffling, and more basic, is the political and social problem with which twentieth-century industrialism confronts us: the problem of developing order and citizenship within the plant, of building a free, self-governing industrial society.

The fact that Henry Ford, after his superb success, failed so signally—that there is today such a grim contrast between his social utopia and our social reality—emphasizes the magnitude of the political task before us. But however treacherous the social jungle of post-Ford, mass-production society, however great the danger that it will fester into civil war and tyranny, the twentieth-century evils which Henry Ford left to us may well be less formidable than the nineteenth-century evils which he vanquished.

CHAPTER NINE

The American Genius Is Political

I

THE GENIUS OF the American people is political. The one truly saintly figure this country has produced, the one name that symbolizes the "fulfilled life" to most Americans, the one man whose very life was dedicated toward directing human activity on to a higher goal, was a politician: Abraham Lincoln.

The phrase which since early days expresses the essence of their own society to Americans is a political promise: the "equal chance of every American boy to become President." One has only to translate the slogan—for instance, into a promise of "equal opportunity for every boy to become Prime Minister"—to see by contrast that it is uniquely American, and this not because the promise of equal opportunities in itself would be absurd, but because the political sphere is the meaningful sphere of social values only in this country.

The American nation itself has been formed out of a multitude of diverse national traditions not by imposing on the newcomer a

First published in *Perspectives,* 1953.

uniform religion, uniform customs, a new culture—not even by imposing on him the American language. It has been formed by imposing on him a common political creed. What makes the immigrant into an American is an affirmation of abstract political principles, the oath of citizenship in which he promises to uphold "the republican form of government."

Above all, the meaning of this country—what it stands for for Americans themselves as well as for the world—is a political meaning. It is a form of government, a social order, and an economic system that are equally in people's minds when they praise America and when they condemn her. And when Americans sing of their own country, they sing of her—in the words of our most popular anthem—as the "sweet land of liberty," which would hardly occur as a definition of one's country and as an avowal of one's identification with it even to the most ardent of European liberals.

We have to go back all the way to the Rome of Augustus with its concept of "Latinitas" to find a society that so completely understands itself in political terms as does the United States. Yet Latinitas was wishful thinking and never became reality, whereas the political meaning of the United States furnishes its essence: its ideal personality, its promises, its power of integration and assimilation. That the American genius is political is therefore the major key to the understanding of America, of its history, and of its meaning.

II

In the political sphere lie the American ideas and institutions which are peculiar to this country and which give it its distinction.

There is, first, the peculiarly American symbiosis of secular state and religious society which is the cornerstone of the American commonwealth. The United States today is both the oldest and the most thoroughgoing secular state. It is also at the same time the only society in the West in which belief in a supernatural God is taken for granted and in which the traditional religious bodies, the churches, continue to discharge, unchallenged, many important community functions. And this coincidence of secular state and religious society is not simply accidental. In the American mind the two serve as each other's main support, if not as each other's precondition. Everywhere else the secular state arose out of a revolt against religion. In this country the secular state owes its existence largely to the demand of the leaders of dominant, indeed of established, religious creeds that civil power and religious society be strictly separated for the greater good of religion and church.

In the political sphere also lies the concept of "constitutionalism" which is the chief organizing principle of American society. Constitutionalism is much more than respect for law; that is something, indeed, for which the American is not renowned. Rather, constitutionalism is a view of the nature and function of abstract principles and of their relationship to social action. It is a belief that power, to be beneficial, must be subjected to general and unchangeable rules. It is an assertion that ends and means cannot be meaningfully separated or considered apart from each other. It is a belief that the validity of actions can be determined by rational criteria. It is, in other words, a political ethics. The Constitution of the Republic is only one application of this fundamental belief. Constitutionalism has been the organizing force in every one of our major institutions. Today, for instance, we see it at work in the industrial sphere fashioning a "common law" in labor-management relations and reinforcing such principles as "federalism" and "legitimate succession" for management inside business enterprise.

Peculiarly American also is the political view of education. This is shown in the insistence of Americans that education, on all levels, be equally accessible to all, if not, indeed, obligatory on all. It is shown in the naïve but general belief that the level of general schooling is a fairly reliable index of civic competence and that any increase in it is a step toward a better and fuller citizenship. Most characteristically, the political view of education is expressed in the definition of the educational goal—the feature that makes understanding the American school system so difficult for the foreigner. American education rejects alike the traditionally European concept of the "educated individual" and the "trained robot" of modern totalitarianism. To both it opposes the demand that the school has to educate responsible self-governing citizens who, in Lincoln's words, "do not want to be masters because they do not want to be slaves." And because the American school is both free from control by the central government and a central political institution, it is bound to be the subject of violent political dispute whenever this country examines the premises on which its society and government rest, as, for instance, during the early days of the New Deal and again today.

Finally, there is the American political party—which has but the name in common with parties in the rest of the Western world. The major purpose of the American party is not to express principles, but to provide at all times a functioning and a legitimate government. It does not express a political philosophy to the realization of which governmental power is to be directed. It expresses the need of the body politic for a strong, a national, and a unifying government. For these reasons no American party has survived unless it succeeded in appealing to all classes and conditions, that is, unless it succeeded in being truly nationwide—which explains why both parties always are moderate in their actions. No party has survived unless it could appeal at once to men on the extreme right and to men on the extreme left. This, in turn, explains why both parties always appeal to the extremists in their campaign oratory. And no party has survived unless it succeeded in sinking differences of interests and principles in the unifying appeal of a common American creed.

III

The real achievement of American history in the first half of this century also lay in the political sphere. It is an achievement so great, so recent, and still so much in a state of becoming as to be almost beyond our vision: the creation of a new industrial society with new institutions—and of an industrial society that promises to be a stable, a free, and a moral society.

We ourselves in this country are prone to discuss our industrial achievements in economic, if not in purely technical, terms. But every single "productivity team" which came to this country from Europe in the forties and fifties to study the causes of American productivity soon saw that economic and technological factors explain less than nothing about the American economy. The key to an understanding lies in the social beliefs and the new social and political institutions that we have developed since the turn of the century. The clue is to be found in our development of the corporation as an organization of joint human efforts to a common goal, or in our new social organ, management, the function of which must be defined in sociopolitical terms, that is, as the organization and leadership of people.

More important even than any single one of these new institutions—more important even than such new ideas as productivity considered as a social responsibility of business, or the concept of the market as something that management through its own actions creates and expands—is the new American theorem as to the relationship between business and society—a theorem as opposed to nineteenth-century laissez-faire thinking as it is to nineteenth- and twentieth-century socialism. Business activity is no longer seen, as it was in laissez-faire theory, as something separate and distinct, without direct relationship to social and political goals. But it is also not seen, as in all socialist creeds, as something which, if it is to be in the public interest, must be controlled and perhaps suppressed by the government. Business activity is seen as a necessarily private activity which, for its own good and its own justification, has to strive for the common good and the stated ends of society. Business enterprise is thus seen as local and autonomous self-government which, by serving the ends of society, serves its own self-interests and guarantees its own survival. This, the most decisive contribution America has been making to the Western world these last fifty years, is unquestionably a theorem of political science.

IV

In the political sphere, once more, lies that peculiarly American form of behavior: voluntary group action. Perhaps nothing sets this country as much apart from the rest of the Western world as its almost instinctive reliance on voluntary, and often spontaneous, group action for the most important social purposes.

We hear a great deal of "American individualism" these days. And there is certainly a fundamental belief in the individual, his strength, his integrity and self-reliance, his worth in the American tradition. But this "individualism" is much less peculiar to this country—and much less general—than its (usually overlooked) "collectivism." Only it is not the collectivism of organized governmental action from above. It is a collectivism of voluntary group action from below.

This shows itself in the way in which people in this country tackle their social and community problems. If the teenagers in a small town get out of control, the local service club, Rotary or Lions, will build a clubhouse for them and get them off the streets. If the hospital needs a new wing, the Woman's Club will get the money for it. American schools are run as much by a voluntary group organization—the Parent-Teacher Association—as they are by the Superintendent of Schools. And when we suddenly have to draft millions of Americans into uniform, we dump the social and community problems that this creates into the lap of voluntary committees and organizations. Even the drafting of young men into the armed forces is left to ordinary citizens who volunteer to serve without compensation on the draft boards of their communities.

Alone among Western countries, the United States knows no "Ministry of Education." But, then, no other country has anything to compare with the power and influence that private groups—e.g., the great foundations—wield over higher education. And yet we take this completely as a matter of course. Every American knows instinctively that this country is actually ruled by thousands of purely voluntary, purely private, mostly local groups. He takes it for granted that it is the easiest thing in the world to get such a group going to meet any local needs whatsoever and that despite its private character it will be responsive to public opinion.

It is not "competition" that characterizes American life, as some social scientists want us to believe. It is the symbiosis between competition and co-operation organized in and through voluntary, private groups. And while the roots of this behavior reach deep into the past—in the brotherhoods of the members of the small religious sects and in their interdependence, as well as in the neighborliness of the frontier—it is just as much at work in our newest institutions. No other feature of our business system is so much remarked upon by visiting management and labor delegates from abroad as the close, highly organized co-operation on policy matters, on technology, on business problems, and so forth that obtains between the most bitter business rivals; or the close, constant co-operation on day-to-day problems that obtains between managers and union officials in a given plant.

V

Americans themselves tend to take it for granted that American genius is political. If they ask at all what explains this, their answer is likely to be: the frontier. Certainly the human explosion which carried settlement and civilization in less than one century from the Atlantic across a wild, hostile, and uncharted continent to the shores of the Pacific is the greatest achievement of the American people and their deepest experience. And yet the frontier and the course of settlement were themselves already results of the American political genius rather than its origins. It was the ability to organize spontaneously for group action, it was the idea of "constitutionalism," that made orderly commonwealths out of the immigrant trains moving over the plains or mountains; it was the ability to adapt, as if instinctively, inherited patterns of social, political, and economic organization to the new and unexpected conditions of the frontier that alone made settlement of the country possible. Above all, the rapid settlement of the continent rested on the country's ability to make, so to speak overnight, Americans out of millions of immigrants from all over Europe. This presupposed the absorption of the alien into American citizenship and his integration into American political institutions.

The formative influence on America's political spirit is something deeper than climate, geography, or even the experiences of our history. It consists in our fundamental beliefs regarding the nature of man and the nature of the universe. To say that the genius of this country is political is to say that America, from earliest colonial times, has refused to split the world of ideas from the world of matter, the world of reason from the world of the senses. It is to say that she has alike refused to grant more than a temporary visitor's visa to the philosophies of Descartes, Hume, or the German Idealists as well as that of Marx—indeed, to the entire body of post-Cartesian philosophy on which modern European thought is founded. For every one of these philosophies denies meaning, if not existential reality, to the sphere of politics.

To the politician, matter can never be unreal, can never be an illusion, can never be base. His task is to use matter for constructive purposes. Nor can he ever consider ideas illusory or unreal. Without them he would have neither direction nor the ability to move toward his goal. The politician must always oppose to the "either-or" of the monistic philosopher—whether idealist or materialist, realist or nominalist, rationalist or intuitionist—the philosophical dualism of "both." He can neither, with the European humanist, divorce "sordid" politics from "pure" intellectual and artistic culture, nor can he, with the European materialist, see in politics simply a rationalization of material conditions or an automatic product of material forces. He can be neither "starry-eyed idealist" and "uplifter" nor the "money-mad chaser of the almighty dollar." He must always combine elements of both extremes in the attempt to find balance and harmony. For to the politician ideas and matter are the two poles of a single world, opposed to each other but at the same time inseparable, mutually interdependent, and each other's complement.

America has insisted—at least since Jonathan Edwards first started philosophizing on these shores two hundred and fifty years ago—that ideas and matter, reason and experience, logic and intuition, must always be held equally real and equally valid. And it is this philosophical world view that alone explains the central position of the political sphere in the American tradition.

In this view politics becomes at once a responsibility of man; it becomes the chief moral duty in human life. Politics becomes a respectable, in fact a creative, sphere of action—creative in the aesthetic meaning of the word—"the endless adventure," as one eighteenth-century politician called it; and creative in the spiritual meaning of the word, as partaking of charity through which man is moved from the pursuit of his own, empty self toward his real mission of making the creation glorify the creator. Politics as the creative, the meaningful, the moral, the responsible, the charitable sphere—that lies at the center of what America believes, what she has achieved, and what she stands for. The great men to whose memory she always turns in the hours of darkness and confusion have been those few political leaders who realized to the full the opportunity and the obligation of politics.

At bottom, the American philosophical position—the position that believes in politics as the human activity through which matter is made to serve spirit—stands on a religious foundation. It is not incorrect to call it "Christian." But actually it is the great contribution of Israel. For it is in the Old Testament that the Lord looked upon his material creation and "saw that it was very good." Yet the creation is nothing without the Spirit that created it. And it is man's specific task, his own mission and purpose, to make manifest the creator in and through the creation—to make matter express spirit.

VI

The challenge that faces this country today is again primarily a challenge of politics. There is, first, the challenge of the Welfare State, of maintaining a free society and a free government under the threat of an indefinite "cold war" under the constant pressure of high taxation, the dangers of sneaking inflation, the tensions and worries of a world neither at peace nor at war.

There is the even greater challenge of the development of a foreign policy that is appropriate to America's power and to her responsibilities. This is doubly great a challenge since foreign policy is the one department of political action in which this country has failed so far. Ours is the third time that the United States has won military victory in a great war only to lose the peace almost immediately.

How we will meet these challenges will decide whether the American experiment has, after all, been nothing more than an episode in the suicidal Western civilization, or whether America will be capable of giving the West political inspiration leading it toward an age of freedom, stable peace, and prosperity. And the outcome of the test will depend not primarily on America's economic wealth or her military strategy, but on her political leadership, her political wisdom, her political maturity. What is on trial today is America's political genius.

CHAPTER TEN

Japan Tries for a Second Miracle

JAPAN WAS ALMOST overrun these last few years by Western economists, bankers, and industrialists who had come to study the "Japanese economic miracle." Arthur Burns, Chairman of the Council of Economic Advisers under Eisenhower, was there in 1963, for instance; he was so impressed, according to reports, that he strongly recommended that President Kennedy adopt some of Japan's tax and money policies to spur our laggard economy. A little later the London *Economist* sent a senior editor on a three months' tour; the result was two book-length supplements in the magazine, the first of which was called "The Most Exciting Example." Dozens of Wall Street analysts poked around Japan looking for "growth" stocks to recommend to American investors who were disenchanted with their own market. And there were industrialists from all over—from Germany, Italy, France, Canada, the United States, and Australia—searching for products to buy, for Japanese partners for joint ventures, or for Japanese markets.

The only people who did not talk about the "Japanese economic

---

First published in *Harper's Magazine,* March, 1963.

miracle" were the Japanese themselves. Their businessmen, economists, labor leaders, and bureaucrats were fretting instead about the threat to Japan's exports and about "excessive competition" at home. They talked about the need to retrench, and they complained about the growing "flood of American imports" that, they said, was about to drive entire Japanese industries to the wall. Most of this was just talking poor, of course. Any competition in the home market is likely to be considered "excessive" in Japan, where for thirty years goods had been scarce. Now, however, with four out of five Japanese families having TV sets, customers no longer stand in line, money in hand, to buy whatever the manufacturers turn out.

But poor talk or not, Japan has fundamental decisions to make on the character and structure of its economy and society and on the nature of its political life—precisely because its economic success has made it the only modern nation outside the West.

The last decades in Japan proved that the methods, tools, and policies of a free economy can generate very fast economic development on non-Western soil. They also proved that with a free economy a non-Western nation can achieve an educated population and a high and rising standard of living. In the next few years, however, Japan will have to demonstrate that the social and political values of a free society (1) can generate effective and well-organized political forces and (2) can resolve the inherited social conflicts of a non-Western culture and tradition. Already a technically advanced and highly educated Great Power—the only non-Western nation to attain this position—Japan now has to prove that it can become the first *society* to be both truly modern and fundamentally non-European.

Cause for Confidence

What has happened in Japan since the end of the American Occupation in April 1952 is the most extraordinary success story in all economic history.

When the peace treaty went into effect and Japan regained her sovereignty, she had just barely worked her way back to her prewar levels of production and income. This was far above any level that could be called "underdeveloped," as witness Japan's industrial output and technical performance in World War II. But the Japan of 1952, like that of 1941, still rated only as a minor industrial country, perhaps twelfth to fifteenth among the industrial nations. Her dominant industries were those that typify the early stages of industrialization: for instance, textiles. Her food shortages were chronic and apparently incurable; the two staples, rice and wheat, were still rationed in the spring of 1952. Even such recovery as Japan had made depended on American orders for the Korean War, and these orders were rapidly drying up. Inflation had been rampant, and labor unrest that came close to armed insurrection was endemic. Joseph Dodge, the Detroit banker who had been the Occupation's economic adviser, said what nearly all the experts thought when he predicted in his final report that the Japanese economy was headed for collapse.

Ten years later, Japan ranked fourth among all nations in total industrial production. Only the United States, the Soviet Union, and West Germany were ahead of her, and she was actually on the point of overtaking the Germans. Since 1952 her national income had tripled and her industrial production and industrial exports were five times what they had been. This means that Japan had achieved an annual average growth rate of 9 percent for national income and almost 20 percent for industrial production and exports. No nation in recorded economic history had ever done this before.

To accomplish this astonishing feat, Japan had in a decade managed to make massive break-throughs on five different and distinct fronts—in new investment, in mass marketing, in agriculture, in education, and in health. Briefly, this is what she accomplished:

First: Year after year the Japanese have put more than a quarter of their national income into new investment. It has been this, primarily, that has made possible the rapid spurt in industrial capacity and production.

Second: At the same time the Japanese created the first genuine mass consumer market outside the Western world. In 1962, for example, the Japanese discovered to their amazement that only the United States had more consumer appliances per family than they had; they were better supplied with TV sets, refrigerators, and washing machines than the British or the West Germans (though the automotive revolution was only just beginning). What is more, along with her mass consumer market, Japan had created a mass stock market, a phenomenon known otherwise only in the United States. In prewar Japan only banks and big industrialists owned shares in industrial companies; in 1963 every tenth Japanese family owned some common shares. (That is not to say that the SEC would have approved of the methods by which these shares were sold.)

Third is the break-through in agriculture. Around 1952 half the Japanese population worked on the land, but Japan could not feed herself. Ten years later only a third of the population was still on the land. But though the Japanese now had to feed a far larger population than they did a decade ago, they were about to acquire that fashionable national disease, an unmanageable farm surplus.

The fourth break-through has been in education. Only the United States and Israel have a larger proportion of their young people in higher education than Japan. Every third or fourth young man of twenty is now in college; this stands in marked contrast to Europe, where the "educational revolution" is yet to come.

And, finally, in one short decade, life expectancy in Japan has risen from less than fifty years (which was high for a non-Western country) to seventy (which is equal to that of the most advanced countries of the West). Furthermore, Japan has managed to cut its birth rate to the Western level so that, alone of all non-Western countries, Japan is not being overwhelmed by "population explosion."

One would expect these achievements to be expensive, but while the Japanese were forging ahead on all these fronts their tax burden did not go up. It has been Japanese budget practice to anticipate the economic growth for the year ahead, figure out what it will mean in higher revenues, and then cut tax rates enough to hold the tax burden down. (It was this, apparently, that so impressed Dr. Arthur Burns.) One might expect such a tax policy to create inflation, but there has been less inflation in Japan than there has been in Europe or America.

Even more surprising, perhaps, the tremendous economic growth in Japan had been accomplished with very little money from abroad. After the Marshall Plan began in 1948, America sent $25 billion in aid to Europe. In the same period Japan (with 95 million people, or one-third the population of all Europe including Great Britain) got at most $1 billion. Furthermore, Japan has been extremely wary of foreign investment, and there has, consequently, been almost none—a marked contrast to Europe, where the five to eight billion dollars of direct American investment have provided much of the fuel for the boom of the last few years.

In 1961 the growth rate in Japan actually hit 15 percent. The government, afraid of inflation, stepped on the brakes—hard—and forced a slowdown. But a Japanese "slowdown" would be a gallop anywhere else—the economy grew by 5 percent in 1962 despite credit restrictions and officially decreed "austerity." (The United States growth *goal* is a rate of 3½ to 4 percent a year!) In 1959 the Japanese government predicted that the economy would double again in the ten years between 1960 and 1970. In September 1962 the Ministry of Finance cut the period to seven years; the growth from 1960 to 1963 alone had already added 40 percent to the 1959 economic level.

Japan, of course, has one very special advantage: a very low defense burden. Though growing steadily, the budget for the Japanese "Self-Defense Forces" still takes less than 2 percent of the country's national income—as against a defense burden of 10 percent of national income in the United States. (Japan and West Germany should be a convincing answer, by the way, to fears of the economic effects of disarmament.) But even after making full allowance for this and a great deal of luck, the Japanese economic achievement is still a real "economic miracle."

This sort of accomplishment ought to make the Japanese smug. On the contrary, they are deeply worried. A good many sane and unexcitable Japanese talk seriously today about what they call "a crisis of self-confidence." Why?

. . . and Cause for Jitters

The immediate cause of Japan's jitters is that in her own self-interest she has to open her domestic market to competition from the West and especially from Europe and the United States. Since 1900, when Japan first began to export manufactured goods in quantity, she has been a tough, aggressive competitor in international markets. But her home market has always been insulated; and neither economically nor socially is Japan prepared for competition in it.

Japan is thoroughly mercantilist. It is, indeed, the one example of successful mercantilism which combines governmental direction with entrepreneurial vigor, and aggressive competition abroad with protectionism and imposed price stability at home. To do away with this protectionism at home is going to mean changing drastically both the entire system of industrial hiring and firing and the long-entrenched but extremely expensive system of distributing goods.

Then why should Japan now, after her economic success, have to let the foreigners come into her domestic market?

Japan's entire postwar expansion has been in the new "advanced" industries—in machinery, synthetic fibers, and plastics; electronics, optics, and pharmaceuticals; trucks and household appliances. The "traditional" industries which dominated prewar Japan are no longer very important in the domestic economy today. Japan depends, for instance, less on cotton-mill employment than does our own Old South. But of her exports half were in 1962 still in "traditional" goods: textiles, toys, footwear. On these exports depends Japan's ability to buy abroad the raw materials—above all, petroleum and iron ore—without which the "advanced" industries could not keep going for one day. And exports of traditional goods are shrinking—fast and inexorably. Japan is already outproduced and undersold in the traditional goods by such new, truly low-low-wage areas as Hong Kong, Singapore, the Philippines, or Pakistan. Within a very few years Japan will have to replace traditional-goods exports by advanced-goods exports. And the only possible buyers of these additional advanced-goods exports are the big markets of the European Common Market and of Great Britain, where Japan today sells practically nothing.

The problem of the traditional exports would have arisen anyhow; no one knew it better than the Japanese. The emergence of the European Common Market as a great economic power, however, brought it to a head a full decade before Japan was ready to face it. Suddenly, in 1962, the Japanese realized—as we and the British did—that they must get into the European market fast or risk being out forever.

There is no economic reason why Japan's advanced products should not sell as well in Europe as they have been selling in the much tougher and much more competitive United States market. But the Japanese cannot even ask for access to Europe unless they offer the Europeans access on equal terms to their own lush domestic market of 95 million prosperous customers—which, after the United States and Western Europe, is the world's third richest market. This, however, means that the Japanese for the first time will have to be able to meet industrial competition on their own home grounds.

To Westerners, who have been used to stories of "Japanese low costs," Japan would seem to have nothing to worry about. It is hard for us to believe, for instance, that Italian or Swiss silks could undersell the Japanese product. Yet Tokyo's largest silk store has for years offered beautiful European silks 30 percent or so below the price of comparable Japanese fabrics, despite a fat Japanese customs duty on such imports. For Japan's is a high-cost economy, except in its most advanced industries, and especially in its advanced export industries. Labor costs run two or three times as high on almost any manufactured item as they do in the West. And the Japanese customer pays almost twice as much for distribution as we pay here, despite our vast distances and high transportation costs. These are costs demanded by the social structure rather than by economic inefficiency and accordingly require social remedies with all their potential political dangers.

Kept On to Do Nothing

Let me explain. The Japanese worker is as productive as any worker in the world. He is better educated and better trained than almost any other worker, and he works cheerfully, hard, and for long hours. Yet, in some Japanese factories it takes six times as many employees to produce the same amount of the same goods as in a comparable American factory. The reason is Japan's traditional system of "lifetime employment," with layoffs or dismissals only for very serious misconduct. As a result most of Japanese industry is grossly overstaffed, and thousands of people for whom there are no jobs are kept on doing almost nothing in the plant or office. Very few Japanese employers know (just as very few American employers know) that it costs three to five times a man's salary to have him on a job—in supervision, in space, in paper work and record keeping, in heat and light, in materials, and so on.

"Lifetime employment," in turn, means that a Japanese over thirty as a rule cannot change jobs. He is paid by his age rather than by the demands of the job he performs. He is assigned, however, to a job on the basis of length of service. A new employee over thirty, therefore, could be given only beginner's work—and would get twice the starting wage. It is small wonder that no one will hire him. But this in turn also means that the firm just keeps him on the payroll and invents work for him.

As a result, older industries and businesses bear the heaviest burden of overstaffing; and the coal mines and railroads, as they are everywhere else, are in the worst shape of all. New industries and new businesses also have high costs because an artificially created "labor shortage" steadily pushes up the wages that beginners can, and do, demand. Starting wages for school graduates have doubled in the last three years.

The younger managerial and professional people in Japan are beginning to move from job to job in increasing numbers, though still only if their original employers permit them to do so. And many different ways to make the manual worker mobile are now being explored.

Some companies are introducing the Western system of paying for the job itself rather than for age and seniority. Others are toying with the idea of splitting between the old and the new employer the wage cost of any worker who changes jobs. The new employer would pay the base wage for the transferring employee; the old employer would pay the difference between that and the wage appropriate to the man's age. The Japanese are beginning to understand that industry has to separate the guarantee of a worker's income—which ought to be maintained—from the stranglehold the job has on him. The worker ought to be freed from the restrictions that penalize him and make it impossible for him to move into a better-paying job in an expanding industry.

But lifetime employment is much more than a matter of money. Until World War II it was almost entirely restricted to white-collar workers. Manual workers didn't achieve it until after the war and then only through bitter labor struggles. To them it represents, therefore, status and acceptance by society. An emotional issue anywhere (as witness our steel strike of 1959 over "featherbedding" or the long and bitter fight of the Flight Engineers), employment security is pure dynamite in Japan. The longest and most violent strike in Japanese labor history took place in the early sixties, when virtually a whole county stayed out for eighteen bitter months in protest against a management decision to retire with a generous severance allowance two thousand coal miners in an exhausted pit. Yet, according to a recent government study, there are another 60,000 coal miners—one-third of the total—for whom there is no real work, though they all have "full-time jobs."

The problem of distribution costs is just as serious, and it, too, is as much a social as an economic problem. The distributive system of Japan is essentially what it was a hundred years ago: it is still a multitude of small middlemen who live on a pittance but who when laid end to end represent a staggering waste.

What adds difficulty to problems of employment security and distribution is the position of these issues on the Japanese political map. On the one hand, employment security is a sure-fire issue for the left—indeed, almost its only domestic issue with mass appeal. On the other hand, the millions of small wholesalers and retailers, who constitute the distribution system, are the solid voting core of the conservative government in power.

Yet these concrete social issues, as full of explosives as they are, frighten the Japanese less than the impact of foreign competition at home on their traditional mercantilism—which has all the force of an unwritten constitution. Opening the home market would surely upset the subtle three-way partnership among government, large business, and small business on which Japan's entire economic development has been based. It would force Japan to abandon the policy under which government prods industries to be productive and competitive for export, while it protects inefficiency on the home market. It would break up the peculiarly Japanese arrangement under which the large producers are hot and hard-hitting rivals, yet maintain a price umbrella for the small fellow. Above all, it would force Japan to let the market decide what should be produced and how it should be priced—questions traditionally decided by political and national considerations.

Old Slogans and a New Generation

Many Japanese leaders believe that their economy must become an integrated part of the world economy anyhow, and fast. They maintain that Japanese industry badly needs the challenge of competition. The costs of automobile production—and with it car prices—would drop a full third, for instance, if Japan's "Toyopet" had to compete with the English Ford, the French Renault, the German Volkswagen, and the American compact car. (Japanese heavy trucks and motorcycles, both export products, are already competitive.) These Japanese believe that their mercantilist economic policy, their employment practices, and their distributive system not only have been made completely obsolete by Japan's economic growth but are fast becoming serious obstacles to further growth. They are convinced that Japan would immediately benefit from economic integration with the West as much as Germany and France benefited from the Common Market. And in all probability they are right. Unless Japan wants to choke off her economic growth and prosperity, she will have to become an open competitive economy. But if she does, tremendous political pressures will build up that will challenge political courage, vision, and leadership.

There are precedents for political leadership of rare ability in Japan's modern history. One occurred in the late nineteenth century when, in one generation, a ruling class of warrior-noblemen voluntarily abdicated, abolished a tribal feudalism a thousand years old, and turned the country into a modern state. No such leadership emerged between 1890 and 1940. But after World War II Shigeru Yoshida, Japan's Prime Minister from 1947 to 1957, again provided leadership of high courage and vision.

But whether similar leadership emerges now or not, the shape of Japanese politics will inevitably change. The defeat of World War II created new institutions and new slogans, but few new values. Even those values of the past that were neither nationalist nor militarist were discredited. The great majority of Japanese found comfort instead in work and its discipline. As in Germany, the job of rebuilding the country became for the time being an end in itself. A much smaller minority, needing absolute beliefs and commitments, took refuge in the only available orthodoxy, which was Marxism. It is no accident that the very same groups that had been the most fanatical nationalists under the old regime—especially students and professors—became the most dedicated Marxists under the new.

Today, the Liberal-Democrats (as the conservative party is called) win every election with a monotonous two-thirds majority. But the static positions bequeathed by the defeat and the Occupation show every sign of breaking up. Japan today gropes for new political values and new political directions. This is true on the right as well as on the left.

Now the job of rebuilding the country has been done. While the great majority wants more worldly goods (and especially wants to be able to buy and drive an automobile), economic recovery is no longer the great national task. And the Marxists in Japan may be where our own American Marxists were in the late 1940's, after the Henry Wallace campaign for President. Their god has been shown to have clay feet.

The president of the Zengakuren—Japan's left-wing and fellow-traveling student federation, which staged the riots against President Eisenhower's visit in 1960—returned in August, 1962, from a "Peace Rally" in Moscow with an amazing tale. The Moscow police, he said, took him and a number of his colleagues behind the Tomb of Lenin on Red Square, gave them a severe beating, and then hung them upside down for half an hour or so. All this for daring to stage a "ban-the-bomb" rally. It is hard to believe that even Communist police could be quite so stupid. But it is even harder to believe that Japanese students could be so naïve as to think that Russia would encourage a demonstration against nuclear testing which condemned indiscriminately United States and Soviet tests. Yet this is what Japan's Marxists (except for their very small core of hardened professionals) really did believe. And this belief is crumbling rapidly under the impact of the ideological conflict between Moscow and Peking which, seen from Tokyo, is hot, bitter, and irreconcilable.

This does not mean that the Japanese left will cease to be anti-American. Indeed, the less dependent on Moscow (or Peking) it is, the more dangerous it may become. It is its subservience to the Communists—and especially to the Russians—which, more than anything else, has kept the left from gaining a majority of the national vote. Should the left ever become genuinely "neutral," it might well get into power, and the consequences for United States strategy and foreign policy in the Far East might be serious.

But if a split opened in the ranks of the governing conservative party—caused, for instance, by a fight over the future of the small retailer—it could be equally serious.

In Search of Certainty

Right and left may, however, look quite different in tomorrow's Japan. The most remarkable political phenomena in Japan today are not political parties or politicians, but two religious sects, both of a strong fundamentalist cast: Ten Rikyo, a kind of Japanese Seventh-Day Adventists, and Soka Gakkai, a schismatic Buddhist sect, somehow reminiscent of both the Mormons and Father Divine.

When the American Occupation took a religious inventory in the late forties, neither sect was even an independent, let alone a major, group. Today each has millions of fanatical members. Ten Rikyo is not directly active in politics, though its members are expected to "vote for what is right." But Soka Gakkai polled four million votes in the Senate elections in July, 1962.

Both sects fully accept modern industrial civilization and are, in general, "for progress"; both are strongly anti-Communist and professedly antinationalist. But they are concerned less with issues than with the ethical, moral, spiritual values of politics and attack all existing parties as unprincipled. Indeed, "Soka Gakkai" means "creation of values." All experience with such movements in other countries would indicate that these two will come to grief as soon as they get into the practical and grubby business of politics—which is probably why Ten Rikyo carefully sidesteps any political responsibility. But such movements are a warning. Their rapid growth and their ability to attract members from all classes—students, for instance, and unskilled recent immigrants from the countryside into the big cities, the maids, chauffeurs, and laundresses—attest both to the yearning for values and commitments and to disenchantment with today's politics and parties.

To meet this real need and opportunity for responsible political leadership in Japan, there is an entirely new generation grown to manhood since the war. But there is also real danger. If Japan fails to integrate herself into the Free World economy—no matter whether it is the West or her own social problems that keep her out—she will be pushed toward close economic ties with Soviet Russia. Especially in Siberia, the Soviet Union has an insatiable appetite for the advanced products Japan has to sell, from chemicals and turbines to railway rolling stock, trucks, and transistors. The only trouble from Japan's point of view is that Russia does not have anything to sell back to Japan, but wants long-term credits which Japan simply cannot give. Yet, if driven to the wall, the Japanese might begin to buy raw material from Russia even though the prices would be high and the supply quite unreliable. Or Russia might use her gold stock to pay Japan.

Trading with Russia would not require that the Japanese sacrifice any of their traditional politicoeconomic practices; they would not have to admit manufactured foreign goods to the home market, or change their methods of employment, or reform their distribution system. It would actually strengthen Japan's mercantilist policy. For these reasons conservative groups, determined anti-Communists at home, send trade mission after trade mission to Moscow, in the hope of finding an "Eastern alternative" to economic integration with the West, which they fear as a threat to their traditional practices and institutions. They are willing to admit that trade with Russia would stop Japan's further economic growth, but they may regard this as a lesser evil.

Such a shift in Japan's economic alignment, even if totally without effect on her foreign and military policies (which, of course, would be quite unlikely), would be a major catastrophe for Japan but an even greater one for the Free World. The balance of economic power, now heavily with the West, would shift sharply toward the Soviet bloc. Worse still would be the psychological impact of such a shift. Japan, as the only non-Western country that has actually accomplished economic development, is the test case for others. If even Japan cannot achieve membership as an equal in the Free World economy, what chance is there for the poorer and far less developed countries ranging from Yugoslavia and Peru to Nigeria and Malaya?

Do We Really Mean It?

There is much the West, and especially the United States, can do to help Japan make the decisions that are right both for her and for the Free World. We can prevent stupidity and racial prejudice (especially of the unconscious and therefore doubly dangerous kind that is so common in Europe) from pushing Japan against her own economic self-interest away from the Free World. If we do not, there is real danger that the Europeans, if only out of widespread ignorance of Japan and of her economic strength, will exclude her.

Even more important is that we recognize Japan's importance to the West. Perhaps because postwar Japan has not been a "problem," our policy-makers have not paid much attention to her—less, for instance, than to India or to the new African nations. We have seen Japan primarily in the light of our own strategy: as a permanent American military base and as a potential military ally. We tend to forget that Japan is also a great power, an ancient culture, and a prime symbol of "economic development" to hundreds of millions of non-Europeans.

"The individual American who shows an interest in Japan—her history, her economy, her arts, her universities, her religion—may do more to tie us to the Free World than all the policies of your government," remarked a prominent Japanese banker, inclined, as a rule, to shrug off such "intangibles."

Finally, we need to realize that Japan is not a "European" country and neither can nor should try to become one. Every responsible Japanese gets the shivers when someone in Bonn, London, or Washington talks of the "Atlantic Community"; he knows that no semantic sleight of hand can make Japan border on the Atlantic or trace her culture back to the "Judeo-Christian heritage" of our college catalogues. No matter how Westernized her economy, how technically educated her people, how advanced her physicians and scientists—her roots of culture and history, art and religion, script, literature, and language are not European, but Asian. A viable modern society in Japan must embrace both her Western civilization and her Asian culture.

There are signs that the Japanese begin to understand this; the appeal of the two religious sects discussed earlier lies largely in the stress they place on both ancient religion and ethics and modern economics, industry, technology, and science. There are signs that Japan can synthesize East and West. At least in painting, Japan's most representative and most truly national art, a whole generation of good young artists are now "abstractionists" in the Western sense and yet unmistakably "Japanese": "calligraphers" in the best Japanese tradition and yet, unmistakably, schooled in Braque, Matisse, or Jackson Pollock. There are other signs of this breakthrough: in the movies, in ceramics, in architecture. The West has never before had to accept a non-European culture and country as an equal, let alone as a leader.

We do, of course, pay lip service to such equality—but Japan waits to find out whether we really mean it.

The big job from now on, however, will have to be done by the Japanese themselves. Of course, their success will depend on an expanding world economy which tends toward being more rather than less liberal. But more important will be Japan's courage and vision in the management of her own domestic affairs—in government, in politics, and in business. Most important: Japan must solve her problems in a manner both "modern" and "Japanese."

Tough as it undoubtedly is, the job is probably neither as big nor as difficult as what Japan has already accomplished since 1952. But it will not only be Japan that will be put to the test in the next decades. Above all, it will be the West and its values that will be on trial in this new "post-Western" world of ours. Modern Japan is both leader and criterion.

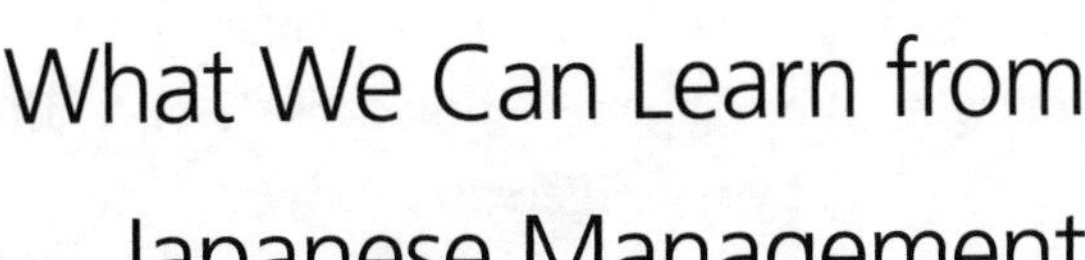

CHAPTER ELEVEN

What We Can Learn from Japanese Management

1. Making effective decisions.
2. Harmonizing employment security with labor-cost flexibility, productivity, and acceptance of change.
3. Managing and developing the young managerial and professional employee.

These three areas surely rank high on any list of management concerns.

In each, Japanese management, and especially Japanese business management, behaves in a strikingly different fashion from Western management, American or European. The Japanese apply different principles and have developed different approaches and policies to tackle each of these problems. These policies, while not *the* key to the Japanese "economic miracle," are certainly major factors in the astonishing rise of Japan in the last hundred years, and especially in Japan's economic growth and performance in the last twenty years.

First published in the *Harvard Business Review,* March/April, 1971.

It would be folly for the West to imitate these policies. In fact, it would be impossible. Each is deeply rooted in Japanese traditions and culture. Each, indeed, applies to the problems of an industrial society and economy values and habits developed far earlier by and for the retainers of the Japanese clan and their relationship with their lord, the Zen priests in their monasteries or the calligraphers and painters of the great "schools" of Japanese art. Yet the principles underlying these Japanese practices deserve, I believe, close attention and study by managers in the West. They may point the way to solutions for some of our most pressing problems.

I

What "Consensus" Means

If there is one point on which all authorities on Japan, Western or Japanese, are in agreement, it is that Japanese institutions, whether businesses or government agencies, make decisions by "consensus." The Japanese, we are told, debate a decision throughout the organization until there is agreement on it. And only then do they make the decision.

This, every experienced manager will say, with a shudder, is not for us, however well it may work for the Japanese. This can only lead to indecision, or to politicking, or at best to an innocuous compromise which offends no one but also solves nothing. And if there were proof needed for this, the history of President Johnson's attempt to obtain a "consensus" would supply it.

But even the most cursory reading of Japanese history, or the most superficial acquaintance with Japanese businesses or government agencies today, shows the opposite to be true in Japan. What stands out in Japanese history, as well as in today's Japanese management behavior, is the capacity for making 180-degree turns, that is, for reaching radical and obviously highly controversial decisions.

No country, for instance, was more receptive to Christianity than sixteenth-century Japan. Indeed, the hope of the Portuguese missionaries that Japan would become the first Christian country outside of Europe was by no means just wishful thinking. Yet the same Japan, in the early seventeenth century, made a 180-degree turn, within a few years completely suppressing Christianity and shutting itself off from all foreign influences—indeed, from all contact with the outside world—for 250 years. Then, some 250 years later, in the Meji Restoration of 1867, Japan executed another such 180-degree turn when it opened itself to the West—again something no other non-European country managed to do.

Or, take some present examples from business and economics. Toyo Rayon, the largest Japanese manufacturer of man-made fibers, made nothing but rayon as late as the midfifties. Then when it decided to switch to synthetic fibers, it did not "phase out" rayon-making, as every Western company in a similar situation has done. It closed its rayon mills overnight, even though, under the Japanese system of employment, it could not lay off a single man.

The Ministry of International Trade and Industry, (MITI), as late as 1966 when I discussed this matter with its officials, was adamantly opposed to any Japanese companies' going multinational and making investments in manufacturing affiliates abroad. Three years later, by 1969, the same officials in MITI, working for the same conservative government, had turned around completely and were pushing Japanese manufacturing investments abroad.

The key to this apparent contradiction is that the Westerner and the Japanese mean something different when they talk of "making a decision." With us in the West all the emphasis is on the answer to the question. Indeed, our books on "decision-making" all try to develop systematic approaches to giving an answer. To the Japanese, however, the important element in decision-making is defining the question. The important and crucial steps are to decide whether there is need for a decision and what the decision is about. And it is in this step that the Japanese aim at attaining consensus. It is, indeed, this step that, to the Japanese, is the essence of the decision. The answer to the question—that is, what the West considers the "decision"—follows.

In this process that precedes the decision, no mention is made of what the answer might be. This is strenuously kept out for an elementary reason. It would force people to take sides; and once they have taken sides, a decision would be a victory for one side and a defeat for the other. Thus the whole process is focused on finding out what the decision is really about, not what it should be. Its result is a meeting of the minds that there is, indeed, need for a change in behavior.*

This takes a long time, admittedly. Indeed, the Westerner dealing with the Japanese is thoroughly frustrated during this period. He does not understand what goes on. He has the feeling that he is being given the run-around.

It is very hard, for instance, for an American executive to understand why the Japanese with whom he is negotiating, say, about a license agreement, keep on sending a new group of people every three months who start what the Westerner thinks are "negotiations" as if they had never heard of the subject, take copious notes, and then go back home, only to be succeeded six weeks later by another team of new people from different areas of the company who again act as if they had never heard of the matter under discussion, take copious notes, and go home in turn. Actually, although few of my Western friends believe it, this is a sign that the Japanese take the matter most seriously. They are trying to involve the people who will have to carry out an eventual agreement into the process of obtaining consensus that a license is, indeed, needed. Only when all the people who will have to carry out the agreement

---

*We actually have a complete account of this process at work, though it is not about a business decision. It is about the decision to go to war against America in 1941. (*Japan's Decision for War,* Records of the 1941 Policy Conferences. Translated and edited by Nobutuka Ike, Stanford University Press, 1967.)

have come together on the need to make a decision is the decision made to go ahead. Only then do negotiations really start—and then they usually move with the speed of lightning.

It is only when the whole group has thoroughly understood what the decision is all about, and when everybody knows that a decision is really appropriate, that the Japanese reach the point we mean when we talk of a decision.

However, they no longer call it a "decision"; they call it (and they are right) the "action stage." At this point top management then refers the decision to what the Japanese experts call "the appropriate people." Who the "appropriate people" are is a top-management decision. And it determines, in effect, what specific answer to the problem will be worked out. For, naturally, in the course of the discussions leading up to consensus, it has become very clear what basic approaches certain people or certain groups are taking to the problem. Top management, by referring the matter to one or the other, in effect, picks the answer—but an answer which by now will not surprise anybody. This referral to the appropriate people is as crucial as the parallel decision in the American political process which so totally baffles any foreign observer of American government: the decision to which committee or subcommittee of the Congress a certain bill is to be assigned. Again, this decision is not to be found in any of the books on American government and politics; yet, as every American politician knows, it is the crucial step that decides whether the bill is to become law and what form it will take. Similarly in Japan, this top-management decision—not mentioned in any Japanese book on government or business, to my knowledge—decides what the actual answer to the question will be.

What are the advantages of this process? And what can we learn from it?

In the first place, it actually makes for speedy decisions, and, above all, for effective decisions. It might seem like a most time-consuming process. Indeed, it takes much longer in Japan to reach a decision than it takes in the West. But we in the West then spend years on "selling" a decision. We make the decision first and then begin to work on getting people to act on it. And, only too often, as all of us in the West know, either the decision is sabotaged by the organization or, which may be worse, it takes so long to make it truly effective that it has become obsolete, if not indeed wrong, by the time the people in the organization actually make it their own behavior, actually make it operational. The Japanese, by contrast, spend absolutely no time on selling a decision. Everybody has been presold. Also, of course, in their process it has become clear where in the organization a certain answer to a question will be welcomed and where it will be resisted. Therefore, there is plenty of time to work on persuading the dissenters or on making small concessions to them which will win them over without destroying the integrity of the decision.

Every Westerner who has done business with Japan has learned that the apparent inertia of the "negotiating stage," with its endless delays and interminable chewing over of the same cud, is followed by a speed of action that leaves him hanging by the ropes. It may take three years to work out that licensing agreement during which there is no discussion of terms, no discussion of what products the Japanese plan to make, no discussion of what knowledge and help they may need. And then, within four weeks, the Japanese are ready to go into production and make demands on their Western partner for data, information, and people which he is totally unprepared to meet. Then it is the Japanese, by the way, who complain, and bitterly, about the "endless delay and procrastination" of the Westerner. For they no more understand our way of making a decision—that is, our way of making the decision first and implementing it later—than we understand the Japanese way which puts making the decision effective *before* making the decision itself.

In fact, the Japanese approach goes to the heart of making effective decisions. This is not what the right answer is, but what right behavior follows from it. It is not derived, as our approach to decision-making is, from mathematics, where the right answer is an end in itself and where *Quod Erat Demonstrandum* ends the decision-making procedure. It is derived from seeing the decision as a process in which the desired end result is action and behavior on the part of people.

The Japanese method is focused on understanding the problem. It almost guarantees that all the alternatives are being considered. It rivets attention to essentials. It does not permit commitment until there is agreement on "what is the decision all about?" As a result, it may come up with the wrong answer to the problem, as was the decision to go to war against the United States in 1941. But it rarely comes up with the right answer to the wrong problem. And that, as all decision-makers have learned, is the really dangerous course, the really irretrievably wrong decision.

Above all, however, the system forces the Japanese to make big decisions. It forces them to make fundamental decisions, not to say radical ones. The system is much too cumbersome to be put to work on minor matters. It takes far too many people far too long to be frittered away on anything but truly important matters leading to true changes in policies and behavior. Small decisions, even if obviously needed, are very often not being made at all in Japan for that reason.

With us it is the small decisions that our process finds easy to make—decisions that do not greatly matter. Anyone who knows Western business or Western government agencies knows that they make far too many small decisions, as a rule. And nothing, I have learned, causes as much trouble in an organization as a lot of small decisions. Whether the decision is to move the water cooler from one end of the hall to the other or whether it is to go out of one's oldest business makes little emotional difference. One decision takes as much time and generates as much heat as the other. One might as well get something for that agony of change in institutional and managerial behavior. This, however, means that one doesn't make small and frequent decisions. One makes the big ones. And this is what the Japanese process achieves.

I once watched a Japanese company working through a proposal for a joint venture received from a well-known American firm—a firm, by the way, with whom the Japanese had done business for many years. They did not even start out by discussing the joint venture. They started out with the question, "Do we have to change the basic directions of our business?" As a result, the consensus emerged into a decision to go out of a number of old businesses and start in a number of new technologies and markets, with the joint venture—which was established and has been doing very well—then as one element of a major new strategy. But until the Japanese understood that the decision was really about the direction of the business, and that there was need for a decision, they did not once, among themselves, discuss the desirability of the joint venture or the terms on which it might be set up.

In the West we are moving in the Japanese direction. At least this is what all the "task forces," "long-range plans," or "strategies" are trying to accomplish. But in the first place, we do not build into the work of these task forces the "selling" which the Japanese process builds in before the decision. This explains in large measure why so many of the brilliant reports of these task forces or long-range planners never develop into action, but remain plans. At the same time, we expect these task forces or long-range planners to come up with "recommendations," that is, to commit themselves to one alternative. To the Japanese, however, quite rightly, the most important step is the understanding of the alternatives available. With us, as every observer of the process knows, the task forces or the long-range planners tend to start out with an answer, that is, with a recommendation, and then try to find documentation for it. The Japanese are as opinionated as we are. But because they discipline themselves not to commit themselves to a recommendation until they have fully defined the question, and because they use the system of obtaining consensus to bring out the full range of alternatives, they are far less likely to become prisoners of their preconceived answers than we are likely to be in our decision-making process.

II

Myths and Realities of "Lifetime Employment"

Just as everyone has heard about "consensus" as the basis for Japanese decisions, everyone, in Japan as well as in the West, knows about Japanese "lifetime employment." And again, most people's concept of lifetime employment is as much a misunderstanding as the common reading of consensus.

To be sure, most employees in "modern" Japanese business and industry have a guaranteed job, once they have come on the payroll.* While they are on the job, not only do they have virtually complete job security, endangered solely in the event of a severe economic crisis or of bankruptcy of the employer. As a rule, they are also being paid by seniority, with pay doubling about every fifteen years, regardless of job.

But instead of a rigid labor-cost structure, Japan actually has remarkable flexibility in her labor costs and labor force. What no one ever mentioned—and what, I am convinced, most Japanese do not even see themselves—is that the Japanese retirement system (or perhaps it should be called the Japanese nonretirement system) not only makes labor costs more flexible than they are in most countries and most industries of the West. It also harmonizes in a highly ingenious fashion the workers' need for a guarantee of job and income and the economy's need for flexible labor costs. Actually most Japanese companies, especially the large ones, lay off

*This, however, requires considerable qualification. Women are always considered "temporary" rather than "permanent" employees. Many of the employees of Japan's "traditional businesses," especially the preindustrial workshop industries such as lacquer-making, pottery work, or silk-weaving, are hired and paid by the hour. And even in modern industry there is a substantial, though slowly shrinking, body of employees—20 percent or so—who by unilateral management decision are considered "temporary" and remain in this category even though they may have been on the job for many years.

a greater proportion of their work force if business slackens than most Western companies are likely or able to do. Yet they can do so in a fashion in which the employees who most need an income are fully protected. The burden of adjustment is taken by those who can afford it and who have alternative incomes to fall back on.

Official retirement age in Japan is fifty-five for everyone except a few who, at age forty-five, become members of top management and are not expected to retire at any fixed age. At age fifty-five, so you are being told, the employee, from floor sweeper to department head, "retires." Traditionally he then gets a severance bonus equal to about two years of full pay.*

Considering that life expectancy in Japan is now fully up to Western standards, so that most employees can expect to live to age seventy or so, this seems wholly inadequate. Yet no one complains about the dire fate of the pensioners. More amazing still, one encounters in every Japanese factory, office, or bank people who cheerfully admit to being quite a bit older than fifty-five and who quite obviously are still working.

The rank-and-file employee, blue-collar or white-collar, ceases to be a permanent employee at age fifty-five and becomes a "temporary" employee. This means, in the first place, that he can be laid off if there is not enough work. But if there is enough work—and of course Japan, these last twenty years, has had an acute labor shortage—he stays on, very often doing the same work as before, side by side with the permanent employee with whom he has been working for many years. But for this work he is now paid at least one-third less than he received when he was a permanent employee.

The rationale of this is fairly simple. The man, the Japanese argue, has something to fall back on: the two-year pension. This, they

---

*Many companies, strongly backed by the government, are now installing supplementary pension payments which, however, by Western standards are still exceedingly low.

freely admit, is not enough to keep a man alive for fifteen years or so. But it is usually enough to tide him over a bad spell. And since he no longer has, as a rule, dependent children or parents whom he has to support, his needs should be considerably lower than they were when he was, say, forty and had presumably both children and parents to look after.

If my intent were to describe the Japanese employment system, I would now have to go into a great many rather complicated details, such as the role of the semiannual bonus. But I am concerned only with what we in the West might learn from the Japanese. The main interest of the Japanese system to us, I submit, is the way in which it satisfies two apparently mutually contradictory needs: the need to provide job and income security, and the need for flexible and adaptable labor force and labor costs.

In the West, during the last twenty-five years, more and more employees have achieved income maintenance that may, in many cases, exceed what the Japanese worker gets under lifetime employment. There is, for instance, the Supplementary Employment Compensation of the American mass-production industries which, in effect, guarantees the unionized worker most of his income even in fairly lengthy layoffs. Indeed, it may well be argued that labor costs in American mass-production industries are more rigid than they are in Japan, even though our managements can rapidly adjust the number of men at work to the order flow, in contrast to the Japanese practice of maintaining employment for permanent employees almost independent of business conditions. Increasingly, also, we find in the heavily unionized mass-production industries provision for early retirement such as was written in the fall of 1970 into the contract of the American automobile industry. Still, unionized employees are being laid off according to seniority, with the ones having the least seniority going first. As a result, we still offer the least security of a job and income to the men who need a predictable income the most, the fathers of young families who, of course, also are the ones who still might have older parents to support. And where we have "early retirement," it means, as a rule, that the worker has to make a decision to retire permanently. Once he has opted for early retirement, he is out and unlikely to be hired back, let alone, at his age, to be hired by another employer. As a result, our labor force—and this is just as true in Great Britain or on the European continent—lacks the feeling of economic and job security which is so outstanding a feature of Japanese society.

In other words, we pay for a high degree of "income maintenance" and have imposed on ourselves a very high degree of rigidity in respect to labor costs. But we get very few of the benefits. Above all, we do not get the psychological security which is so pronounced in Japanese society: the deep conviction of a man of working age that he need not worry about his job and his income. Instead, we have fear—fear of the younger men that they will be laid off first, just when the economic needs of their families are at their peak; fear of the older men that they will lose their jobs in their fifties and then be too old to be hired. In the Japanese system there is confidence, instead, in both age groups—confidence of the younger men that they can look forward to a secure job and steadily rising income while the children are growing up; confidence on the part of the older men that they are still wanted, still useful, but also not a "burden."

In practice, of course, the Japanese system is no more perfect than any other system. There are plenty of inequities in it; and the treatment of the older people in particular leaves a great deal to be desired, especially in the small workshop industries of preindustrial Japan and in the multitude of small service businesses. But the basic principle which the Japanese have evolved—not by planning rationally, but by applying traditional Japanese concepts of mutual obligation to employment and to labor economics—seems to make more sense and works better than the expensive patchwork we have applied to symptoms of the problem without, however, coming to grips with the problem itself. Economically, it might be said, we have greater "security" in our system; we certainly pay more for it. Yet we have not obtained what the Japanese system produces: the psychological conviction of lifetime employment, that is, of job and income security.

There is today talk, and even a little action, in American industry of "reverse seniority" to protect newly hired blacks, who have little or no seniority, in the event of a layoff. But we might also consider applying reverse seniority to older men past the age of greatest family obligation, now that so many labor contracts provide for "early retirement" after age fifty-five. And the pressure for such early-retirement provisions will predictably rise as the number of young men entering the labor force for the first time goes up sharply in the next few years. Men who have the right to an early-retirement pension may be expected to be laid off first; today their seniority gives them all but absolute job security. By the same token, however, these men might have the right, today normally denied them completely, to come back out of early retirement and be rehired first when employment expands again. Indeed, some such move that strengthens the job security of the younger, married employee with his heavy family burdens might well be the only defense against pressures for absolute job guarantees that could otherwise impose on America the rigid labor costs with which folklore endows the Japanese economy.

But even more important as a lesson to be learned from the Japanese is the need to shape benefits to the needs and wants of specific major employee groups. Otherwise they will be only costs rather than benefits. In the West, and especially in the United States in the last thirty years, we have heaped benefit upon benefit to the point where the "fringes" run up to a third of total labor cost in some industries. Yet practically all these benefits have been applied across the board, whether needed by a particular group or not. The one exception I can think of is maternity leaves. But teenage girls, who want to stay only till they find a husband, are made to pay into retirement plans due at age 65. Health insurance, whether Blue Cross or private carrier, does not, as a rule, provide any protection against the costs of illness to an employee out of work, just when he needs such coverage the most. But a majority of the plans provide full benefits to the nonworking dependents of an employed worker even though, with today's wages, most employees, when fully employed themselves, could well pay for routine illness in their families, despite soaring health-care costs. In fact, underlying our entire approach to benefits—with management and union in complete agreement, for once—is the asinine notion that the work force is homogeneous in its needs and its desires. As a result, we spend fabulous amounts of money on "benefits" which have little meaning for large groups, sometimes even the majority, of employees, and leave unsatisfied genuine needs of other, equally substantial groups. This is in itself a major reason why our benefit plans have produced so little employee satisfaction and psychological security and why an increase in one kind of benefit leads immediately to demands for new and different benefits to "equalize" the benefit position of some other group—the old or the young, the skilled or the unskilled, and so on.

What management and union alike might learn from the Japanese experience is to mold benefit plans so that the same amount of money can provide the maximum, flexibly, in true benefit for different employee groups with different needs and desires according to their stages in life and family cycle. It is this psychological conviction that underlies also what might be an important "secret" of the Japanese economy: cheerful willingness of the employee to accept continuing change in technology and process, and the acceptance of increasing productivity as good for everybody.

There is a great deal written today about the "spirit" of the Japanese factory. But far more important than the company songs workers in big factories sing at the beginning of the day is the fact that Japanese workers show little of the famous resistance to change which is so widespread in the West.

The usual explanation is "national character"—always a suspect explanation. That it may be the wrong one is indicated by the fact that acceptance of change is by no means general throughout Japan. The Japanese National Railways, for instance, suffer from resistance to change fully as much as any other railway system, including the American railroads. But the numerous private railways which crisscross the densely populated areas of Japan seem to be relatively free from it. That the Japanese National Railways are as grossly overstaffed as any nationalized industry in the world may be part of the explanation; the workers know that any change is likely to create redundancy. More important is the fact that the industries in Japan which, like the Japanese National Railways, suffer from resistance to change are also the ones that are organized according to Western concepts of craft and skill. The industries which apply Japanese concepts, as do the private railways, as a rule, do not suffer from resistance to change, even though their employees also know that the company is overstaffed rather than understaffed.

The secret may lie in what the Japanese call "continuous training." This means, first, that every employee, very often up to and including top managers, keeps on training as a regular part of his job until he retires. This is in sharp contrast to our Western practice where we train a man, as a rule, only when he has to acquire a new skill or move to a new position. Our training is "promotion-focused"; the Japanese training is "performance-focused." But also the Japanese employee, on all levels, is generally being trained not only in his job but in all the jobs on his job level. The man working as an electrician will automatically attend training sessions in every single skill area in the plant. But so will the man who pushes a broom. Both of them may stay in their respective jobs until they die or retire. In fact, their pay is independent, in large measure, of the job they are doing and is geared primarily to the length of service, so that the highly skilled electrician may well get less money than the floor sweeper. But both are expected to be reasonably proficient in every job in the plant which is, generally speaking, on the same level as their job (which in a plant means all rank-and-file blue-collar jobs, for instance). The accountant in the office is similarly expected to be trained—or to train himself through a multitude of correspondence courses, seminars, or continuation schools available in every big city—in every single one of the professional jobs needed in his company—such as personnel, training, or purchasing. And so it goes all the way to top management.

The president of a fairly large company, who once told me casually that he could not see me on a certain afternoon because he attended his company's training session in welding—and as a student rather than as an observer or teacher—is, of course, the exception. But the company president who takes a correspondence course in computer programming is fairly common. And the young personnel man does so as a matter of course.

It would need a thick book on Japanese economic and industrial history to explain the origins of this system—although in its present stage it is just about fifty years old and dates back to the labor shortages during and right after World War I. It would take an even thicker book to discuss the advantages, disadvantages, and limitations of the Japanese system; and the limitations are very great, indeed. The young technically trained people, the young scientists and engineers, for example, resent it bitterly and resist it rather successfully. They want to work as scientists and engineers and are by no means delighted when being asked to learn accounting or when being shifted from an engineering job into the personnel department. Also, such highly skilled and highly specialized men as papermakers, running a large paper machine, or department-store buyers are not, as a rule, expected to know other jobs or to be willing to fit into them. But even these specialists continue, as a matter of routine, to perfect themselves in their own specialty, long after any "training" in the West would have ended; indeed, normally, for the rest of their working lives.

One result of this practice is that improvement of work and process is built into the system. In a typical Japanese training session, there is a trainer. But the real burden of training is on the participants themselves. And the question is always: "What have we learned so we can do the job better?" Most of the participants, in other words, know the job—have, indeed, been doing it for many years. As a result, the new, whether a new tool, a new process, or a new organization of the work, comes out as "self-improvement" week after week, month after month. A Japanese employer who wants to change the process to introduce a new product or a new machine does so in and through the training session. As a result, there is usually no resistance at all, but acceptance. Indeed, Americans in the management of joint ventures in Japan always report that the "bugs" in the new process are usually worked out, or at least identified, before the new goes into operation on the plant floor.

A second benefit from this is a built-in increase in productivity. In the West we train until a learner reaches standard performance. Then we conclude that he has mastered the job and needs new training only when he moves on or when the job itself is being changed. Our "learning curve" reaches the "standard," after which it stays on a plateau. Not so in Japan; and the Japanese understanding is more realistic, more in tune with all we know about learning. The Japanese, of course, also have a standard and a learning curve leading up to it. Their standard, as a rule, is a good deal lower than the corresponding standards in the West; the productivity norms which have been satisfying most Japanese industries in the past are, by and large, quite low by Western measurements. But the Japanese keep on training. And sooner or later their learning curve starts breaking out of the plateau which we in the West consider permanent. It starts to climb again, not because a man works harder, but because he starts to "work smarter." In the West we are satisfied if the older worker does not slacken in his productivity. This is a problem, too, in some Japanese industries; young women assembling precision electronics, for instance, reach the peak of their finger dexterity and their visual acuity around age twenty and, after twenty-three or twenty-five, rapidly slow down. (This is one reason why the Japanese electronics industry works hard to find husbands for the girls and to get them out of the factory by the time they are twenty-one or twenty-two.) But by and large the Japanese would say that the older employee is more productive; and their figures would bear this out. With pay based on seniority, the output per yen may be much higher in a plant in which the work force is largely new and young. But output per man-hour is almost invariably a good deal higher in the plant that has the older work population—almost the exact opposite of what we in the West take for granted.

In effect, the Japanese apply to work in business and industry their own traditions. The two great skills of the Samurai, the members of the warrior caste which ruled Japan for three hundred years until 1867, were swordsmanship and calligraphy. Both demand "lifetime training." In both one keeps on training after one has achieved mastery. And if one does not keep in training, one rapidly loses one's skill. Similarly the Japanese schools of painting, the Kano school, for instance, which dominated Japanese official art for three hundred years until 1867, taught that even the greatest master spends several hours a day copying, that is, keeps in continuous training. Otherwise, his skill, and above all his creativity, would soon start to go down. And the greatest judo master still goes through the elementary exercises every day—just as, of course, the greatest pianist in the West does his scales daily. "One difference that I find hard to explain to my Western colleagues," said one of the leading industrial engineers of Japan to me one day,

> *is that we do exactly the same things that the industrial engineer does in Detroit or Pittsburgh; but it means something different. The American industrial engineer lays out the work and the worker. We just lay out the work. In respect to the worker, we are teachers rather than masters. We try to teach how one improves one's own productivity and the process. What we set up is the foundation; the edifice the worker builds. Scientific management, time and motion studies,*

materials flow—we do them all, and no differently from the way you do them in the States. But you in the States think that this is the end of the job; we here in Japan believe it is the beginning. The worker's job begins when we have finished engineering the job itself.

Continuous training in Japan goes a long way toward preventing the extreme specialization and departmentalization which plague us. There are no craft unions or craft skills in Japanese industry. (The most significant exception is the Japanese National Railways, which imported craft specialization from Great Britain and Germany, together with their steel rails and locomotives, and which are perhaps even more fragmented by craft and jurisdictional lines than American or British railroads are.) Craftsmen, in the early days of Japanese industrialization, flatly refused to work in the new factories, which therefore had to be staffed by youngsters, fresh from the farm, who had no skills and had to be taught whatever they needed to know to do the job. Still, it is not really true, as Japanese official doctrine asserts, that "men are freely moved from job to job within a plant." A man in a welding shop is likely to stay in a welding shop, and so is the fellow in the next aisle who runs the paint sprays. There is much more individual mobility in office work, and especially for managerial and professional people. A Japanese company will not hesitate to move a young manager from production control into market research, or into the accounting department. Yet the individual departments in the office tend to be rigidly specialized and highly parochial in the defense of their "prerogatives." The tunnel vision that afflicts many people in Western business is, however, conspicuously absent in Japan. The industrial engineer I quoted earlier insists meticulously on the boundaries between industrial and other engineering or industrial engineering and personnel. He himself never worked in any other function, from the day he graduated from engineering school to the day when, at age fifty-five, he was made president of an affiliated company in his group. Yet he knew the work of every other function. He understood their problems. He knew what they could do for his industrial engineering department and what, in turn, the industrial engineer had to do for them. He is the purest of specialists in his own work, and yet he is a true "generalist" in his knowledge, in his vision, and in the way in which he holds himself responsible for the performance and results of the entire organization.

This he himself attributes to the fact that—as he laughingly admits, very much against his will in the earlier years—he was subjected all along the way to continuous training in all the work going on at his job levels. When he was a junior industrial engineer, he took part in the training sessions of all juniors, whether engineers, accountants, or salesmen, and so on, all the way through until he became a member of top management. And then he joined, voluntarily, a top-management group which met two evenings a week, usually with a discussion leader from the outside, to train itself in the work of top management.

We in the West emphasize today "continuing education." This is a concept that is still alien to Japan. As a rule, the man or woman who graduates from the university never sets foot on campus again, never attends a class, never goes back for "retreading." Normal education in Japan is still seen as preparation for life rather than as life itself. Indeed, Japanese employers, even the large ones including government, do not really want young people who have gone to graduate school. They are "too old" to start at the bottom. And there is no other place to start in Japan. They expect to work as specialists and to be experts rather than submit to training by their employer. Indeed, the resistance to the highly trained specialist is considered by many thoughtful management people in Japan to be a major weakness of Japanese business, and even more of Japanese government. There is little doubt that, in the years to come, continuing education will become far more important in Japan than it now is and that, at the same time, the specialist will have to become far more important as well. But at the same time, Japan's continuous training has something to teach us. We in the West react to resistance to change and productivity largely along the lines of Mark Twain's old dictum about the weather. We all complain, but no one does anything. The Japanese at least do something—and with conspicuous success.

Continuous training is not completely unknown in the West. A century ago it was developed by the fledgling Zeiss Works in Germany and applied there to *all* employees in the plant even though most of them were, of course, highly skilled glass blowers and opticians with many years of craft training behind them. The world leadership of the German optical industry until World War I, if not until World War II, rested in large measure on this policy which saw in high craft skill a foundation for, rather than the end of, learning. With craft jurisdictions in the United States (and even more in Great Britain) frozen in the most rigid and restrictive union contracts, probably this could be done today, however, only in mass-production industries with plant-wide or, at least, department-wide seniority.

But it could be done—and should be done—with the nonunionized, the clerical, supervisory, professional, and managerial employees. But here, where union restrictions cannot be blamed, managements are today busily working at creating departmentalization, specialization, and tunnel vision. To be sure, there is a good deal of continuous training; many companies not only have massive training programs themselves but encourage, through tuition refund, for instance, their younger technical, professional, and managerial people to keep on going to school and to continue their education.

But in all too many cases, the emphasis in these programs is on a man's becoming more specialized and on *not* learning the other knowledges, skills, and functions. In most of the training programs I know—and I know quite a few—the emphasis is entirely on the one function in which a young man already works; at most he is being told that "other areas are, of course, important." But then he is enjoined to learn more in his own field, whether market research or tax accounting or industrial engineering. As a result he soon comes to consider the other areas as so much excess baggage. And when we have to introduce something truly new—the computer is the horrible example—we bring in a whole corps of new specialists, with the predictable result that the newcomers are both ineffectual, since no one knows what they are trying to do, and resented, because they present a threat to everybody. Surely this management-imposed departmentalization and narrowness has been one of the major reasons for the difficulties we are having with the computer, let alone with the computer specialists.

And when it comes to education outside, in evening courses at the local university, for instance (practically all my students tell me that), a young man's supervisor will push his subordinate into taking more work in his specialty and away from anything else. To be sure, company policies invariably make no such distinction in offering tuition refund; but the supervisor, as a rule, has to approve the young man's program before the company will pay for it.

The rule should be the opposite: once a young man has acquired the foundations of a specialty, he should be systematically exposed to all the other major areas in the business, whether in his company's training courses or in continuing education outside. Only in this way can we hope to prevent tomorrow's professional and managerial people from being as departmentalized, as riven by "jurisdictional demarcations," as confined in their vision to yesterday as we have encouraged the skilled worker to become.

III

The Care and Feeding of the Young

The House of Mitsui is not only the oldest among the world's big businesses; it dates back to 1637, half a century before the Bank of England was founded. It also was the largest of the world's big businesses until the American Occupation split it into individual companies (and today, when these companies have come back together into a fairly close confederation, it may well be again the world's biggest business). In all its three hundred years of business life, Mitsui never had a single chief executive (the Japanese term is "chief *banto*," literally "chief clerk") who was not an outstanding man and a powerful leader. This accomplishment no other institution can match, to my knowledge; neither the Catholic Church, nor any government, army, navy, business, or university.

If one asks how to explain such an amazing success in executive development and selection, one always gets the same answer:

> *Since earliest days the chief* banto*—himself never a member of the Mitsui family but a "hired hand"— had only one job: manager development, manager selection, and manager placement. He spent most of his time with the young people who came in as junior managers or professionals. He knew them. He listened to them. And as a result, he knew, by the time the men reached thirty or so, which were likely to reach top management, what experiences and development they needed, and in what job they should be tried and tested.*

At first sight, nothing would seem less likely to evolve strong executives than the Japanese system. It would rather seem to be the ideal prescription for developing timid men selected for proven mediocrity and trained "not to rock the boat." The young men who enter a company's employ directly from the university—and by and large, this is the only way to get into a company's management, since hiring from the outside and into upper-level positions is practically unknown—know that they will have a job till they retire, no matter how poorly they perform. Till they are forty-five, that is, for the first quarter-century of their working life, they will be promoted and paid by seniority alone. There seems to be no performance appraisal, nor would there be much point to it when a man can be neither rewarded for performance nor penalized for nonperformance. Superiors do not choose their subordinates; the personnel people make personnel decisions, as a rule, often without consulting the manager to whom a subordinate is being assigned. And it is, or so it seems, unthinkable for a young manager or professional to ask for a transfer, and equally unthinkable for him to quit and go elsewhere.* Indeed, every young managerial and professional employee in Japanese organizations, whether business or government, knows that he is expected to help his colleagues look good rather than stand out himself by brilliance or aggressiveness.

This goes on for twenty to twenty-five years, during which all the emphasis seems to be on conforming, on doing what one is being asked to do, and on showing proper respect and deference.

Suddenly, when a man reaches forty-five, the Day of Reckoning arrives, when the goats are divided from the sheep. A small—a very small—group is picked to become Company Directors, that is, top management; they can then stay on well past any retirement age known in the West, with active top-management people in their eighties by no means a rarity. The rest, that is, from Department Director on down, stay till they are fifty-five, usually with at best one more promotion. Then they are retired; and unlike the case of rank-and-file employees, their retirement is compulsory.†

To an outsider who believes what the Japanese tell him, namely, that this is really the way the system works, it is inconceivable on what basis this crucial decision at age forty-five is made; yet it results in the emergence of the independent and aggressive top managers

---

*This is changing, especially for highly trained technical people, but very slowly. It would still be almost unheard of for a young man to take a job in another company except with the express permission of his previous employer.

†There is a third category which, while very small in numbers, is of great importance and highly visible. Some members of upper middle management, that is, department heads, when they reach fifty-five, are moved into the top management of a subsidiary or affiliate, where they can then stay on without age limit. This is reserved for senior men who, while outstanding in their own work, are too narrowly specialized to move into the top management of the parent company. It explains, by the way, though only in part, why large Japanese companies have so many ostensibly independent subsidiaries and affiliates.

of Japan's businesses who have pushed Japanese exports all over the globe and in the space of twenty years have made Japan the third ranking economic power in the world, although at the eve of World War II, Japan was not even among the first dozen.

It is precisely because Japanese managers have lifetime employment and can, as a rule, neither be fired nor moved, and because advancement for the first twenty-five years of a man's working life is through seniority alone, that the Japanese have made the care and feeding of their young people the first responsibility of top management. The practice goes back at least four hundred years, to the time of Hideyoshi, the military dictator who organized the retainers of the military clans, the Samurai, in tight hereditary castes, with advancement from one to the other officially not permitted. At the same time, the government of the clan had to find able people who could run the clan's affairs and who had to get opportunities at a very early age and without offending higher ranking but less gifted clan members.

Today, of course, it would be impossible for the chief *banto* of Mitsui to know personally the young managerial people, as his predecessor did a few generations ago. Even much smaller companies are much too large and have far too many young managerial and professional employees in their ranks. Yet top management is still vitally concerned with them. But it discharges this concern through an informal network of senior middle-management people who act as "godfathers" to the young men during the first ten years of their career in the company.

The Japanese take this system for granted. Indeed, few of them are conscious of it. As far as I can figure out, it has no name, the term "godfather" is mine rather than theirs. But every young managerial employee knows who his godfather is, and so does his boss and the boss's boss. The godfather is never a young man's direct superior and, as a rule, not anyone in direct line of authority over the young man or the young man's department. He is rarely a member of top management and rarely a man who will get into top management.

Rather he is picked from among those members of upper middle management who will, when they reach fifty-five, be transferred as top management to a subsidiary or affiliate. In other words, these are people who, having been passed over at age forty-five for the top-management spots in their own company, know that they are not going to make it in their own organization. Therefore, they are not likely to build a faction of their own and to play internal politics. At the same time, these are the most highly respected members of the upper middle-management group, the people who are known, trusted, and looked up to by the entire organization.

How the individual godfather is actually chosen for a young man, whether by formal assignment or by informal understanding, no one seems to know. The one qualification that is usually mentioned is that he be a graduate of the same university from which the individual young man graduated himself: the "old school tie" binds even more tightly in Japan than it ever did in England. ("The Harvard Business School Alumni Association is the only truly Japanese institution outside of Japan," a Japanese friend of mine often says, only half in jest.) But everybody inside the company knows who the godfather of a given young man is and respects the relationship. During the first ten years or so of a young man's career, he is expected to be in close touch with his godchild, even though he may have in a large company a hundred such godchildren at any one time. He is expected to know the young man, see him fairly regularly, be available to him for advice and counsel, and in general look after him. He has some functions which godfathers outside of Japan don't normally have, such as to introduce the young men under his wing to the better bars on the Ginza and to the right bawdyhouses. But learning how to drink in public is one of the important accomplishments the young Japanese executive has to learn. If a young man gets stuck under an incompetent manager and wants to be transferred, the godfather knows where to go and how to do something which officially cannot be done and "is never being done." Yet nobody will ever know about it. And if the young man has been naughty and needs a good spanking, the godfather will give it to him in private. By the time a young man is thirty, the godfather knows a great deal about him.

It is this godfather who sits down with top management and discusses the young people. Again, this may be completely "informal." Over the sake cup, the godfather may say quietly, "Nakamura is a good boy and is ready for a challenging assignment," or "Nakamura is a good chemist, but I don't think he'll ever know how to manage people," or "Nakamura means well and is reliable, but he is no genius and better not be put on anything but routine work." And when the time comes to make a personnel decision, whom to give what assignment and where to move a man, the personnel people will quietly consult godfather before they make a move.

A personal experience of mine may illustrate how the system works. A few years ago, I found myself, by sheer accident, a temporary godfather.

One of my ablest students in twenty years at New York University's Graduate Business School was a young Japanese; let me call him Okura. The son of a diplomat, he went to Oxford for his undergraduate work and took the Japanese Foreign Service examination, which he passed with honors. But then he decided to go into business instead, came to our Graduate Business School in New York, and went to work for one of Japan's big international companies. A few years ago, while I was in Japan, he came to see me. I said, "Okura, how are things going?" He said, "Fine, but I think I may need some help; this is why I have come to see you. Not having gone to school in Japan, I do not really have anyone in my company who feels responsible for me. All our management people have gone to school in Japan. As a result, there is no one in upper management who can tell the personnel people that I am ready for a managerial job in one of our branches abroad. I know they considered me when they filled the last two vacancies in South America, but no one knew whether I wanted to go there, whether I was ready, and altogether what my plans were. I know that you are going to have lunch with our Executive Vice President in a day or two, and, having been my professor, you can speak for me." I said, "Okura, won't your Executive Vice President be offended if an outsider interferes?" He said, "Oh, no. On the contrary; he'll be grateful, I assure you." And he was right. For when I mentioned Okura's name to the Executive Vice President, his face lit up and he said, "You know, I was going to ask you to do us a favor and talk to Okura-san about his plans. We think he is ready for a big management assignment abroad, but we have no way of talking to him; none of us went to the same university he went to." Three months later Okura was posted to head the company's branch office in a fairly important country in Latin America.

In the West, where relationships are far less formal, the godfather as a source of information on the young people may not be important. But we need, just as much as the Japanese—if not more so—the senior manager who serves as a human contact, a human listener, a guide for the young people during the first ten years or so in business. Perhaps the greatest complaint of the young people in the large organization today is that there is nobody who listens to them, nobody who tries to find out who they are and what they are doing, nobody who is their godfather. The idea which one finds in all our management books that the first-line supervisor can actually fill this role is simply nonsense. The first-line supervisor has to get the work out. All the sermons that the "supervisor's first job is human relations" won't make it so. Above all, a supervisor will, of necessity, hang on to a good man, rather than let him go. He will not say, "You have learned all there is to learn in this place." He will not say, "You are doing all right, but you really don't belong here." He will not ask a young man, "And where do you want to go, what kind of work do you want to do, and how can I help you to get there?" In fact, the supervisor is almost bound to consider any hint of a desire to change or to transfer on the part of a young and able managerial and professional subordinate a direct criticism and an attack on himself. As a result, the young managerial and professional people in American business and industry (but also in Europe) "vote with their feet." They quit and go elsewhere. The absence of the human contact, the guide, the counsel, the listener, is a main reason for our heavy turnover among young educated employees. Whenever one talks with them, one hears, "The company is all right, but I have nobody to talk to." Or, "The company is all right, but I am in the wrong spot and can't get out of it." "I need someone to tell me what I am doing right and what I am doing wrong, and where I really belong, but there isn't anybody in my company to whom I can go." They do not need a psychologist. They need a human relationship that is job-focused and work-focused but still available to the individual, accessible to the individual, and concerned with the individual. And that the Japanese—precisely because of the impersonal formality of their rigid system—have had to supply a long time ago. Because they cannot admit officially that this system exists, they have set it up the right way. For it is clearly the strength of their system that this godfather function is not a separate job, is not a part of personnel work, and is not entrusted to "specialists," but, on the contrary, is discharged by experienced, respected, and successful management people.

But it is not only the young people in the American or European company who need a point of human contact, a counselor, a "guide for the perplexed." Today senior managers need even more to establish communications to them from the young. The influx of the young, educated people is only beginning, for it is only now that the combined effect of the postwar "baby boom" and of the "educational explosion" is beginning to hit the management ranks. From now on, for ten years or so, the number of young entrants into technical, professional, and managerial work (i.e., of young men and women with a higher degree) will be very much larger than it has been so far when the college-educated still came largely from relatively low-birth years. The babies of the first really high-birth year, 1950, will be graduating from college in the very early 1970's. And however little we really know about the young, we do know that they are different—in their expectations, their experiences, their knowledge of the world, and their needs.

In a number of companies, especially a few large ones, with which I have been working these last few years, the attempt has been made to have senior executives meet, fairly regularly, with younger men, outside of office hours and without respecting lines of function or authority. In these sessions the senior man does not make a speech, does not "communicate." Rather he asks: "And what do you have to tell me—about your work, about your plans for yourselves and this company, about our opportunities and our problems?" These meetings have not always been easy going. But the young people, though at first highly suspicious of being patronized, after a while came to look forward to these meetings, indeed, to clamor for them. The real beneficiaries, however, have been the senior executives. The godfather concept of the Japanese may be too paternalistic for us in the West; it may even be too paternalistic for the young Japanese. But that the young managerial and professional people should be the special concern of senior men is an idea which we might well use, especially in this age of the "generation gap" and of the change from a manual work force to a highly educated knowledge work force.

Any Japanese executive who has read this piece will protest that I grossly oversimplify, let alone that I omitted most of the salient features of Japanese management. Any Western student of Japan who has read so far will accuse me of being uncritical. But my purpose in this article was not to give a scholarly analysis of Japanese management or even to attempt an explanation of Japan's managerial performance. I am fully aware of the many frustrations of the young manager in Japan, and altogether of the tremendous tensions in Japanese economy and society created by the Japanese economic achievement—tensions which are so great as to make me highly skeptical about all those current predictions that the "twenty-first century will be Japan's century." (Indeed, if I were a Japanese, this prediction would scare me out of my wits.)

Whether anyone can learn from other people's mistakes is doubtful. But surely one can learn from other people's successes. The Japanese policies discussed here are certainly not "The Key" to Japan's achievement; but they are major factors in it. They are equally not "The Answer" to the problems of the West. But, I submit, they contain answers to some of our most pressing problems, help for some of our most urgent needs; and they point to directions we might wisely explore. It would, indeed, be folly to imitate the Japanese; but we might well try to emulate them.

CHAPTER TWELVE

Keynes: Economics as a Magical System

THE INFLUENCE AND reputation of John Maynard Keynes are not explained by his having been a great economist, nor did his importance lie primarily in his economic theories. He was, indeed, a very great economist, in all likelihood the last of the "pure" economists of the classical school, at once the legitimate heir and the liquidator of Adam Smith. But he was, above all, the representative political thinker of the interwar period; he expressed perfectly its attempt to master what it knew to be a new world by pretending that it was the old one. Keynes's work was built on the realization that the fundamental assumptions of nineteenth-century laissez-faire economics no longer hold true in an industrial society and a credit economy. But it aimed at the restoration and preservation of the basic beliefs, the basic institutions of nineteenth-century laissez-faire politics; above all, it aimed at the preservation of the autonomy and automatism of the market. The two could no longer be brought together in a rational system; Keynes's policies are

---

First published in *Virginia Quarterly Review*, Autumn, 1946.

magic—spells, formulae, and incantations to make the admittedly irrational behave rationally.

Keynes's theoretical analysis of the new social and economic reality is a masterpiece that will endure. His conclusions from this analysis proved wrong, however; the economic policies which gave him his reputation and influence have failed. When he died in the spring of 1946 he was apparently at the peak of success and power: the chief financial adviser of his government, a peer of the realm, the almost undisputed master of the schools, especially in this country. But his very disciples, while using Keynesian terms, methods, and tools, were actually abandoning fast both his economic policies and his aim.

I

Keynes, who could write prose of a rare lucidity if he wanted to, chose to present his theories in the most technical and most jargon-ridden language, but his central ideas are quite simple.

Classical economics knew neither money nor time as factors in the economic process. Money was the "universal commodity," the symbol of all other commodities, but without any life or effect of its own. It was convenient and necessary, but only an accounting unit to keep track of what went on in the economy of "real" goods and "real" labor; price was simply the rate at which one commodity could be exchanged against all others. The money of classical economics is very much like the ether of classical physics: it pervades all and carries all, but it has neither properties nor effects of its own. And the classical economist was also very much like the physicist of his age in his concept of time: while everything happens in time, time itself is not a factor in the events themselves. This is no accident; classical economics were patterned consciously on the model of Newtonian physics, in structure as well as in its basic assumption of a mechanical and static economic universe.

Keynesian theory is based on the assertion, axiomatic in an industrial age, that the economic process is not only in time but largely determined by time and that the economic expression of the time factor is money. To the classical economist, money was the shadow of existing goods. Actually money, especially the bank deposits which are the money of a credit economy, is created and comes into being in anticipation of goods to be produced, of work to be performed. This means that money is not determined mechanically and according to economic rationality, but psychologically and socially on the basis of confidence in the future. Time thus enters into every economic transaction in the form of fixed money obligations for the investments of the past on which the present is based. These money obligations for the past actually are the largest factor in the economic transactions of every member of an industrial society; for the cost of everything we use, whether a house, a loaf of bread, or a hired man's labor, is made up very largely of the money obligations for the past. Money, instead of being an inert and propertyless expression of economic transactions, influences, molds, and directs economic life; changes in the money sphere cause changes in the "real" economy. We live at the same time in two closely interwoven but distinct economic systems: the "real" economy of the classics—an economy of goods, services, and labor, existing in the present and determined mechanically; and the "symbol" economy of money, heavy with the obligations of the past and determined psychologically by our confidence in the future.

It is no belittling of Keynes to say that these insights did not originate with him, but were the work of a whole generation of economic thinkers before him, especially of his two countrymen Hawtrey and Withers, of the Swedes Cassel and Wicksell, and of the German Knapp. But Keynes synthesized their isolated observations and thoughts into one system and developed a theory of the dynamics of the economic process from them; and it is this theory we usually mean when we talk of "Keynesian economics."

The assumptions of the classics had made it virtually impossible for them to understand how a depression could ever happen except as a result of physical catastrophes such as an earthquake or the destruction of war. Also, they were entirely unable to explain how a depression could last; if only left alone it had to correct itself. With the new understanding of the autonomy of the monetary sphere as his starting point, Keynes could give the first adequate theoretical explanation of the vital phenomena of depression and unemployment.

The first answer was Keynes's most famous theory—the theory of oversaving. Any saving is by definition a surplus of productive resources—goods, labor, equipment—over current consumption. For the classics that meant that, unless physically destroyed, any saving must automatically be "invested," that is, used for future production. This, however, ceases to be true as soon as we bring in money as autonomous, as having an economic reality of its own. Then it becomes possible for savings not to be invested but to become mere money savings, with the productive resources they represent left unused and unemployed. Keynes asserted that the modern economy has an inherent tendency toward oversaving.

Of even greater importance was his explanation of the unemployment of a chronic depression. In the universe of classical economics a long-term depression simply could not happen; before a maladjustment could reach depression proportions it would have been corrected by the infallible and automatic mechanism of falling prices and falling costs. Yet long before 1929 long-term depressions had become far too familiar for their existence to be denied except by the most bigoted academician. Hence, orthodox economics had to engage in a search for the criminal conspiracy that prevented "natural" adjustment and correction. Price monopolies, unions, government intervention through relief payments, subsidies, and tariffs—these and all the other measures by which society seeks to protect itself against the social destruction of a depression—became diabolical forces; and the resulting persecution mania of the economists who saw the cloven hoof in the mildest attempt at controlling economic forces soon made it impossible to base economic policy on the classical theories, even though these theories themselves were still generally accepted. From 1870 to 1930 economic policy was without proper theoretical basis. The ruling theory could not justify any of the measures actually taken; and as any economic policy that was possible politically was open to condemnation on theoretical grounds, theory furnished no guidance to distinguish between beneficial and destructive policies. Out of social necessity every economist in office had to do things he opposed in his writings; the resulting blend of cynicism and bad conscience finally gave us that evil genius of old-school financial economists, Dr. Schacht.

But with money a factor, the automatic and infallible adjustment becomes the exception rather than the rule. In a credit economy prices and wages cannot adjust themselves very readily; they must be comparatively inflexible. For a very large—indeed, the largest—part of all costs is the money obligation for the past. This obligation is unaffected by changes in the present value of money as the goods and services it represents were produced in the past at past prices and wages. We may add—though this may be going beyond Keynes—that prices and wages are also hard to adjust downward because money has a social meaning, independent largely of its purchasing power; it buys not only goods but prestige. This is especially true of the lower income levels where the weekly money wage represents a definite social position.

For these reasons, the adjustment in a depression will not, in the modern economy, take the form of lower prices and lower wages. Prices and wages will tend to stay up. Hence the adjustment will take the only form possible: lower employment both of men and of capital equipment. And, unlike the adjustment through lower prices and wages, unemployment not only does not tend to correct the depression; it tends to make the disequilibrium permanent.

Actually, under modern conditions prices will fall, though not as evenly as they should—and with significant exceptions in the capital-goods fields. But wage rates will not go down. In the first place, the wage earner has usually much less margin between his income and his fixed obligations than the industrialist; hence the economic factors militate against wage cuts. Second, the political pressure of organized labor is much more effective in modern society than the economic power even of the strongest monopolist. Hence the maladjustment will not only not be corrected in the "normal course of events"; it will become worse. The point at which new investments again become profitable will recede into the distance. From this follows one of Keynes's most important and, at first sight, most paradoxical conclusions: that we have to raise prices in a depression in order to obtain the very effect orthodox economics expected to get from falling prices.

II

These general theories have been justly criticized for their narrow emphasis on the monetary phenomenon to the exclusion of everything else. The monetary factor is probably only one of the causes of a depression, though perhaps a central one, rather than, as Keynes asserts, always and everywhere the only cause. But aside from this not unimportant question of emphasis, the Keynesian theories have been almost universally accepted. And with these basic theories a great many economists also accepted at first his economic policies. But, as most of the disciples have begun to find out, Keynes's economic policies do not follow from his basic theories; indeed, they are hardly compatible with them. His policies were really dictated by his political aim, not by his economic observations. His attempt to bring the two together into one whole, to make the policies emerge as the inevitable conclusion from the theories, may very well explain the tortuous and tortured style of his later writing, his increasing reliance on purely formal arguments, and his uncritical use of mathematical techniques.

According to Keynes the economic theorist, the level of business activity is determined by the amount of investment in capital goods, which in turn is determined by the confidence which leads businessmen to borrow for expansion. Business activity depends in the last analysis on psychological, that is on economically irrational, factors. According to Keynes the economic politician, the very confidence which creates credit is itself strictly determined by credit. Keynes offers two answers to the question of what causes confidence. He asserts that confidence is a function of the interest rate: the lower the rate, the greater the confidence. He also asserts that confidence is a function of consumer spending: the higher consumer purchases, the higher the investment in capital goods. In his theories Keynes seems to have wavered between these two answers; politically, it does not make too much difference, however, which explanation is preferred. Both lead to pretty much the same conclusion: the quantity of money or credit available determines the degree of confidence, with it the rate of investment, and thus the level of business activity and of employment. Hence Keynes's monetary panacea for booms and depression: in a boom, prevent maladjustment through "draining off" purchasing power into a budget surplus; in a depression, cure maladjustment by creating purchasing power through budget deficits. In either case the quantity of money automatically and infallibly regulates confidence.

Keynes starts out with the statement that human behavior in economic life is not, as the classical economists assumed, determined by objective economic forces, but that, on the contrary, economic forces are directed, if not determined, by human behavior. He ends by asserting as rigid an economic determinism of human behavior and actions as any Ricardo or Malthus ever proclaimed. By this assertion Keynes's entire economic policy stands and falls. And it is this assertion that was conclusively refuted by the experience of the New Deal. The New Deal—at least from 1935 to 1939—was based on deficit spending which created consumer purchasing power and forced down the level of interest rates. Neither brought about a resumption of investment or a significant cut in unemployment. With the credit pumped into the banks, business promptly repaid its old debts instead of borrowing for new investments; and the money paid out by the government to the consumers flowed back to the banks almost at once to become "oversavings."

The faithful Keynesians have been hard pressed to explain away what happened. Their favorite argument is that political opposition to the New Deal offset the economically created confidence. But this defense is not permissible, let alone convincing. Either confidence can be created by creating credit and purchasing power regardless of the way business or any other group feels about governmental policy, or Keynes's economic policies are wrong. And confidence has been conclusively proved not to be producible by a check-writing machine.

Most of the disciples of the earlier years have drawn the conclusions from this experience. They are still Keynesians in their theoretical analysis, but no longer so in their policies. They continue to express their thoughts in monetary terms, but they no longer talk about the interest rate or even about budget deficits or surpluses. Consumer purchasing power and "confidence" have all but disappeared from their vocabulary. The program of the most influential group of Keynesian economists in this country—as written by Alvin Hansen of Harvard into the original draft of the Full Employment bill—provided that, in times of depression and unemployment, the government shall *produce* capital goods through public works and government orders in a quantity sufficient to bring the total capital goods production to a level which gives full employment. Whether this is done with or without a deficit, at a high or at a low interest rate, is of very minor importance; what matters to the neo-Keynesian of today is not monetary policy, but capital-goods production. This shift denies both Keynes's economic concepts and his over-all political goal.

In fact, this shift even caught up with Keynes himself. Ironically enough, the very event which brought him official recognition and honors showed up the shortcomings of his theories and policies. In the course of the war, Keynes became the official financial adviser to his government, a director of the Bank of England, a member of the peerage. For the first time his native country officially adopted Keynesian ideas as the basis of its financial policy; the measures outlined in his little pamphlet, *How to Pay for the War*, were adopted almost unchanged by the British government. But the war also showed, especially in Britain, that monetary policy is quite subordinate and that, by itself, it achieves very little. England's war production was obtained not by directing the flow of money, credit, and purchasing power, but through physical controls of men, raw materials, plant equipment, and output which could have worked almost as well with a different monetary policy; in Nazi Germany they worked without any monetary policy at all.

III

In the popular mind Keynes stands for government intervention in business. This may well be a correct evaluation of the ultimate effect of Keynesian economics; but if so, Keynes achieved precisely the opposite of what he intended to achieve. For the one passionate aim of his policies was to make possible an economic system free from government interference, a system determined exclusively by objective and impersonal economic forces. "The free market is dead, long live the free market," would be a fitting motto for his entire work.

Keynes's basic insight was the realization that the free market of the classical economists fails to adjust itself automatically as predicted because the economic forces of demand and supply, cost and price, are overridden by the psychological forces of money and credit. From this basis several conclusions as to economic policy would have been logically possible.

Keynes could have argued that conscious political action had to achieve by breaking through the money wall what the market forces should have achieved by themselves. That would have been an economic policy of direct government intervention into *production* through public works and public orders rather than a policy of credit creation; and it is precisely what most of the neo-Keynesians have advocated. Such a policy would restore the supremacy of the "real" system, but at the price of its political independence.

Keynes might also have arrived in logical development from his premises at a policy in which governmental action is used only to induce private business to build up reservoirs of capital-goods production for use in a depression, for instance, through a system of tax rewards for building up reserves in good years to be coupled with stiff tax penalties incurred if these reserves are not used for employment—creating new investments in a depression. He might even have come to the conclusion that the proper policy is psychological rather than economic, i.e., propaganda to create confidence; the German economist Knapp, whose ideas had great influence on Keynes, actually gave this answer.

The one conclusion which logically and theoretically it seems impossible to derive from Keynes's premise is the one he actually did derive. But it was the one and only conclusion which gave Keynes the desired political result: the maintenance of a laissez-faire political system in which only objective economic factors determine the economy and in which man's economic activities are entirely under the control of the individual, not under that of the government.

If the liberal state of nineteenth-century laissez faire was a night watchman protecting the peaceful and law-abiding burgher against thieves and disturbers of the peace, Keynes's state was a thermostat protecting the individual citizen against sharp changes in the temperature. And it was to be a fully automatic thermostat. A fall in economic activity would switch on credit; a rise would cut it off again; and in a boom the mechanism would work in reverse. In contrast to the nineteenth-century state, Keynes's state was, indeed, to act positively; but the actions as well as their timing were to be determined strictly by economic statistics, not subject to political manipulation. The only purpose of these actions was to restore the individual's freedom in the economic sphere, that is, the freedom from all but economic factors, from all but economic considerations—with "economic" referring to the "real" economy of the classics.

The economic system of orthodox economics had been a machine built by the "divine watchmaker," hence without friction and in perpetual motion and perpetual equilibrium. Keynes's system was a clock, a very good and artful clock, but still one built by a human watchmaker, and thus subject to friction. But the only actions required of the watchmaker were to wind, to oil, and, where necessary, to regulate the clock. He was not to run it; he was only to make it fit to run itself; and it was to run according to mechanical laws, not according to political decisions.

Keynes's basic aim of restoring by unorthodox methods the orthodox automatic market system, his basic belief that his methods were objective, nonpolitical, and capable of determination by the impersonal yardstick of statistics, show best in his last major work: the "Keynes Plan" of an international currency and credit system proposed in 1943. This plan projected his policies from the national into the international sphere. It proposed to overcome international depressions and maladjustments by the adjustment of prices and purchasing power through international credit creation. The agency which was to be in control of this international currency and credit was not to be a world government, but an international body of economic statisticians governed by index numbers and almost entirely without discretionary power. The result of this international system and its main justification was to be the restoration of the full freedom and equilibrium in international trade and currency movements.

Critics have rightly pointed out that Keynes was naïve, to a degree amazing in such an accomplished and experienced political practitioner, in believing that his system could really be immune to political manipulation. It may be possible to obtain objective statistics. But to be meaningful, statistics have to be interpreted by human beings; and interpretations will differ radically with the political beliefs and desires of the interpreter—as witness the widely accepted 1945 forecast of ten million unemployed in the United States by the spring of 1946, made in good faith by government experts interested in setting up a planned economy. Also, even impersonal and objective control is still control; and it is an old political axiom that a government that controls the national income, i.e., the livelihood of the people, inevitably controls the souls of the people. Keynes's political system, in which the state has the power to interfere in the individual's economic activities but refrains from using it, is thus a very different thing from his ideal, the state of nineteenth-century liberalism which was without power of interference.

But the decisive criticism of Keynes's argument is not that there are flaws in it, but that it is an irrational argument. It says in brief: we have proved that the factors that control economic activity are economically irrational, i.e., psychological factors; *therefore* they themselves must be controllable by an economic mechanism. But this "therefore" is not of the vocabulary of reason, not even of that of faith; it is the "therefore" of magic. It is on this very belief—that the admittedly irrational can be controlled and directed by mechanical means—that every system of magic is based. The Keynesian "policies," in spite—or perhaps because—of their elaborate apparatus of mathematical formulae and statistical tables, are spells. Because of this, the fact that they failed once, in the New Deal, means that they have failed forever. For it is of the nature of a spell that it ceases altogether to be effective as soon as it is broken once.

But it was precisely its irrationality that made Keynes's policy so convincing to the generation of the long armistice. After World War I the Western world suddenly awakened to the realization that the basic nineteenth-century assumptions no longer applied. But it refused to face the necessity of new thought and decision. The timid pulled the featherbed of normalcy over their eyes and ears to sleep on a little longer. The courageous accepted the new situation, but attempted to avoid facing it by finding a formula, a mechanical gadget, a spell, in other words, which would make the new behave as if it were the old. One example would be the labor policy of the New Deal. It started with the realization that social and political relationships, rather than the purely economic nexus of the paycheck, are the essence of modern industry. But it concluded that the mechanical device of "equal bargaining power" on economic issues would do the trick. Another example is in the field of international relations. Here World War I had clearly shown that peace cannot be based on the concept of equal sovereign states whose internal and external policies are nobody's business but their own. The answer was a strictly mechanical formula, the League of Nations, which represented nothing but the equal sovereign states in their fullest equality and sovereignty, which was neither a supergovernment nor a supercourt, not even an alliance of the Great Powers, but which was expected, in some magical way, to overcome sovereignty.

We can trace this desire for a mechanical formula to make the new function like the old, to make what was irrational in the old assumptions again behave rationally, into fields far removed from politics. It explains, for instance, the tremendous appeal of Freudian psychoanalysis as a cure-all. Freud had had the insight to see the fallacy of traditional, mechanist psychology—the same psychology on which the classical economists had based themselves, incidentally. He realized that man is not a bundle of mechanical reflexes and reactions, but a personality. But he avoided facing the problem—a philosophical or religious one—by asserting that this personality is determined biologically, that it operates through the grossly mechanical forces of repression and sublimation, and that it can be controlled by the mechanical technique of analysis.

But the area in which the desire for a magical system was greatest was that of politics. And in the political field Keynes's economic policy was the most accomplished, the most brilliant, the most elegant attempt to make the impossible again possible, the irrational again rational.

IV

In the field of economic thought, Keynes was both a beginning and an end. He showed that classical economics no longer apply and why. He showed that economic theory has to give an answer to a new problem: the impact of man, acting as a human being and not as an economic machine, on the economy. But he contributed little or nothing to the solution of these new problems; he himself never went beyond the classical methods and the classical analysis. Indeed, it may be said that he held back economic thought. Before he came to dominate the scene we had made promising beginnings toward an understanding of the human factor in economic life in such books as Knight's *Risk, Uncertainty, and Profit* and Schumpeter's *Theory of Economic Dynamics,* both written around World War I; and at the Harvard Business School, Elton Mayo had begun his pioneering studies of the relationship between worker and production. Keynes's influence, his magnetic attraction on young men in the field, made theoretical economics again focus on the mechanical equilibrium and on a mechanical concept of economic man determined by impersonal and purely quantitative forces.

Keynes's main legacy is in the field of economic policy. He has formulated our tasks here; even the term "full employment" is his. But his only contribution to a solution—by no means an unimportant one—was to show us which way we cannot go; we cannot, as he did, assert that economic policy is possible without a political decision. We may decide perhaps that the state has to assume direct economic control of production—the decision of most of the neo-Keynesians. This decision raises the question of how political freedom can be maintained in such a state. It also brings up the equally difficult question of what the state is to produce and who is to decide on it; so far no state, whether capitalist, fascist, or socialist, has been able to overcome unemployment by direct government intervention except through producing armaments and armaments plants, that is, through a war economy.

Or we can decide that the state has to create by political means the conditions in which a free-enterprise economy will itself prevent and overcome depressions. Such a policy is not impossible to devise on paper. We would need a fiscal policy that recognizes that industrial production extends over the business cycle, rather than one based on the fiction of the annual profit. We would need a policy of definite encouragement of new ventures and of capital investment in bad years. And we would need a labor policy which, while restoring the flexibility of wages through tying them in with productive efficiency and with business profits, gives security through such employment guarantees as an annual wage. But all this raises the question of how such policies, which demand of all groups that they subordinate their short-term interests to the long-term good of the whole, can be realized in a popular government based on sectional groups and subject to their constant pressure.

But Keynes himself cannot help us to make these decisions, or to answer these questions.

CHAPTER THIRTEEN

The Economic Basis of American Politics

I

Why is there not one single American among the "great economists"? From its earliest days this country has had more economists than any other country. It has led in the development of the tools of economic analysis. Economists are everywhere—in government, in business, in the universities, in the labor unions. In no other country, indeed, is a knowledge of economics considered part of ordinary education; in the United States, however, we have for many years been trying to combat "economic illiteracy" in the secondary schools. And certainly there is no country in which popular interest in economics is greater and in which economic issues are more prominent.

Yet we conspicuously lack the Great Economist, the economist who changes our ideas about economics and gives us new approaches to the interpretation and direction of economic events.

Or, rather: the great economists America has produced are not

First published in *The Public Interest,* Winter, 1968.

known as such, are not recognized as such. Alexander Hamilton and Henry Clay certainly deserve being considered very great economists: Hamilton, at the very dawn of systematic economics, created a basic theory of economic development which has not been much improved since; Henry Clay's "American System" is the font and origin of all welfare economics. Yet their very names are rarely mentioned in histories of economic thought, whereas the German Friedrich List, who repeated what Clay had taught him, usually occupies a prominent place in these books.

Of course, neither Hamilton nor Clay really wanted to be known as an economist. Their own ambitions were elsewhere: Hamilton on becoming the Commanding General of a victorious United States Army, Clay on being elected President. To both men, their economics were totally incidental to their politics and a tool thereof. For both Hamilton and Clay, economic policy was clearly a means to a political end. And when their economic views are discussed, they are correctly treated as part of their political theories and political strategies.

The explanation for this state of affairs would seem to be this: Economics is too important to American politics to be left to the American economist. Economics has a political role to fulfill that transcends its own subject matter. For well over two hundred years it has been the unifying impulse in this country's political process. Since colonial days, "economic interests" have been used systematically to create political forces and political alignments and, above all, to unite regional and sectional groups behind one leader and one program. The names of these economic interests have changed; but whether we speak of the "manufacturing interest," the "farming interest," or the "silver bloc," the idea itself has not changed. Similarly, for well over two centuries, economic issues—such as the tariff, the currency, or free soil—have been used to overcome and neutralize ideological cleavages and conflicts that otherwise might have torn apart the nation. During all of our history, fundamental rifts in the country have been bridged by polarizing politics on economic issues; these are issues on which a compromise, distributing dollars and cents, is always possible. The classical example is, of course, the compromise over the "Tariff of Abomination" between the South and Andrew Jackson that postponed the conflict over slavery for thirty years. All along it has been good American political manners to talk dollars and cents when we really mean political decisions. The way in which Robert McNamara, as Secretary of Defense in both the Kennedy and Johnson administrations, used budgetary control radically to alter strategic concepts and military organization is another good example.

Perhaps most revealing is the way in which we have used the economic sphere to think through and work out basic issues of the relation of government to society. Big business is far more powerful in France or Germany, for instance, than it is in the United States. But only in the United States has the relationship between "government and business" come to be considered the key issue for a fundamental discussion of the role and power of government in society. Indeed, our public discussions for a century now have led many a naïve foreign observer to conclude that in the United States there are no noteworthy social institutions other than business institutions.

The Great Themes of American History

The result of this peculiar role of economic issues and economic controversy in the American political process is most paradoxical. On the one hand, economics in this country appears to be far more prominent and far more important in the political life than in any other country. American history seems to be dominated, at first sight, by economic conflict. Indeed, it is possible to overlook the fact that the great themes of American history have all along been moral and constitutional: slavery, the industrial versus the agrarian society, and federalism in the nineteenth century; racial equality, the role and function of the central government, and America's place in an international society in this century. In sharp contrast to countries whose politics have an ideological organization and pattern, such as all European countries, these great themes are barely mentioned in day-to-day, year-to-year American politics, where the slogans are primarily economic. It is, therefore, only too easy to mistake the appearance for reality. It is thus possible to argue, as a whole school of historians did, that the Civil War was an "unnecessary conflict" and could have been avoided by paying a few hundred million dollars to the slaveowners. It is possible, as Arthur M. Schlesinger, Jr., did in his brilliant *Age of Jackson,* to overlook completely that the central theme and the crowning achievement of the Jackson administration was to establish the sovereignty of the national government over all regional or sectional interests; instead, Mr. Schlesinger made economic and class interests paramount. It is even possible, as Charles Beard did in a long life as a historian, to see the whole of our history as determined by, and subordinated to, economic interest. But Beard lived long enough to find out that any attempt to predict the course of American history and American political behavior from economics is bound to misfire.

Every American politician must, indeed, know how to use economic measures for political ends. If he aspires to a national role, he must be a master of finding and creating economic alignments that unify diverse groups across the nation. Even John C. Calhoun, the most nearly "metaphysical" of our political thinkers, spent the last two decades of his life in an abortive attempt to bridge the moral gulf of slavery between South and West by means of their common economic interest as farmers.

So it is that, despite its appearance of centrality, economics in the American experience is actually a subordinate means to predominantly noneconomic ends. Our values are not economic values, nor is our economics autonomous. Politics even decides what economic issues are allowed to appear on the stage of American history. For, to be "available" as a political vehicle an economic issue must fit into our political logic. It must mobilize national energies and must unify large masses across regions for joint political action and for the conquest of the central political power that is the Presidency.

This explains the absence of the Great Economist. Such a man must assume the autonomy of the economic sphere in human life. He must assume the reality of economic values. If he is interested at all in politics (as few of them were), he must treat politics as a handmaiden of economics and as a tool for achieving economic purposes. These assumptions make no sense to the American experience. What flourishes in this country, therefore, is economic technicians of skill and renown, economic analysts, and expert fashioners of economic tools. We have political economists and economic politicians galore. But the climate is most uncongenial to the Great Economist. Such a man must assume an autonomous economic reality, of which the political issues are merely a reflection. In our American experience, however, economics is the conventional shorthand and the lingua franca for issues and decisions which are not economic, but political and moral. One might, indeed, formulate a basic rule of American politics to read: *If at all possible, express a political issue and design a political alignment as an economic issue and an economic alignment.*

II

The insight that economic interests can be used as the hinge of politics is commonly traced to the famous No. 10 of the *Federalist Papers* in which James Madison (following Harrington's *Oceana* and John Locke) concluded that power follows property. But, when Madison wrote, American political life had already, for a century, been habitually organized around economic issues and in economic alignments. Madison only codified what had been fairly general American experience during the colonial period.

Colonial legislatures had, indeed, no alternative if they wanted to be effective at all. The matters that now occupy a legislature—public order and law, the administration of justice or education—may have been of very great interest to them, but were normally not within their reach. They had, perforce, to be left to the individual local communities, the towns and counties. In colonial America, distances were too great, population too sparsely settled, for any central authority to be effective. If the local community would not look after its own internal affairs, nobody else could. The major burning issue for the colonial legislature was relations with the mother country. And those turned on economic problems and economic questions: taxes and tariffs, coinage and credit, and so on. It was in these matters, above all, that the colony's Royal Governor was interested; for in eighteenth-century theory and practice, an overseas colony was an economic asset. Of course, such recurrent disturbances as Indian risings or the endemic war with the French occupied a good deal of the time and attention of the colonial politician. But his main job was to represent the colonist before and against the economic power represented and exerted by the Governor. His very *raison d'être* was economic. And only by identifying and organizing economic interests could the eighteenth-century colonial politician create unity in the electorate he represented—an electorate which, as the century wore on, became increasingly diversified in its other characteristics (religious beliefs, ethnic origins, and so on). There never was much need to do for the eighteenth-century politician, in the state houses of Boston, Philadelphia, and Williamsburg, what Sir Lewis Namier had to do in our century for his English counterpart: to seek out and identify his economic affiliations and interests. That was the one fact about the politician in colonial America that was always clear, evident, and known to everybody.

But to Madison—and to all the brilliant politicians who, in the first quarter-century of United States history, established the political conventions and the political processes for the infant country—should be given credit for one fundamental insight: Economic interests could be used to *unify*. They could be used to overcome the pernicious "factions," the cleavage of society into ideological camps divided by their basic beliefs, which the founding fathers rightly feared as incompatible with nationhood and political stability.

The Uses of Economic Conflict

This is a political view of economics—a view which explains economic events in terms of human behavior. This, more than anything else, distinguishes the traditional American approach to economics from the approach of the economist. The economist understands the behavior of commodities. And if he is naïve (as our present-day neo-Keynesians tend to be), he believes that human beings behave as commodities do. But even at his most profound and skeptical, he is likely to consider ordinary human behavior as economically nonrational behavior. In fact, the economist has, all along, been either suspicious or at the least contemptuous of the politician who, so it seems to him, subordinates the clear logic of economic rationality to the murky unreason of human emotions and vanities. From this starting point, the classical economists essentially arrived at a denial of politics. To them there was a pre-established harmony in the economic system, with economic self-regulation automatically producing the optimum for all groups and classes in society. Marx himself was no less contemptuous of the politician: no longer accepting the classical doctrine of harmony, but instead accepting the reality of economic conflict, he deduced therefrom the inevitability, beyond any politician's contriving, of class war and revolution.

The political economists of the American tradition never for one moment believed in pre-established economic harmony. Economic conflict was much too obvious for that. It had, after all, characterized relations between the infant colonies and the mother country, culminating finally in a violent upheaval of the political order in the Revolution. But at the same time, they saw in economic conflict their means to prevent the more dangerous ideological conflict. And they saw in economic conflict the means to establish order—*not* harmony, which they did not expect on this earth. Above all, they saw that economic conflict was the one clash within the body politic that could be managed. It could be managed because economic interests are divisible, whereas political or religious beliefs are not. One can always split an economic difference in two—and while half a loaf is better than no bread, half a child, as King Solomon long ago perceived, is no good at all. The same goes for half a religion, half a philosophy, or half a political principle.

Above all, their experience, unique at that time and quite at variance with what "common sense" would have taught elsewhere, had convinced the founding fathers that, unlike all other cleavages, economic conflicts tend to become less acute with time. They may not be self-healing, but they are capable of amelioration. If the fight is over "who gets how much," then one can satisfy both sides if the amount available for distribution increases. And their experience as colonists on the virgin continent had taught them that the economic pie is, indeed, capable of being increased by human action, rather than being fixed forever.

They may not have consciously thought this through. But Alexander Hamilton started out from the assumption that it is possible to increase the economic resources available. This assumption explains in large part why his countrymen, no matter how much they distrusted his politics, took to his economics at once, but also why he never attained full respectability as an economist. For the economist traditionally—until well past World War II—took it for granted that economic resources are given and limited, so that the problem is their most effective distribution in a system of equilibrium. In this respect Keynes, however much he otherwise might have differed from his predecessors, was as traditional as anyone. It was not until the most recent decades, until the advent of "economic development" as a goal of economic policy—with President Truman's "Point Four" declaration of the early 1950's being the crucial date—that proper economists accepted the purposeful creation of dynamic disequilibrium as possible and meaningful.

To the American—no matter how faithfully he repeated the teachings of the economist, no matter how faithfully he himself taught them in the classrooms of his colleges—it was obvious that in his country the economic resources had been proven to be capable of almost infinite expansion through human and, in large measure, political action. He may have agreed with the economist that this was purely the result of the rarest of accidents: the existence on this continent of vast areas of empty soil, ready for the plow, ready to be appropriated and to be converted into an economic resource. But very early we find in the actual political behavior of the American strong evidence that, deep down, he knew differently. He knew what Hamilton had known in the last decade of the eighteenth century: that there is an economic dynamic and that economic resources are the creation of man rather than of Providence. This underlies quite clearly such bold measures as the Morrill Act of 1865 which, in creating the land-grant colleges, clearly assumed that the application of knowledge creates economic value and productive capacity well beyond that given in the existing resources. It underlay, from the beginning, all American trade-union movements. American "business unionism" assumes not only that the economic pie can be made greater but, above all, that the fight over the division of the pie is by itself likely to produce a larger pie—that, in other words, economic conflict by itself leads to economic growth and therefore, at the same time, to political and social unity.

III

There can be little doubt that the American concept of "economic interest" as an effective and unifying political force has served this country exceedingly well.

In fact, it is questionable whether there could have been an American nation without it. With the wisdom of hindsight, we have come to see in the frontier a source of strength. But, in reality, the experience of the frontier must have been an almost unbearable strain, as witness all other countries that have undergone a similar experience. It was not only the kind of strain on the physical resources and on the political energies which rapid, turbulent expansion produces. Above all, it was a strain on the unity of a country in which the new tidal wave of immigrants of different social background, national origin, and religious allegiance always arrived long before the preceding wave of immigrants had been absorbed. In such a country, growing at a frenetic speed, ideological, philosophical, or religious cleavages might have been fatal.

One should not forget that the immigrants, by and large, had themselves no tradition of self-government or even of political activity; it was not, after all, the respectable or well to do who arrived in the holds of the immigrant ships. And yet these vast heterogeneous masses had to become a nation under one government and with one set of basic values practically overnight, or else the American experiment would have floundered. If economic interests had not been available as the political organizer, it would either have been necessary to impose the most rigid authority on the population or else pluralism would have organized itself *against* the nation and its unity—with every imported tradition of religion and culture, every imported political value and belief, the focus of an ideology alien, if not hostile, to American nationhood (as is so clearly the case in Latin America).

The great phenomenon of the nineteenth century is not, after all, the rise of the American economy. It is the creation of the American nation. For a nation, as we are now finding out the world over, is not something one can easily create. It is, on the contrary, usually the fruit of long experience and of historical forces operating over many centuries. Neither the nations of Europe nor Japan were created overnight. That nationhood is difficult and takes a very long time to create is proven by the fact that, outside of these old nations—and of the United States—very few, if any, nations have yet come into being. In all of Latin America, for instance, despite centuries of political identity, only Mexico and, to a lesser extent, Brazil, can be said to be "nations"—and, in both, nationhood has come only in this century. But the United States achieved nationhood in a few short decades, or, at the most, within a century. This it owes to a very large extent to the tradition which used economic interests and their clashes and conflicts as the foundation for political issues, political alignments, and political conflicts. This has enabled the United States to tolerate, if not to encourage, pluralism in all other spheres, to survive the fiercest of civil wars, and to attain a unity of allegiance and of basic commitments which represent as strong a common bond and communion as centuries of common history, common language, and common experiences have given to any of the older nations.

The Bias Toward "Bipartisanship"

But the convention of economic interests has not only tended to prevent ideological issues from arising. It has forced the American political system into a nonpartisan approach to noneconomic problems.

A noneconomic issue threatens the existing political alignments. It is not easily encompassed within the American political system. The American politician shuns ideological stands, for the simple reason that they are certain to alienate a large proportion of a constituency brought together and held together by economic interests. Any noneconomic ideological stand would have at once, for instance, exploded the alliance between the lily-white, fundamentalist Protestant, and proudly Anglo-Saxon South and the cosmopolitan, largely Catholic or Jewish working class in the big cities on which the Democratic party was based for so long. The only thing that could hold them together—and could thereby get a Democratic politician into federal office—was their economic opposition to the manufacturing interest.

This built into the American political process a powerful incentive to handle noneconomic issues on a "bipartisan" basis, that is, to remove them essentially from party politics. Indeed, the greatest praise in our political system is reserved for the "patriot" who turns a potentially disruptive noneconomic issue into bipartisan consensus. It is for this act of patriotism at the expense, legend has it, of his Presidential chances that American history primarily remembers Henry Clay. And a century later, Arthur Vandenberg earned himself a permanent place in the American political pantheon by similarly making American foreign policy after World War II "bipartisan," thereby again sacrificing whatever chance for the Presidential nomination of his party he might ever have had. A great many voters repudiated Barry Goldwater in 1964, not because they disagreed with his views, but because his decision to take a partisan stand on noneconomic issues seemed to them a greater threat to the Republic than a wrong, but bipartisan, consensus on the issues. And, in the context of the American political process, they were right.

Foreign affairs, religion, education, civil rights, and a host of other areas which, in any other country, are the bread and meat of party politics and political organization are, therefore, as much as possible, treated as "bipartisan" in the American political system. This does not mean that they are not controversial. It means that the system, as long as it works, uses them to bring together otherwise warring factions rather than to create new factions on each side of the controversy. In fact, we much prefer not even to tackle such issues unless there is available for them a broad coalition cutting across our conventional political alignments. Again and again, initiative in such an issue is left, as if by passive agreement, to the one body in the American political system that is outside the established party alignment, the Supreme Court. That in both the great constitutional issues of the recent years, civil rights and reapportionment of voting districts, a Supreme Court decision took the place of political action in these politically crucial areas was in full accord with the tradition that goes back to John Marshall's Court. For a Supreme Court decision is the "law of the land" and thus establishes its own consensus.

The Limitations of "Consensus"

There are obvious and real limitations to the effectiveness of the convention of economic issues in American politics. Not every noneconomic—that is, ideological, political, or moral—issue can be either made to appear as economic or organized as "bipartisan." Indeed, the most important issues and decisions in the life of a nation cannot be handled in this fashion. The great example is slavery, of course, for in this country slavery did not primarily serve an economic function (as it did, for instance, in the plantation economy of Brazil). At least by the second quarter of the nineteenth century, the main function of slavery was to endow the "poor white" in the South with a feeling of human superiority, no matter how wretched his physical or moral condition. Even if slavery in its origin and spread was an economic institution, by the time it became an issue, that is, after 1820 or so, the main beneficiary was no longer the slave owner, but rather the non-owner who derived the psychic benefits of a slave society without having to carry the increasing economic burden of maintaining the slaves. In other words, the Abolitionists, as we now know, were right: slavery in this country was a sin rather than a crime. And for this reason the abolition of slavery by itself, without true civil rights for the blacks, settled so very little.

And for this reason, too, slavery could not be camouflaged as an economic issue, no matter how hard the politicians of the early nineteenth century tried. Moreover, as a truly "irreconcilable" issue, that is, as a spiritual and moral one, there could be no "consensus" on it, even though the Supreme Court of the time tried to establish it in the Dred Scott decision. Nor could the existing political organization handle such a noneconomic issue—and probably the political system of no country, no matter how organized, could have handled it. On the issue of slavery, then, the American political system floundered and sank into Civil War, almost destroying the country with it.

But even in less crucial and less sensitive areas, the American political system is not geared to handling the noneconomic issue. This is particularly true whenever foreign policy cannot be organized on the basis of "consensus" and "bipartisanship." Any such failure leaves deep and long-lasting scars. For any such failure endangers national cohesion. This was true of the War of 1812. It was true of the bitter foreign-policy conflict that preceded our entry into World War I. But for the Japanese attack on Pearl Harbor, the rift over foreign policy in the years before World War II might similarly have proven incapable of being organized within the American political system and might have torn apart American national unity. Today, Vietnam poses a similar threat.

But then there is also always a danger that our politicians may forget that the economic issue is a convention and fall into the error of believing that economics really controls politics. In domestic affairs, the danger is not very great. It is a very stupid politician who will not intuitively realize the limitations, as well as the uses, of the convention. Certainly no strong President—Jackson, Lincoln, the two Roosevelts, or Truman, for example—ever believed that economic interests and economic policy were by themselves sufficient, or that they necessarily prevailed. But in foreign affairs we have made this mistake again and again—and have paid dearly in every case. Again and again we have fallen for the illusion of "economic sanctions" as an effective tool in foreign affairs. And again and again we have found that they are ineffective. This holds true for the belief of the South that "King Cotton" would force the North to its knees and constrain Europe to ally itself with the Confederacy, but also for the balancing belief of the North that the Confederacy could be defeated by economic blockade. And we now also know, from the diaries of Pro-Western Japanese leaders, that the economic sanctions which the United States and Great Britain imposed on Japan in 1940 and 1941 only strengthened the war party and deprived the moderates of all influence, just as the blockade of Germany in World War I emasculated the moderates in the German government and made the military extremists all-powerful. Ironically, we now also know that economic sanctions did not even work in the one case in which they seemed to have been successful—the case which probably explains the blind American belief in this policy: the "economic sanctions" of the American colonists against the first British attempt to tax them, a decade before the American Revolution. Recent historical research has made it reasonably certain that the British Cabinet used the American boycott as an excuse for a retreat from a policy which had proven exceedingly unpopular among powerful backers at home, and not primarily for economic reasons.

The convention of economics as the ground of political action and organization is, in other words, just a tool. Like every tool, it has to be used with judgment. And like every tool, it has limitations. Whoever mistakes the convention for reality pays the heavy penalty one always has to pay for deceiving oneself.

But while not perfect, not infallible, and not a panacea by any means, the convention has served the American people remarkably well.

IV

The question, however, is not really how well the convention has served in the past. It is: is it still useful, still serviceable? Can the common, ordinary, political business of the American people still be ordered by the traditional rule to formulate issues, as far as possible, as economic issues and to define alignments, to the greatest extent possible, as economic alignments?

It is just barely possible that this traditional convention of domestic American politics has a major future role to play in foreign and international affairs. But at the same time, it may be at the end of its usefulness at home.

Every one of the many new countries that have come into existence in the last two decades has yet to become a nation. Every one is less well equipped for this task, by history and tradition, than was the infant American Republic two hundred years ago. In every one, the cleavages between tribes, between religions, between races, run deep—and will have to be bridged fast if the country is to survive. No one of them could survive a conflict of ideologies. In this situation, a good many of them, if not all, will predictably take recourse in the elimination of politics—the vain promise of every dictatorship. Equally predictably, this will only worsen the conflicts and make them even less tractable. Predictably also, some of them at least will seek escape in braggart nationalism, if not in conquest abroad. This, too, history amply teaches, will not succeed. Only an approach to politics which allows conflicts to be productive and to create unity across the dividing line of tribe, religion, tradition, or race would seem to fit the needs of the new countries. In the traditional American approach, which makes politics turn on economic interests and economic issues, the new countries might well find what they need, ready-made and well tested.

Indeed, this approach might become increasingly more important for the international community altogether. The world today is threatened by a danger even greater than that of class war in the nineteenth century. It is threatened by the danger of a worldwide race war of the poor and largely colored majority against the largely white minority of the rich. At the same time, this is an infinitely smaller world than was that of the eighteenth century—a world in which everybody is everybody else's neighbor and in which, therefore, there is no alternative to living together. In such a world, a political concept which allows for productive conflict, but which also organizes unity beyond the ideologies and traditions that divide, might be of the greatest importance.

We are obviously very far from any such accomplishment; the "Alliance for Progress" in President Kennedy's original version was probably the closest to it. But, in retrospect, the development efforts of the 1950's and 1960's may well one day appear as the first uncertain and faltering steps toward a new, nonideological, and yet unifying concept of international order, different alike in its flexibility and effectiveness from the world anarchy of sovereign states which has become a hopeless anachronism, and a world government which, if at all feasible, could today be only a world-wide tyranny.

The Need for Innovation

But at the same time, it seems likely that in domestic politics the traditional economic convention has come to the end of its usefulness. It is not that we are dissatisfied with it or that we hanker after ideological politics. It's just that the problems and challenges of American life no longer can be cast easily, if at all, into an economic mold. The civil-rights issue, in all likelihood, is typical of the issues that will be central to American politics from now on: the problems of the metropolis; the structure, values, and relationships of a society increasingly organized in large and powerful institutions; or the role, function, and limitations of science and technology. These questions cannot be converted into economic issues. Nor, despite President Johnson's attempts at "consensus," are they likely to admit of "bipartisanship." Bipartisanship is effective when the answers are known, at least in broad outline. But great political innovations, such as we need, are rarely the children of compromise.

And yet these are also issues which the traditional ideological alignments, the alignments of European politics, cannot tackle. To do as so many foreign and domestic critics of the American political system have urged us to do for well over a century—to organize our political life on the basis of "liberal" and "conservative," or "right" and "left"—would only add to the confusion. What is "liberal" in respect to the government of the metropolis? Or in respect to the relationship between the individual and the large organizations on which he depends for effectiveness, but on which he must not depend if he wants to be free? And what does it mean to be a "conservative" on these issues? There is obviously going to be violent disagreement in respect to these issues; in fact, there is need for such disagreement and for a diversity of approaches to their solution. But ideological alignments are bound to be as irrelevant to these issues as the traditional alignment by economic interests. The "New Left" is thus bound to be sterile and to be condemned to total frustration.

If, indeed, the world will permit us the luxury of domestic affairs in the next half-century or so, we will not only have to face up to new issues. We shall have to devise a new approach to domestic politics altogether. This signifies a greater upheaval in our political life, a greater strain on political sanity and stability, than the new issues themselves could possibly mean and a greater opportunity for creative political thought and effective political leadership than this country has known since the days of the founding fathers.

In seizing this opportunity, we may well have to abandon the traditional reliance on economic interests and economic issues as symbols of political intercourse and as means of political organization. I hope that we will not give up with them the principle underlying them: the mobilization of conflict to create unity, and the appeal to interest against the fanaticism of ideological faction. It is not only a civilized concept; it is a principle that makes politics productive for the common good. It has served the American people well—so well that doing without the Great Economist seems a very small price, indeed.

INDEX